This Is Not Your Father's Stockpicking Book

This Is Not Your Father's Stockpicking Book

Profiting from the Investment Clues Found in Everyday Life

DERRICK NIEDERMAN

TIMES BUSINESS

RANDOM HOUSE

All stock-price charts courtesy of
Securities Research Co.
A Division of Babson-United Investment Advisors, Inc.
101 Prescott St., Wellesley Hills, MA 02181

Library of Congress Cataloging-in-Publication Data
Niederman, Derrick.
This is not your father's stockpicking book: profiting from the
investment clues found in everyday life /
Derrick Niederman.
p.   cm.
Includes index.
ISBN 0-8129-2216-6
1. Stocks.   2. Speculation.   I. Title.
HG4661.N45   1995   332.63'22—dc20   95-2485

Manufactured in the United States of America

9   8   7   6   5   4   3   2

First Edition

To my family

PREFACE

Why did the drought of 1988 cause dozens of stocks to plummet and then rebound? How did the stock market react when Clara Peller first shouted "Where's the Beef?" What did Bill Clinton do that made the bond market so afraid of him? And how can you use these anecdotes from the past to make better investment decisions in the future?

The aim of this book is to come up with investment ideas by connecting familiar aspects of the everyday world with their not-so-familiar effects on public companies. In five chapters, we will cover everything from advertising to weather, from the presidency to television, even fads, taking a new look at subjects that are familiar to anyone with a pulse but whose investment content has gone largely unexplored.

Why do investors tend to ignore these highly visible arenas? Probably because popular culture seems far too frivolous to influence something as serious as an investment decision. To many, investment success can only come from an encyclopedic mastery of such items as accounts receivable, profit margins, and debt/equity ratios. No surprise that the stock market remains a forbidding place, where someone else always has the advantage.

I must confess that it took me many years in the money management business to realize that the real advantage held by top professional investors is simpler than you'd think. It doesn't come from high-level mathematics, nor is it derived from years of training in obscure financial accounting methods. The one trait common to all successful investors is the ability to see potential in situations that others view with either skepticism or a yawn.

By the time you finish this book, you're going to have that trait as well.

The situations we're going to investigate will be as ordinary as a new advertising campaign, a television series, or a winter storm. In many cases there will be no obvious investment connection, but that's the point: Making that connection is what will give us our advantage.

Of course, it's easy to reject clues plucked from the popular culture —on the grounds that they can't possibly tell you everything you need to know to make the proper investment decision. But it is extremely rare for any one indicator to tell you everything you might want to know about a given stock. All you really need is *enough* information to point you in the right direction.

What this book will do is help you decide which indicators should be acted on, which should be investigated, and which should be ignored altogether. With advertising, for example, I would argue that the Federal Express ads of the late seventies told you about 80 percent of what you needed to know to make one of the great investments of that era. In the context of the stock market, an 80 percent indicator is a rarity and something that should be heeded—rather than lamenting the other 20 percent! By comparison, IBM's Charlie Chaplin campaign of the early eighties was not an outright buy signal (as I'll explain in a later chapter), but it still carried some positive messages; it wasn't the end of an investment decision, but it could have been the beginning of one. We'll see many more examples like these before we're through.

I should tell you up front that my methodology may differ from what you are accustomed to seeing in an investment book. Rather than force-feeding you my own personal vision of how to succeed in the market, I'm going to dive headfirst into the examples, because that's where the action is. In many cases, you and I will be reacting to the examples at the same time. I'll set up theories and test them on these very pages. Sometimes the initial theories won't hold up perfectly, so we'll have to revise and modify. But we'll move through it together.

If you've never invested in a stock before, I suppose I should also admit that this book isn't entirely devoid of financial jargon and other tricks of the trade, because some complexities can't be avoided. However, it is my fervent hope that any new terms will arise in the context of familiar examples that should ease any would-be learning pains.

Finally, to those who have already developed investing styles of your own, rest assured that I'm not asking you to change anything. If you prefer to invest in turnaround situations, that's fine with me. If you lean toward companies that are more growth oriented, all the power to you. But where do you suppose the clues to those turn-arounds come from? And where can you find the characteristics that lead to above-average growth? Often the answers come from the popular culture—often enough to fill your portfolio several times over.

ACKNOWLEDGMENTS

Writing a book is such a solitary process, I sometimes forget that dozens of people have helped me as I—well, let's be honest—as I ruined the past three years of my life. The truth is that I have been aided by some of the best minds in publishing and on Wall Street, and I am only too happy to acknowledge these many contributions.

My earliest debts go to the terrific crew at the old Fidelity Publishing Group, where the ideas that formed this book started to take shape. Thanks go to Leo Dworsky, my next-door office neighbor for seven years, whose trained eye helped me on numerous occasions; to Melanie Shaw, who cheerfully edited my columns and feature stories; to Kathy Johnson, Charlene Niles, and Laurie McCartney, whose research efforts made those articles that much easier to write; to Gina Pelosi and Sharon Qualls of the Fidelity Library, for some timely fact-finding; most of all, to John Boyd, the man who started it all, whose confidence in me has never been forgotten.

When *Worth* magazine debuted in 1992, a whole new group arrived, and my indebtedness would only grow. I'd like to acknowledge

Bob Clark and Tom Weber, for the until-now thankless task of editing my columns. Jim Melloan, fact-checker extraordinaire, has bailed me out many, many times. Alison Parks has been an enthusiastic backer of my various efforts over the years. And I'd like to offer a special thanks to our CEO Randy Jones, who was never too busy to hear out the thoughts and concerns of a humble scribe. It was appreciated.

I've also received valuable support from Fidelity Capital, our parent organization. I'd like to thank Jim Curvey for always stopping by as he made his rounds. And Karen Ernst and Laurie Watts had a knack for being generous at crucial times.

Denise Russell, Karen O'Toole, and Bob Hill of Fidelity's technical services department got me started as I compiled the stock charts for the book. Fiona Dadswell of Datastream provided price data for some hard-to-get-at companies. Donald Jones and Michael Gmitter of Securities Research Corporation spent many hours producing the final, camera-ready copies.

I'd also like to pay special tribute to Geoff Shandler, my editor at Times Books, who graciously and methodically improved the manuscript well beyond the original submission. Nancy Inglis and Naomi Osnos did beautiful work down the home stretch, and the book is much the better for it. To Karl Weber and John Mahaney, the driving forces behind the new Times Business Books imprint, let me say how much I've appreciated your support. Doe Coover, my agent, put in many hours on my behalf, hours that didn't go unnoticed. Thanks to all.

For the vast legions of Wall Street analysts and corporate spokespeople who granted me their time and insights, let me give a blanket thanks. I don't have the space to provide everybody's corporate affiliation in the list that follows. (Not to mention the fact that you people move around a lot!) However, assuming you know where you are, I hope you find your name on this long list. Specifically, I'd like to thank Tim Reiland, Harold Vogel, Paul MacRae Montgomery, Ron Nordmann, Cliff Butler, Juris Pagrabs, Fred Ward, Paul Handler, Mike Smolinski, Marie Ziegler, Clive Shallow, Bob Malloy, Dick Wood, Tom Burns, Dick Vietor, Jay Nelson, Nick Filippello, Walt Casey, Dean Haskell, Ken Heebner, Jane Shickich, John McMillin, Danielle Seitz, Ed Gordon, Brenda Landry, John Swendrowski, John Pazurek, Brian Taber, Marshall Hopkins, Kay Norwood, Dick Lilly, Joanna Scharf,

Sharon Lewis, Jonathan Gray, Paul Szczygiel, Bonnie Wittenburg, David Barron, Jack Trout, Al Ries, Frank Rolfes, John Casesa, Alan Gould, Paul Mackey, Pat McCormack, Michael Elling, Robin Maynard, Gregg Villany, Nomi Ghez, Roy Burry, Tim Ramey, Gloria Vogel, Michael Corasaniti, Candace Browning, David Londoner, Herb Schlosser, Jessica Reif, Alan Gottesman, Michael Niemeira, Ed Comeau, Lee Tawes, Dorothy Lakner, Harry Katica, John Curti, Louise Yamada, John Rohs, Janet Mangano, Joe Buckley, Gareth Plank, Skip Wells, and David Leibowitz.

With these many debts behind me, I trust that I will be forgiven as I save my final and deepest acknowledgment for that person without whom this book would never have been conceived, much less written, someone who has been there for me during the many ups and downs of the past three years, and someone, I am delighted to say, who is still there today. That person, of course, would be Peggy.

CONTENTS

This Is Not Your Father's Stockpicking Book

1 ❏ Investor's Almanac

Talk about volatile combinations. The weather and the stock market are two of the least predictable fields you could possibly find. And they are unpredictable in entirely different ways. Meteorologists, despite our cynicism, have a reasonably good shot at telling you about tomorrow's weather, but they haven't the vaguest clue what the weather will be ten years from today. Securities analysts, on the other hand, have no idea what the market will do tomorrow, but they know with reasonable certainty that in ten years the market will be higher than it is today.

Not surprisingly, when people try to make connections between the weather and the direction of the stock market—like those who insist that sunspots and market behavior are somehow related—they aren't taken all that seriously. However, by shifting the focus from the overall market to individual stocks, we will discover that many of the seemingly unpredictable ups and downs of individual securities are actually *explained* by the ups and downs of the weather. Best of all, some reliable patterns start to emerge.

These patterns aren't exactly well known. If you ask a typical Wall Street analyst how investments in his or her industry are affected by the weather, the first response is generally a laugh—not a sneering, derisive laugh, mind you, but a laugh nonetheless. Analysts will remind you that they aren't paid to predict the weather, so they can't exactly take it into account when making earnings estimates. In other words, these conversations don't start well. I should know. I've had dozens of them.

But in a few moments, they just might come up with an example of how a rainstorm or a heat wave affected one of the companies they follow. Then that example will lead to another, and the ball is rolling.

So what are these examples all about? How could an investor possibly benefit from weather patterns? The answers don't come from predictions; they come from common sense. If you've ever decided not to go shopping because it's raining outside, you know that the retailing business is weather dependent. So, for that matter, are industries such as insurance, transportation, farming, energy, even amusement parks. It's a long, long list.

The list is so long that coming up with industries that *aren't* affected by the weather is the harder task. The semiconductor industry, for one, seems immune but isn't: Chip making is a water-intensive process, which made the multiyear California drought of particular interest to Silicon Valley. Catalog retailers, unlike storefront retailers, would also appear to be immune. But when Sears discontinued its 108-year-old catalog business in 1993, the company was reacting in part to the immense losses its Allstate insurance subsidiary had suffered the year before because of Hurricane Andrew. Weather is everywhere.

It is tempting to believe that weather is fleeting, and that long-term investors can afford to disregard it. But as we will see, a single weather episode can influence corporate performance for many years. Perhaps the most important point to be made—and one that will surely be repeated before these pages are through—is that you don't have to predict the weather to profit from it. Buying opportunities often emerge months after the weather in question has come and gone.

Mark Twain claimed that "everyone talks about the weather, but no one ever does anything about it." Well, here's your chance.

The Drought of 1988: A Prototype for
Weather-based Investing

Weather-based investing wouldn't get very far if the weather never changed, and it should come as no surprise that the occasions of greatest interest to us are those where Mother Nature has truly gone awry. Fortunately, the stock market's response to any extreme meteorological condition—whether it be rain, snow, heat, or wind—tends to fall into a couple of easy-to-recognize patterns. A good example is the midwestern drought of 1988.

The First Leg: 1988

When foul weather strikes, an investor's first task is to identify industries that are positioned to benefit; these are what we will call "first-leg" winners. Being early always helps on the first leg, and in 1988 our role model was celebrated commodities trader Paul Tudor Jones.

That January, Jones told the annual *Barron's* magazine investment roundtable: "If there is a problem planting this spring, you could really see grains soar. That is a trader's speculation I definitely want to make." The "problem planting" Jones was speculating on is now known as the drought of 1988.

The drought began modestly enough: April produced 2.2 inches of rainfall on the corn belt, below the 3.6 inch average but not alarmingly so. But May produced just 1.7 inches of rain versus the accustomed 4.0, and June came in at 1.2 versus the average of 4.2. In late June, *Barron's* revisited the story and asked veteran soybean trader John Tocks to summarize the prevailing view in the commodities pit. Quipped Tocks, "[Traders believe] it will never rain again in your or my lifetime." The attitude showed: Between April and the end of June, corn futures rose 80 percent, while wheat gained 49 percent and soybeans 69 percent.

Our task is to make money without speculating in futures contracts (the mechanism whereby investors bet on the short-term price of grains, metals, and other commodities) and without forecasting the foul weather months ahead of time. It can be done. Remember, Jones didn't *know* there was going to be a drought—he simply knew what to do when one actually occurred. That type of preparedness works just as well on the stock market.

In the early summer of 1988, one place to look was among fertilizer stocks. The investment thesis was fairly straightforward: As the crop disaster unfolded, it became clear that farmers would spend the next year trying to rebuild their flagging crop inventories. To achieve this goal, they would have to utilize previously idled (and therefore nutrient-depleted) land, land that required extensive fertilizing. The increased fertilizer demand—both real and anticipated—pushed up the price of staple fertilizers such as diammonium phosphate (or DAP), which rose from $157 per ton in May to over $170 per ton by the end of the year.

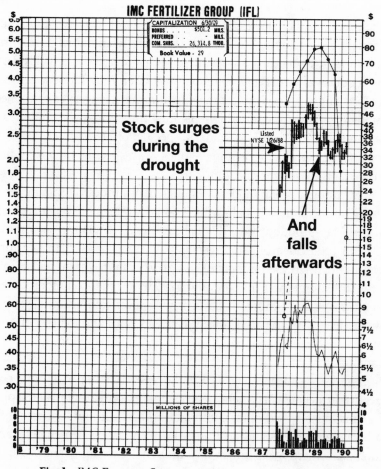

Fig. 1 IMC Fertilizer Chart (Courtesy of Securities Research Co.)

A $13-per-ton gain in DAP prices may not set your heart aflutter, but the earnings of commodity producers, whether of fertilizer or anything else, are extremely sensitive to changes in that commodity's price. It therefore made sense to invest in IMC Fertilizer, a major DAP producer—and the sooner, the better. IMC stock moved from $30 to $43 in June alone, and was at $50 by the end of 1988, an overall gain of 66 percent. The shares of Freeport-McMoran Resources, another leading fertilizer producer, advanced 50 percent during the same period.

Riding first-leg winners doesn't always require split-second timing; in fact, investors are often well advised to spend some extra time understanding the story. A case in point in 1988 was Valmont Industries, a Nebraska-based manufacturer of mechanized irrigation equipment.

It may seem obvious that an irrigation company would prosper in drought conditions, but the situation wasn't that simple. After all, the farm economy had been downright lousy for several years prior to 1988, and many farmers weren't in a position to buy irrigation equipment even if they desperately needed it.

However, farmers who did have crops that year stood to do unusually well because of the higher commodity prices. It turned out that farmers in Nebraska and Kansas went virtually unscathed in 1988, the brunt of the drought being felt in Iowa, Indiana, and Illinois. Conveniently for Valmont, Nebraska and Kansas were its prime territories! (If you think I knew that *before* the drought, you're crazy. That's where the extra research time came in handy.) Anyway, these farmers were in a position to bolster themselves for the upcoming year, and they greatly increased their irrigation orders.

This increased demand for Valmont's products didn't end with the summer. Year in, year out, irrigation demand relates more to the farmers' mind-set than to the actual weather (recognizing that this mind-set is of course weather dependent). The drought of 1988 created such a vivid and enduring image of destruction that Valmont's orders stayed strong well into the second half of the year, ordinarily a slow period. And this surge in orders flowed straight to the bottom line: The company's earnings (or net profits) for 1988 came in at $1.38 per share, a 79 percent increase from the $0.77 per share earned in 1987. As for the stock, Valmont shares doubled in 1988 alone. So, for that matter,

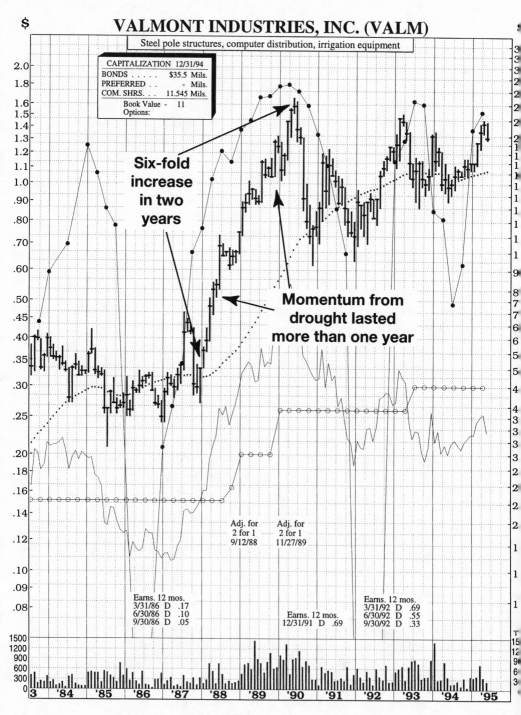

Fig. 2 VALMONT INDUSTRIES CHART (Courtesy of Securities Research Co.)

did those of Lindsay Manufacturing, another Nebraska-based irrigation manufacturer—quite a feat, given that the company didn't go public until September.

The Second Leg: 1989

As a weather event such as the drought comes to a close, the first-leg winners often lose their luster, for essentially three reasons: (1) they've gone up a lot, (2) bad weather doesn't last forever, and (3) market forces begin to change the fundamentals of the companies themselves. Here's how those things played out in 1988.

On the futures market, corn, wheat, and soybean prices did not stay up indefinitely, despite the substandard 1988 harvest. The main reason was that the grain supplies left over from the 1987 harvest— the so-called carryover—proved a more-than-adequate buffer; though the carryover was reduced substantially in the drought year, it never became dangerously low, and the plentiful crop of 1989 pushed it back up to comfortable levels. In effect, the high commodities prices could only have been sustained by a drought in *1989*, something that never materialized.

Among the fertilizer makers, the good news was short-lived for a somewhat different reason. As fertilizer prices rose in 1988, companies such as IMC and Freeport greatly stepped up their production (this is one of those "market forces" I was talking about). Unfortunately, although overall plantings did increase in 1989, the amount of the increase was far less than expected, and fertilizer demand was not enough to match the extra production. The net result was a glut that caused fertilizer prices to fall across the board in the summer of 1989. By the end of that year, both IMC and Freeport shares had literally given up all of their gains.

Irrigation-equipment companies enjoyed somewhat longer prosperity, because, as suggested earlier, farmers continued to want protection from drought conditions long after 1988. Valmont Industries' irrigation sales rose from $126 million in 1988 to $158 million in 1989, an increase of 25 percent; meanwhile, earnings were up 29 percent. At Lindsay Manufacturing, domestic irrigation sales were so strong that they accounted for 58 percent of total revenues by 1989, up from only 28 percent in 1987. Between the end of 1988 and the middle of 1990, both stocks doubled again.

But the real second-leg investment winners were companies that started off as *victims* of the drought. In general, stocks that go down in response to extreme weather can be the most important ones to identify. For starters, they have the potential to go up dramatically when the weather reverses itself (as it always does). Better still, the window of opportunity stays open a lot longer. In 1988, you had several months to see that packaged-food stocks would become terrific second-leg investments.

The force that drove these stocks down in the first place was higher commodity prices. To food companies that use grain as a raw material, the higher commodity prices of mid-1988 translated into higher costs, which Wall Street reasoned would lead to lower profit margins. On these fears, shares of General Mills, Sara Lee, and McDonald's each dropped over 15 percent between the spring and summer of that year.

These drops were actually major buying opportunities in disguise, because a couple of important factors pointed to a rebound. First, grain prices had already peaked by midsummer, in semipredictable fashion—that much the charts could tell you. Second, most of these companies weren't suffering as much as the stock market would have had you believe. "[The drought] didn't really affect us much," said Cliff Butler of Pilgrim's Pride, a major poultry producer whose profits would seemingly have been hurt by the doubling of feed costs that year. The reason for Butler's indifference was that the public's preference for chicken over beef made it easy for poultry producers to raise prices, thereby passing their higher costs on to consumers.

The price-conscious consumers of today might have rebelled, but back then the brand-name packaged food companies had pricing power on their side, and they took full advantage. Cereal manufacturers such as Kellogg and General Mills found that the higher grain costs could be offset by a price hike on the order of 4 to 5 percent, which was enacted without consumer resistance.

Now for the investment kicker. When the more normal 1989 harvest brought grain costs back down, did these same companies reduce their prices? Not on your life. As a result, those nominal-looking 4 to 5 percent price hikes flowed straight to the bottom line, fueling earnings gains of 20 percent or even more. With profitability rendered stronger than ever, our initially penalized stocks of General Mills, Sara Lee, and McDonald's were up an average of over *50 percent* by summertime 1989.

Even some less well positioned companies provided rebound opportunities, simply because the stock market overreacted to the problem at hand. Archer Daniels Midland, the nation's leading processor of agricultural commodities, was a stock to avoid throughout the summer of 1988. Archer Daniels makes ethanol, a corn-based gasoline substitute, which was caught in a price squeeze: Not only were costs higher because of higher corn prices, but the company's ability to pass these higher costs on to consumers was limited by the relatively low price of gasoline. Ethanol is an important product for ADM, so investor concern was understandable.

Securities analysts, fearful of even more price squeezing as the drought progressed, sharply lowered their 1988 earnings estimates for Archer Daniels—from a pre-drought consensus estimate of $2.40 per share to as low as $1.60 by August—and the stock remained weak throughout the summer (as stocks will when earnings estimates are being slashed 33 percent).

At times such as these, the investor has to remind him- or herself that the estimate reductions are taking place in an atmosphere of pure panic (remember those traders who thought it would never rain again). In the words of Oppenheimer's Lee Tawes, "the anticipation was much worse than the event." The ethanol price squeeze was only temporary, and actual per-share earnings for the year came in at the $2.30 level, well above the summer trough. In the twelve months starting in August 1988, ADM shares doubled.

Finally, rebound potential applies even to a company that has created its own problems. Chubb, otherwise a highly regarded insurance company, lost millions during the drought by essentially insuring against weather conditions that had already taken place—but the stock became a second-leg winner anyway.

Chubb had dabbled in selling rain insurance to farmers even before the drought year of 1988, but that year it took the fateful step of empowering a firm called Good Weather International to issue rain insurance policies on its behalf. Good Weather turned out to be a misnomer in every sense. First of all, despite Chubb's intended limit of

$3 million, GWI issued policies for $350 million. Making matters worse, $275 million of this coverage, issued to some 6,600 farmers, was written in mid-June, by which time the drought had already done its damage—hence the surge in applications.

By the time Chubb discovered its underwriting gaffe, the company had a public relations nightmare on its hands. Thousands of farmers had to be told that their applications had never been approved by Chubb and therefore would not be honored. The stock market quaked at the potential class action liability, and within three days the stock dropped from $58 to $53, a decline of almost 10 percent.

But that's as bad as the story ever got. When Chubb settled the potential class action with a $48 million payment to the shortchanged farmers, investors found their nerve, and the stock made up all of its lost ground and more in a few short months.

Experienced investors will recognize the second-leg approach as a variant of the age-old strategy of buying quality companies during periods of temporary distress. There is never any precise way of determining when second-leg stocks will make the transition from loser to winner, but that's the nature of rebound investing. The fact that most of them bottomed out somewhere around August of 1988 is important for another reason: The drought first made headlines in the spring. Second-leg stocks are the ultimate example that you don't have to predict the weather in order to profit from it.

PROFITING FROM YEAR-TO-YEAR WEATHER CHANGES

Investors tend to like favorable year-to-year comparisons. All other things being equal, when a company's earnings for a given period are better than they were for the same period of the prior year, it bodes well for the stock. Something good must be happening.

That's where weather enters the picture. Common sense tells us that the weather can greatly influence year-over-year earnings comparisons for a wide range of companies. What isn't as obvious is how Wall Street reacts to these fluctuations. It is perfectly possible for the market to disregard or look beyond a near-term meteorological calamity, just like any other near-term calamity. However, those cases of market indifference aren't nearly as numerous as you might think. When a company produces substandard earnings, not all investors have the time or energy to find out that the shortfall may be weather-related, nor do they necessarily have the courage to act against the prevailing winds.

Furthermore, not all weather-based investing requires conditions as freakish as the drought. Happily, stock market opportunities can arise from much more mundane circumstances—as mundane as one year's weather differing from that of the prior year.

This creates opportunities for those who pay attention to the weather. It turns out that the best places to capitalize on year-to-year weather changes are among retailing and natural gas stocks.

Retail Stocks: An Opportunity Every Month

Retail stocks are a great source of "weather plays" because of the frequency of their financial reporting. Whereas any public company must issue earnings reports each quarter, retailers take this one step further by reporting *each month* their so-called same-store sales figures. These figures tell how sales compare to the year before (at least, among those stores that have been open at least a year). In the near term, retail stocks go up and down on the basis of these figures.

If these reports were made only four times per year, weather wouldn't be much of a factor, because its effects would tend to get canceled out. But twelve times per year is a different story, because it means that a single weather episode can cast a shadow over an entire reporting period.

If you've ever put off a potential shopping spree because of a thunderstorm, you've provided evidence that the consumer mentality is highly weather dependent. Even a sunny day can be a deterrent, in that people can find more interesting things to do than shop. These sorts of decisions seem individual and/or anecdotal, but in the aggregate they can and do affect the stocks of the nation's biggest retailers.

Case in point: Wal-Mart. In September 1989, the weather in the south central United States—Wal-Mart's prime selling area—was substantially colder than normal, a favorable backdrop for the sale of fall merchandise. As a result, Wal-Mart's same-store sales growth for the month came in at an astonishing 16 percent, well above the company's

already industry-leading average of 11 percent. The stock rose 8 percent during the first few trading days of October (before the release of
the sales figures, but *after* September's weather had been logged into
the record books; again, no forecasts necessary).

Fig. 3 WAL-MART: WHAT A DIFFERENCE A YEAR MAKES

	1989	1990
Average September temperature in Arkansas (*Normal: 74.3°*)	71.2°	77.5°
Wal-Mart's September same-store sales growth (*Normal: 11%*)	16.0%	8.0%
Stock price change during first week of October (when results are announced)	+7.0%	−14.0%

The earlier the new season begins, the better it is for retailers, especially when it comes to
apparel. A cold September in 1989 enabled Wal-Mart to sell much more fall merchandise; a hot
September the following year produced the exact opposite result. (The weather in Arkansas was
indicative of the weather throughout the South Central United States, Wal-Mart's most important
selling area.)

The next year—1990—that same area of the country witnessed
one of the hottest Septembers on record. This time around, Wal-Mart's
same-store sales growth came in at only 8 percent: great for anyone
else, but not up to Wal-Mart's standards. The stock dropped 14 percent in the first week of October.

Understanding these fluctuations is vital even if you never intend
to make a short-term weather-based trade in retail stocks. Suppose
you had actually owned Wal-Mart during the bad-weather patch in
1990. As you watched the stock drop from $29 to $25 in a matter of

days, wouldn't you have been curious about what was going on? It's human nature to get a little panicky at times like these, as in "What's wrong with Wal-Mart?"

Knowing that the substandard results were merely a function of the weather would have made it much easier not to panic—and, therefore, not to sell. The fact that the stock went down as far as it did suggests that a lot of people didn't reach the same conclusion. Which is too bad, because Wal-Mart stock went on to double in the next twelve months.

In general, if you remember what the weather was like the year before (during the month in question), you have a better perspective for assessing sales and earnings comparisons. Of course, it could be argued that you'd have to be some kind of nut to keep weather in your mind that way. However, that's the reason the approach still works: Not many people are doing it.

If the prospect of tracking weather twelve months a year seems too exhausting, consider reducing your load to the four months that begin the four seasons—specifically, September, December, March, and June. The notion of "good retail weather" for these months can be described by a simple rule: When the new season comes early, retail sales tend to go up—and, on balance, so do retail stocks.

The weather during seasonal transitions is especially important to *apparel* retailers. For example, a cool September helps apparel retailers because it makes the fall selling season longer, and because stores get an early look at what is selling and what is not. This renders the reordering process that much more efficient. To the extent that fewer items end up going on sale at the end of the season, well, that's yet another positive. In this way, one month's extreme weather has the potential to affect operations—and earnings—for a much longer time.

Here's a precipitous case of this principle in action. In December 1990, things looked quite grim for a shoe retailer called J. Baker. The company's specialty was (and is) operating shoe departments for major department stores, which in theory can be a highly profitable niche business. Unfortunately, J. Baker wasn't living up to its potential because of the poor financial health of its biggest customer, Ames Department Stores. In April 1990, Ames filed for Chapter 11 bankruptcy protection and announced several store closings. The uncertainty of the Ames-related damage moved J. Baker stock down from the high teens to just $7 per share by mid-1990. I recommended the stock at that time, thinking that things couldn't get any worse.

The bad news is that things got a lot worse before they got better. The good news is that a weather-related consideration saved me from selling at the absolute low.

Remember that in late 1990 the country was completely enveloped by the onset of recession and the crisis in the Persian Gulf. Investors were selling stocks pretty much indiscriminately, and percentage losses among single-digit stocks were particularly high. By December, J. Baker had moved from $7 down to $5—a decline of almost 30 percent. When the company announced lousy sales figures for December, the stock got knocked down 40 percent further, to $3. When you've recommended a stock at $7 and it declines to $3 within nine months, you start to wonder how you're going to talk yourself out of the whole thing.

But those sales figures, however crummy and however poorly timed, were partly the result of an unusually warm December; without snow, boots don't sell. No snow in December is especially bad, because it means more boots will end up in the post-Christmas markdown bins. This simple explanation suggested that panic was in the stock price and it was no time to sell. So I held on, and in fact recommended the stock again at $4 per share.

I didn't know that the Gulf War resolution would lift the market the way it did in early 1991, nor did I predict that J. Baker's return to financial health would come as swiftly as it did. And neither of these factors was related to the weather. Nonetheless, a simple observation about the weather is what saved me from selling at the absolute bottom. Good thing. The stock hit $20 in late 1991.

Natural Gas Stocks: The "Two out of Three" Principle

Aside from retailing, the other main source of year-over-year weather plays is the energy sector. To most people, an "energy stock" means a familiar name like Exxon, Texaco, Mobil, or any of the major international oil companies. In terms of weather-related opportunities, though, the companies to watch are those that deal in natural gas—

companies like Anadarko Petroleum, Burlington Resources, Cabot Oil and Gas, Enron Oil and Gas, Noble Affiliates, and Plains Petroleum.

Natural gas has been widely heralded as the energy source of the future, what with its clean burning characteristics and consequent approval by environmentalists. Many analysts believe that the demand for natural gas will push prices considerably higher in the next five or ten years, reason enough to consider an investment in this industry. However, anyone who expects the price of natural gas to track an orderly, constant climb doesn't understand the impact of the weather.

Seasonality is the most important short-term factor in determining gas prices. Natural gas is used primarily as a winter heating fuel. Summertime use comes from so-called peaking plants, which are put into service when electricity demand, notably for air conditioners, exceeds what can be supplied by other, cheaper power sources, notably coal. An increase in demand, whether arising from a cold winter or a hot summer, will ordinarily translate into a higher spot price of natural gas (the spot price is what you have to pay for immediate delivery). The higher spot price in turn tends to push natural gas stocks higher.

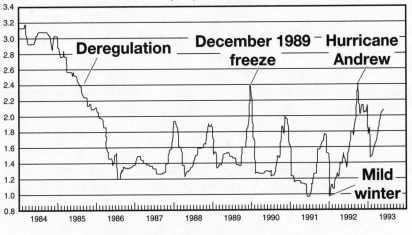

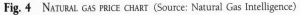

Fig. 4 Natural gas price chart (Source: Natural Gas Intelligence)

As the long-term price chart suggests, the spot price of natural gas is wildly volatile. (Note: The price is measured in dollars per million Btu's, where "Btu" stands for British thermal unit, an energy measure.) Typically, prices rise with the onset of winter, as buyers—utilities, refiners, whoever—build their inventories for the cold season. Once inventory levels are deemed satisfactory, demand and price tend to fall off sharply.

Rest assured that natural gas stocks aren't nearly as volatile as the spot price. However, they still can have significant ups and downs based on the weather. The classic contrarian strategy is to buy immediately after unfavorable weather strikes, then wait for an improvement.

A case in point was the banner year of 1992, during which Anadarko rose 22 percent, Burlington 33 percent, Cabot 45 percent, and so on through the alphabet. What happened was that the winter of 1991–92 was unusually mild. As utility companies saw this mildness unfolding, they realized their winter supplies were adequate and therefore cut back on their natural gas purchases earlier than usual. As a result, the spot price fell from $1.80 in November to under $1 in January, during which time natural gas stocks dropped an average of 17 percent. The worst casualties were Apache Oil & Gas and Noble Affiliates, each of which nose-dived over 30 percent.

The stock market wasn't crazy in pushing these stocks down, because natural gas producers could not make money at these depressed price levels. Hopes for a rebound in natural gas stocks centered on two possibilities: first, that producers would rein in their output, thereby tightening the "supply" of the supply/demand equation; and second, that the weather would become an ally—even if that meant its getting worse!

Both of these events took place within the year. The reduced supplies of natural gas by themselves facilitated a price rise that lasted most of 1992. This trend became a surge in September, when Hurricane Andrew arrived. Andrew temporarily knocked out about 10 percent of the gas-producing capacity in the Gulf of Mexico (the Gulf accounts for some 25 percent to 30 percent of total U.S. production). Under this near-term supply disruption, prices reached $2.40 per million Btu's, almost three times the January low. Between January and September, Noble rose 66 percent and Apache 83 percent. This trading opportunity would not have been possible without the prior winter's unseasonably warm weather.

To exploit such opportunities in the future, we should remember that natural gas stocks tend to move in accordance with the *expectations* for gas prices, rather than the spot price. We could figure out these expectations by studying the price trends of natural gas futures, which by definition quantify expectations. But for a less technical approach we can consider the "two out of three" principle —the brainchild of First Albany energy analyst Mike Smolinski. The basis of Smolinski's principle is that the behavior of the purchasers of natural gas during a given year is to a great extent predicated on the previous year's weather. It's a familiar theme, with unusually specific results.

If, for example, one winter was especially mild, buyers might be reluctant to build inventories the following year—after all, wasn't the most recent problem that inventories were too high? The result is that a weather reversal—in this case, a cold snap—would cause them to scramble for natural gas, bidding up prices. That's exactly what happened during the Christmas freeze of 1989, which pushed the gas price to almost $2.40 per million Btu, a level that wasn't exceeded for almost three years. That month, the Standard & Poor's Natural Gas stock index moved from 456.68 to 489.13, an increase of over 7 percent.

The principle could also have been invoked in February and March of 1993, when a series of storms brought an abrupt end to what had been a second consecutive mild winter. The cold temperatures made natural gas prices reverse their negative trend and turn sharply higher. Natural gas stocks rose 19.6 percent in the first quarter of that year, compared with a 2.9 percent rise in the S&P 500. Knowing the effect of these weather reversals was central to participating in these gains.

Where does the "two out of three" come in? It's simple. For any given period, there are only three possibilities for the weather: hotter than normal, normal, and colder than normal. The greatest year-to-year changes in weather—and, therefore, in buyers' psychology and the potential for price swings—occurs when the prior year's weather was at one extreme or another. And that happens in two out of three cases.

The principle does *not* say that a warm winter must automatically be followed by a cold one. What it does say is that *if* the following winter is cold (or even has a single frigid patch), you have the one-extreme-to-the-other type of swing that is most conducive to a dramatic change in the gas price. That's the sort of situation that an investor in natural gas stocks should be waiting for. Best of all, these situations should continue to be created as long as human nature governs the purchasing of natural gas.

LOCATION: THE FORGOTTEN VARIABLE

I almost scrapped the following pearl of wisdom because it seemed too obvious: When analyzing a weather episode for investment purposes, you have to pay close attention to *where* the extreme weather is taking place. The importance of location isn't entirely new to us (recall Nebraska's insulation from the 1988 drought), but there are many other variations on the theme.

Take another look at the companies in your portfolio. If they sell something, where do they sell it? If they make something, where do they make it? The less geographically diversified a company is, the more likely it is to be disrupted by a single weather episode, and knowing where your vulnerabilities are before the weather strikes can be a big advantage.

The financial markets don't understand location as much as you'd think. For example, when California experienced a surprising freeze in December 1990, orange juice futures were pushed sharply upward. But California oranges are grown to be *eaten,* not to be used for juice, so a California freeze should have no bearing on futures prices. Recognizing the market's folly made money for those savvy traders who were willing to bet that the market would realize its error and retreat. It did. (By the way, now that Brazil has supplanted Florida as the leading supplier of juice oranges, even Florida freezes won't have the effect on juice futures that they once did.)

Our discussion of the 1988 drought illustrated a different sort of misunderstanding of location. One of the excuses for investor distress that year was the fear that there could be another drought in 1989. And drought conditions in successive summers aren't that unusual.

But successive *midwestern* droughts come around about once a century —a nice fact to tuck away as others are panicking. As we saw, the return of a more normal harvest in 1989 brought with it the resurgence of many stocks that had been victimized by panic selling in 1988.

Distinguishing between different companies in the same industry is perhaps the most common application of location. Within the utility industry, for example, there is a simple distinction to be made between summer-peaking and winter-peaking utility companies. The former are in the South, where the demand comes from air-conditioning, and the latter are in the North, where the emphasis is on winter heating. Knowing these patterns is essential to understanding the seasonality of financial results.

Among retailers, we have already seen a case where unseasonable weather helped push down the shares of Wal-Mart, the industry leader. For smaller, regional retailers, the effects of a weather incident can be far more pronounced: Boston-based Filene's Basement was hit particularly hard by the big winter storm of March 1993, likewise for Des Moines–based Younkers during the midwestern floods of that summer. Both companies lost a significant amount of business because of their respective disasters, and both stocks slumped to new lows in the aftermath.

On a more positive note, location can also be the reason for a particular company's advantage over its peers. When Southwest Airlines sprang up out of Dallas in the early 1970s, it posted performance numbers that were unheard of in the airline industry. One of the company's secrets is a quick-turn strategy that gets its planes to and from destinations several times per day. Southwest's planes routinely go from landing to takeoff faster than anybody else's: At one point they were averaging 9.3 departures per day, compared with 5.7 at Delta and 4.6 at American. This means that they can get by with fewer aircraft than the competition, which in turn makes them profitable with lower fare levels.

Lost in the impressive financials is that Southwest's quick-turn approach is a fair-weather strategy (if they were Northeast Airlines instead, there is no way that they could have pulled it off). But Southwest's dominance in fair-weather markets alone was enough to make it the most admired airline in the country, and at times it has been *the* stock to own in an industry that has so often been a frustrating place for your investment dollars. For example, between January 1, 1991, and January 1, 1994, the S&P Airline Index struggled to a 22.5 percent gain; meanwhile, Southwest Airlines rose 500 percent.

Within the gaming industry, although the spread of casinos across the country reduces the impact of location, a good first step for an investor is to understand the fundamental weather differences between Atlantic City and Las Vegas. Namely, of the two, only Vegas has a reliable climate, enabling it to attract an entirely different clientele. Many Vegas visitors are there for a weekend holiday and are perfectly content to lose money along the way, whereas Atlantic City has a greater incidence of day-trippers, whose sole purpose is to make money. Add to that advantage a superior convention business, and it is not surprising that Las Vegas casino operators like Circus Circus have been more productive long-term investments than Atlantic City's Bally's or Resorts International.

Even the Nevada desert isn't immune from the weather, though. When rains made the California highways impassable in early 1993, first-quarter earnings estimates for Circus Circus came down a nickel, from $0.43 to $0.38, and the stock dropped from $40 all the way to $28 in just one month. But Vegas investors have a tradition of over-reacting to rain: Bugsy Siegel, the mobster visionary who got the town rolling, was gunned down by his buddies after freak rainstorms plagued the first days of the Flamingo, the very first Vegas hotel. As we know, the Flamingo recovered. So did Circus Circus: The stock was back up to $48 by October, a 70 percent gain off its low.

Finally, an awareness of location will also help sort out occasions when two different companies report entirely different weather experiences for the same period. I've looked at such situations and wondered how it could be both dry and rainy at the same time, until I realized that the companies in question were based hundreds of miles apart. In today's world of international expansion and global brands, it is easy to forget that there are a lot of regional enterprises out there. Don't. Some profitable weather plays may be riding on it.

TEST CASE: AMUSEMENT PARKS

How far can the simple themes of year-to-year change and location take us? Judge for yourself as we tackle the amusement park industry. It has been chosen purely for simplicity, as there are essentially only three publicly traded entities in the business: Disney, EuroDisney, and Cedar Fair.

Only the last of these three companies may need an introduction. Cedar Fair is a master limited partnership, traded on the New York Exchange. Its primary properties are the Cedar Point amusement park in Sandusky, Ohio, and the Valley Fair park in Shakopee, Minnesota.

As a master limited partnership, Cedar Fair passes on most of its earnings to shareholders in the form of a cash dividend. The yield on the stock is therefore an important investment consideration, as is the stability of the dividend. No one had any reason to question Cedar Fair's dividend until the company was met with a rash of soggy weekends in the early summer of 1990. It was the first weather crisis of many that the industry would encounter in the new decade.

As Cedar Fair spokesman Juris Pagrabs explained, "About 75 percent of the registered shares are held in Ohio. People probably just looked at our [wet and empty] parking lot and sold their shares." During that summer, the stock fell 20 percent, from $13 to $10½—a steep decline for a stock that was thought to be a stable high-yielder.

The weekend washout was a new wrinkle on some of the themes we encountered in looking at the 1988 drought. In this case, the issue was the *timing* of the foul weather. As Fred Ward, a Lexington, Massachusetts–based weather consultant, pointed out, "A lot of companies do their planning on the basis of monthly weather data, but a dry month with wet weekends can often be worse than a wet month with dry weekends."

Despite the July washout, Cedar Fair's tight cost controls put the company in a position to salvage the summer with even minimal cooperation from the weather. When the sun returned in August, fun-starved vacationers again flocked to the parks and Cedar Fair became a classic second-leg winner. Although total summer attendance was down 4 percent (relative to a weather-aided 1989), the company posted level earnings for the year, increased its dividend, and watched the stock make up all its lost ground in a matter of months.

Any company that can produce level earnings with terrible weather conditions must be doing something right. Cedar Fair was not only a rebound candidate (the stock was back to the $13 level by 1991), it was also a company worth owning for the long term. The stock pierced $35 by 1993.

With Disney, you won't ever get such a "rain play." Average annual rainfall is just four inches in Anaheim, and a similar amount in Orlando. But weather made its way into the Disney investment equation in the fall of 1989, as EuroDisney made its stock market debut.

For those intrigued by EuroDisney's prospects, it would theoretically make sense to invest directly in EuroDisney shares rather than dilute the investment via the parent company. And, for a while, many investors were doing precisely that. Between late 1989 and the spring of 1992, Walt Disney shares advanced a respectable 20 percent, but EuroDisney's shares moved from $11 to $28—a gain of over 150 percent. And the park hadn't even opened yet.

One of a stock market investor's tasks is to ferret out situations where the anticipation of an event exceeds the likely reality. EuroDisney was one such case—a rather big one at that. As we know, attendance was disappointing from the very beginning, and those who did come didn't spend enough. The result was that the heavily indebted company lost $0.20 per share in fiscal 1992 and $0.90 per share in 1993. By the end of calendar 1993, the stock had dropped over 80 percent from its 1992 highs.

A location-oriented weather investor wouldn't have been tempted in the first place. Although the company's fall was the result of many factors, the mere fact that EuroDisney is located at almost 50 degrees latitude—as high as Gander, Newfoundland—put the park at a permanent disadvantage. The chilly weather that greeted customers on the first day—April 11, 1992—was a sign of bad things to come.

In general, a park that has a weather-defined season will always have a weather component to its financial results, and this has to be factored out if you want to assess the progress of other developments, such as a new ride or attraction.

The length of the season is by itself a big swing factor in year-over-year comparisons. Publicly held S-K-I Limited is not an amusement park—it operates such ski resorts as Killington in Vermont and Bear Mountain in California—but the company must also cope with a limited season. So must shareholders. Since 1988, the stock's performance for the second half of the year has correlated almost perfectly with the opening date at Killington. In 1991, when Killington opened on October 21 (later than usual), the stock was off 12 percent for the second half of the year. In 1992, helped by a record early start of October 1, the stock was up 31 percent for the same time period.

But the final word on seasons belongs to Cedar Fair. In 1992, when 1990-like rains created the possibility of another down year, the company came to a surprising realization. As the summer neared an end, customers were coming *despite* the bad weather, because it was now or never. On top of that, the stock continued to be strong throughout the fall, as investors became excited about the company's acquisition of a water theme park—ironically, the sort of park that fared least well in that summer's drizzle. There's not much you can do except applaud.

DETAILS THAT MAKE A DIFFERENCE

Just because the weather can lead us to some reasonable conclusions about amusement park stocks does not mean that it is a stand-alone investment tool. Some naive statements do hold up, though. All else being equal, when a company's earnings are inflated because of favorable weather, any associated stock-price rise should make you lean toward selling (IMC Fertilizer, 1988). Conversely, if earnings are under pressure purely because of unfavorable weather, any price decline should make you lean toward buying (Cedar Fair, 1990).

But what constitutes unfavorable weather? The answer isn't always as straightforward as you might think. Even when companies are in the same industry, their vulnerabilities to the weather may be entirely different. To get the most out of weather-based investing, we must therefore incorporate more details about the specific industries we're dealing with. A look at the food/agriculture industry will show that a few simple details can produce a wealth of opportunities.

Recall that during the summer of 1988, stocks such as General Mills and Sara Lee—or any company that used grain as a raw material —were brought down because of the higher grain prices that the drought produced. If that created the impression that food companies don't like bad weather, I am sorry. Companies that use *vegetables* as a raw material (Heinz, Campbell) can be perfectly happy with a bad crop.

Here's how it works: Prior to the actual planting season, these companies agree to purchase a specified amount of product—tomatoes, potatoes, green beans, whatever—at a specified price. Already, this means that their costs are independent of the harvest, unlike the situation we saw for grain-using companies. (Grains can be stored; vegetables cannot.) Theoretically, this independence is a good thing. However, it turns out that overly abundant harvests can work to these companies' competitive disadvantage.

The competition comes in the form of so-called private-label producers—the people that make "generic" or store-brand merchandise. Suppose that the major brand-name producers have contracted out for 1 million pounds of tomatoes, and the harvest is well above that—at, say, 1.2 million pounds. This leaves farmers with 200,000 pounds to get rid of, which allows the private-label manufacturers to move in and negotiate a lower price than the majors contracted for in the first place. Obviously, this enables the private-label people to sell their ketchup, or whatever, much more cheaply. The ultimate result is that the brand-name makers have to keep their prices down, for fear of losing market share.

This possibility is more than theoretical. Already, the nineties have seen several such plentiful harvests, and the private-label business has flourished. Meanwhile, Heinz has at times been stymied; the company's 1993 earnings of $2.04 per share were only 7 percent higher than its 1990 earnings of $1.90 per share. The stock traded at $36 in 1990; three years later, it was available at the same price.

Of course, to hear the media talk, the entire private-label success story was attributable to a consumer trend away from high-priced brand-name merchandise. What no one mentions is that, at least for these food categories, the private-label producers happened to have enjoyed a weather-related advantage—one that could easily go the other way.

The potential attractiveness of bad weather is even greater for companies that *sell* the food in question (as opposed to the Heinzes and Campbells of the world, to whom the foods represent a raw material). There is a good reason why bad weather can help the bottom line of food sellers: *What they lose in volume they more than make up for in price.* If you're looking for the single most important theme in weather-based food-stock investing, well, you've just found it.

In the banana industry, for example, the relevant locale would be Central America, where the bulk of the crop is grown, and bad weather would be defined as rain, which bananas hate. When conditions are unusually damp, the bananas are prone to acquire a fungus infection (the dreaded black sigatoka disease) and become unmarketable. When the resulting short supply shows up in the form of higher banana prices, it's bullish for Chiquita Brands, even if they have to deal with tons of ugly, black, rotten bananas in the process.

Blowdowns can also be a blessing in disguise for banana growers. In 1983, winds took down enough of the crop to make banana prices soar, creating a sharp reversal in these companies' fortunes. Chiquita (then United Brands), which had omitted its dividend in late 1982 in an effort to cut costs, earned over $2.50 per share in 1983, and the stock moved from $7 to $28. Shares of Castle & Cooke (Dole) rose from $7 to $19 during the same period.

In 1991, Costa Rica and Panama experienced an earthquake that not only damaged banana crops but also uprooted rail lines that would bring the crops to market. The resulting strong pricing enabled Chiquita to post record earnings of $128 million; its stock price doubled between mid-1991 and the end of the year, reaching an all-time high of $50 per share.

The theme of higher prices through scarcity is by no means restricted to bananas. For example, ConAgra, based in Omaha, is one of the nation's biggest and most diversified food/agribusiness companies. Successful, too: Between 1975 and 1993, its stock appreciated 144-fold, buoyed by a string of well-planned acquisitions. But a little-known fact is that the single biggest surge in ConAgra stock over that entire period was the result of lousy weather, not corporate dexterity.

The year was 1980, and all you need to know about the weather was that the summer was oppressively hot. As a result, chickens didn't eat, and their mortality rates grew. At ConAgra, poultry volumes were down (a negative), but prices were up sharply (a positive that more than compensated). Best of all—at least according to the twisted logic at hand—the chicken shortage wasn't just a three-month circumstance. The hot summer temperatures also caused fertility problems in

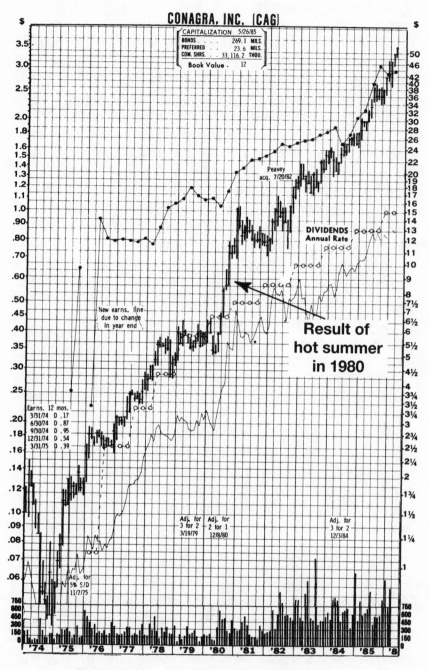

Fig. 5 CONAGRA CHART (Courtesy of Securities Research Co.)

adult chickens, which made for a lingering short supply. The sustained higher chicken prices caused ConAgra's earnings to surge a surprising 25 percent for the year. The stock, whose steep discount reflected the company's supposedly dreary earnings prospects, *tripled* in the last nine months of 1980. The sharp upward spike you see in the middle of ConAgra's long-term stock chart is that very move.

Such a move is certainly something to aspire to, but it comes with a warning. Although many of yesterday's weather plays are terrific models for what *might* happen, they needn't literally repeat themselves. Some situations that look like replay candidates differ from the model in one or more key respects, and investors should think twice before buying shares.

One such trap occurred in the beef industry in early 1993. Harsh winter weather slowed the development of calves on outside feed lots: Not only was it difficult to feed the cattle in the first place, but more of their energy was spent combating the cold, which made it difficult for them to gain weight. In turn, this slow development reduced supplies and raised cattle prices in the near term. ConAgra happens to be a major beef processor: Do you buy its shares again?

No—because a simple detail made this situation the exact opposite of 1980. What made the 1980 surge possible was the *vertical integration* of the chicken business, meaning that ConAgra owned its chickens and, therefore, benefited from higher prices. With beef, the situation is just the opposite. Beef processors generally have to buy their beef from someone else, which means that if weather conditions raise the price of beef, earnings will turn down, not up. In 1993, higher beef (and pork) prices contributed to a 25 percent decline in ConAgra shares during the first quarter of the year.

Knowledge of details could also have saved food-stock investors in 1992. That year, there was a lot of the cool, wet weather that banana companies are supposed to love—because it produces a scarcity of bananas and hence higher banana prices. Yet 1992 was the worst year in Chiquita's history. What gives?

The problem was too much of a good thing. Black sigatoka disease ruined some 25 to 30 percent of the crop, well beyond the range of prior experience. And much of the fruit was already en route to market when it became damaged; the issue was therefore not a shortage of bananas but rather a glut of spoiled ones. (Meanwhile, there were ample crops of competing fruits.)

In addition, the European Economic Community was in the process of setting quotas for banana producers, causing many growers to overproduce in the hope that the quotas would merely return them to a normal level. That hope may sound fanciful, but not only did so-called ACP producers (Africa, Caribbean, Pacific) end up receiving proportionately more generous quotas than Chiquita, their overproduction forced Chiquita to endure the double whammy of rotten bananas *and* poor prices for those they did sell. In this worst of all worlds, the company's earnings dropped from $2.52 per share in 1991 to a $3.10 per share *loss* in 1992. Chiquita stock fell from its high of $50 to below $15, and continued to flounder there for the next two years.

Some investors look at a complicated example like Chiquita and conclude that weather shouldn't be heeded unless it is certifiably the number-one influence on a company's earnings and stock price. But weather can (or should!) play a decisive investment role even when much more important events are taking place. That was true in 1990, when an enormous investment opportunity developed behind the scenes.

That summer, the Dow Jones Industrial Average reached 2999.75, a level that looked tantalizing but was in fact quite precarious. In late July, Saddam Hussein began lining up tanks at the Kuwait border. Back home, a recession was beginning, though we didn't realize it quite yet. By the end of the year, the country was on the verge of war and no one could argue with the fact that a recession was under way. The Dow had dropped below 2400.

Two leading chemical companies, Monsanto and American Cyanamid, were hit especially hard. If you want to be cruel enough to count from the absolute high to the absolute low, they declined 35 percent and 32 percent, respectively, during the year, quite a bit worse than the Dow's already severe high-to-low drop of 20 percent. Of course, given what can happen to economically sensitive stocks during recessions, the underperformance didn't seem to require any additional explanation.

Were the stocks buys at these lower levels? In retrospect, yes, but if you waited for the recession to officially end, you would have missed the rebound. Knowing the weather details made it much easier to get back in. Let's reexamine the story from a weather perspective.

In the summer of 1990, far away from the headlines, the herbicide business experienced a massive swing in fortunes. Monsanto's Roundup is the world's best-selling herbicide and the single most profitable product in the company's history. It is a "nonselective" herbicide, meaning that it kills just about anything green that it touches. But its sales are also weather-sensitive. If conditions are too dry, not only will demand be down because of fewer weeds, but Roundup's efficacy will be reduced, in that it tends to work better on healthier weeds.

In 1990, drought conditions in California and Europe created one of the worst years on record for Roundup. Operating earnings at Monsanto's entire agricultural division dropped 25 percent, from $432 million in 1989 to $327 million in 1990. It was also a difficult year for American Cyanamid and its Pursuit and Scepter brands (herbicides tend to have creative names). Cyanamid's problem was the wettest season in fifty years in the grain states (Iowa, Kansas, Illinois, Indiana, et cetera). With many farmers unable to get into the fields at all, planted acreage was down for the year, and so were Cyanamid's agricultural earnings. As the year played out, Monsanto stock fell from $60 to $39, and Cyanamid from $61 to $42.

It is of course absurd to suggest that the weather alone made the stocks decline; hundreds of securities took it on the chin in the horrendous macroeconomic climate of late 1990. However, for these two companies in particular, the weather made for downbeat sales and earnings reports at a time when the market was in no mood to shrug the whole thing off. That combination suggested the market had overreacted on the downside—your cue to get back in.

Admittedly, it took a fair amount of fortitude to invest in *anything* that particular year, given that war was in the air and the recession seemed bottomless. And perhaps focusing on the weather at that time would have seemed unpatriotic as well as economically ignorant. Yet the onetime character of these two companies' herbicide problems gave the stocks a built-in rebound potential.

As it happened, the market rallied strongly amid the Persian Gulf euphoria in 1991, finally piercing the 3000 level in April. No one could have predicted the exact timing of the market's recovery, but the fact remains that between the 1990 low and the 1991 high, herbicide makers easily outperformed the market: American Cyanamid gained 64 percent, while Monsanto doubled.

CORPORATE MISTAKES THAT CAN HURT YOUR PORTFOLIO

Has it occurred to you that something is missing? Until now, we have looked at various weather events with an eye to how *the market* is reacting. Meanwhile, *companies* are reacting to the same weather. In many cases, their responses are what an investor should be paying attention to, because the wrong response can be an automatic sell signal.

Chubb's ill-fated rain insurance scheme during the 1988 drought was the most glaring corporate weather mistake we have encountered so far, but the mistakes we're really interested in are of a different breed. Typically, the worst mistakes are made in good times, not bad: *When management behaves as if past beneficial weather will repeat itself, it makes the company extremely vulnerable.*

For example, in the early eighties, a Florida-based company called American Agronomics harbored ambitions of becoming a giant in the orange juice business: Why be a mere supplier when you can process and sell the goods to consumers yourself? The opportunities seemed big enough to withstand a bloating of the cost structure—new packaging facilities, corporate jet, et cetera.

All of which made for a thunderous fall from glory in the mid-eighties, when a series of winter freezes invaded Florida groves previously thought to be out of harm's way. The result was a massive shift in orange production to Brazil, and with it a 50 percent decline in juice prices. Admittedly, none of the publicly owned domestic orange grove companies—including such exotically named entities as Alico and Consolidated Tomoka—has had an easy time of it since the freezes set in. But at least these companies are still afloat. As for Agronomics, an investor did well to recognize that the company's excesses gave it no margin for error when the harsh weather arrived. The owners were eventually forced to sell out in distress.

Now for the classic example of corporate mismanagement that investors ought to find a place for in their memory banks: The company in question is Toro, based in Minneapolis. Here's how a sell signal emerged from the best of times.

Looking at the long history of the Toro company, it's hard to believe that *winter* weather almost did it in. Toro began operating in 1914 as a lawn mower manufacturer, and for many years specialized in equipment for golf course care. Obviously those lines of business prosper only in the summer, and sometime in the fifties the company responded to the seasonality problem by branching off into snow-thrower production. For twenty-plus years, snowthrowers were a perfect complement to Toro's product line, a small, niche business requiring little in the way of marketing or innovation. Then came the fateful winters of 1978 and 1979, when heavy snowfalls nationwide gave Toro the opportunity of the century—but almost killed the company.

Without question, the weather was anomalous. In Boston, where I live, the blizzard of '78 remains the storm against which all others are measured. Mile after mile of cars became stranded along the beltway we call Route 128, having literally been stopped in place because of the snow. Then-governor Michael Dukakis declared a snow emergency, grounding every vehicle that wasn't a fire engine, an ambulance, or part of the cleanup operation. Plows pushed snow to levels of eight to ten feet along many major roads. Nothing like it has happened since; even the major storm of March 1993 pales by comparison.

Within this anomaly, industrywide snowthrower sales surged as never before, moving from $60 million in 1977 to $94 million in 1978 to $250 million in 1979. (The 1978–79 winter was rough in its own right, and people throughout the northern part of the country were determined not to shovel the way they had in 1978.) At those levels, Toro's snowthrower sales exceeded the company's entire sales of just ten years before. Earnings tripled in two years, from $1.07 per share in 1977 to $3.22 per share in 1979, and Wall Street seemed to approve: Toro stock flew from $6 per share in 1977 to $30 per share in early 1979.

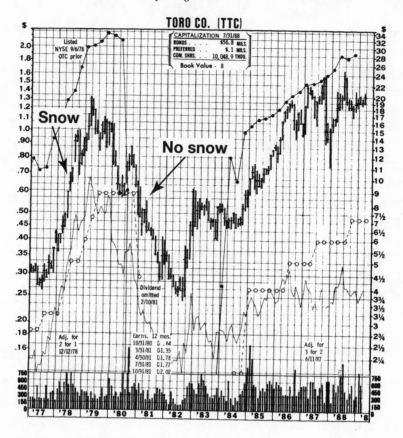

Fig. 6 Toro chart (Courtesy of Securities Research Co.)

So far, so good, but trouble was around the corner. Lured by the snowthrower surge—even though a second Ice Age would have been required to sustain it—Toro bought a new office building and hired a swarm of new middle managers; in other words, the profit gains masked some reckless additions to the company's overhead. That in itself needn't have been a tragedy, but when Toro aggressively built up inventories for the following winter, licking its chops at the thought of another bonanza, the company had set the stage for its own undoing. For the investor, it was time to step back and ask, "What if it doesn't snow?"

The correct response was to sell. Or, for those who like the idea of profiting from a stock's decline, you could have sold Toro stock short, because it was a disaster waiting to happen. (I won't go into detail about the mechanics of short selling, but the process involves selling shares you have in essence borrowed from your broker; once you do that, you're rooting for the stock to fall, in hopes of buying the shares back—or "covering" your position—at a lower price.)

The winter of 1979–80 was the winter that wasn't: no snow for skiing, no snow for snowballs, no snow to be hurled off driveways. The United States Small Business Administration even offered low-interest loans to dozens of struggling ski-related businesses in New England and the Midwest. The impact on Toro was nothing short of disastrous. Snowthrower sales plummeted from $130 million to $40 million in a single year. By February, the company resorted to rebates to move the merchandise, but it was too little, too late. Said analyst Frank Rolfes of Minneapolis brokerage Dain, Bosworth, "Toro and all its distributors choked on unsold snowthrowers."

Earnings dropped from the 1979 peak of $3.22 per share to just $0.90 per share in 1980 and a loss of $2.64 per share in 1981. The stock dropped from $30 in early 1979 to just $5 by 1982. Over a thousand employees, some 25 percent of Toro's workforce, had to be laid off or let go. Among those losing their jobs were company chairman David McLaughlin and president John Cantu.

It is easy to say that management was being greedy, but greed was also evident at the dealer level—so much so that management couldn't see its own. What the company did see was that dealers were pressuring them to produce more, and they couldn't resist. Said chairman McLaughlin in *Business Week,* "We could have said no, but when you're the market leader, that's hard to do unless you want to open the door to competition." Added John Cantu, "One of the cardinal sins is to give away market share."

In other words, whether Toro overproduced or not, dealers would have stocked too much merchandise for the winter of 1980. Unfortunately, by caving in to dealer pressure, Toro's management simply insured that the unsold merchandise would be theirs. Adding insult to injury was the fact that dealers, having exhausted their inventory dollars on these unsold snowthrowers, had to scale back on Toro lawn mowers when summer rolled around.

One of the most important lessons of the Toro debacle is how difficult it is for a typical shareholder to assess the quality of corporate management. In an interview with *Forbes* in November 1978, Toro chairman McLaughlin looked altogether rational as he emphasized the importance of the company's outdoor line: "The grass will normally grow," he said, "but it doesn't have to snow." Yet within a year, McLaughlin's company acted as if the snow would never stop.

There is a final piece to the Toro puzzle. Why didn't investors see the folly of all this earlier? Why did Toro stock get so high in the first place?

There are a couple of explanations. First of all, many investors played along for the simple reason that success begets success; when a company increases earnings the way Toro did, it's human nature to assume "they must be doing something right"—and, in a very near-term sense, they were.

Another reason the risks may not have been appreciated was that Toro shares didn't seem expensively valued—at least not by conventional measures. It is not unusual for the stock of a fast-growing company to be valued at twenty or even thirty times its earnings per share; in Toro's case, however, even at its absolute peak of $30, the stock was trading for less than ten times what the company actually earned in 1979 ($3.22 per share). This ratio of stock price to earnings, called the price/earnings ratio, or P/E, is the simplest gauge of investor sentiment toward a particular company. A high P/E indicates that Wall Street is excited about the company's future earnings prospects, whereas a low P/E indicates that Wall Street understands that the earnings gains may be temporary.

Given Toro's low multiple, investors may have deluded themselves into thinking that the stock market was already well prepared for a weather reversal. But (let me pause here for emphasis) *when a company's fundamentals totally fall apart, a low P/E isn't going to save you.* In many cases—Toro's included—earnings can disappear altogether. And so can the would-be protection of a low P/E.

I don't mean to pick on Toro. It's a great company, and it has certainly learned its lesson. The more important point is that other corporate managements can and will fall into the same trap. Remember the sequence: the right kind of weather, financial success, excessive inventories, and, finally, the wrong kind of weather. When the wrong weather hits, run for cover.

HURRICANES AND INSURANCE STOCKS: A PERPLEXING CASE

Thus far we have had a pretty good success rate in extracting patterns from various weather events, but we're about to meet our match. Strange as it seems, it is almost impossible to give a simple answer to the question "What do hurricanes do to insurance stocks?" But we can try.

What everyone agrees on is this: Hurricanes have the potential to cause damage, this damage leads to insurance claims, and these claims can cost insurance companies a lot of money. In recent years, however, the stock market has reacted to different storms in completely different ways. Two hurricanes from the eighties shed light on the bizarre riddle of insurance-stock psychology.

The "logical" storm, if you want to call it that, was 1985's Hurricane Gloria. The investment logic, which began as the storm moved its way up the East Coast, was that Gloria might have enough steam to reach the metropolitan Northeast and therefore could be unusually destructive. On these fears (at some point, panic replaced logic), insurance stocks started to lose ground. Aetna, for example, dropped from $45 to $43 in a couple of trading sessions—the drop would have been worse, except that fear about Gloria's arrival in New York caused the New York Stock Exchange to shut down altogether!

From my personal perspective, Gloria *was* a destructive storm; it dropped a maple tree on my house at an angle that would have made Pythagoras squirm. Relative to the entire metropolitan Northeast, however, Gloria was a flat-out dud, meaning that the before-the-fact damage estimates were way too high. The stock market quickly understood that its prior panic was misplaced. Not only did Aetna stock immediately make up the couple of points it lost, it continued on to the mid-60s by early 1986 on the basis of otherwise favorable industry trends. In other words, within the bull market for insurance stocks of 1984–86, Gloria provided a rare pullback buying opportunity.

In the 1986–87 period, however, the fundamental outlook for the insurance industry took a very bad turn. Insurance companies, in their quest to write more policies (and thereby get their hands on more money to invest in the then-roaring bond market), entered into what turned out to be an enduring price war. Policy underwriting became widely unprofitable—meaning that insurers' profits were reduced to whatever returns were available from the financial markets, if that. The result was a sharp decline in industry profitability and a multiyear bear market in insurance stocks. The only rallies within this bear market came at times when investors had reason to believe that the price wars might be coming to an end.

This "rally rationale" sounds logical enough, but it has a strange corollary. Ever since investors have focused on the underwriting cycle —and when it might take a turn for the better—damaging hurricanes have been seen as a *positive* for insurance stocks.

Hurricane Hugo was a perfect case in point. Arriving in September 1989, Hugo was at that time the most frightful storm of the century. It racked up damages in excess of $4 billion, over $2 billion of that in South Carolina alone. Yet insurance stocks rose ghoulishly during the week of Hugo's assault, with many attaining postcrash highs: Investors were clearly hoping that Hugo-related losses would force insurers to reconsider their self-destructive price wars.

It didn't work out that way. Competition remained fierce, and profitability at virtually all the major multiline insurers remained stuck in a downtrend. When the recession hit in the fall of 1990, the once-staid insurance shares were among the major casualties. Aetna, which had pierced the $60 barrier in the Hugo rally of 1989, fell to under $30 per share. CIGNA dropped from $65 to $34. And Travelers, which cut its dividend by 30 percent as losses mounted in 1990, saw its shares plummet from $44 all the way down to $12.

PUTTING IT ALL TOGETHER: WEATHER INVESTING IN REAL LIFE

When writing about investing, you have the luxury of picking examples from different years to support different parts of your strategy. The actual practice of investing isn't as accommodating. Everything happens at once, and you never know which past example you might have to draw upon.

I began putting weather-based investing to the test in 1992, one year after developing the basic principles. Even though no two stock market situations are ever precisely alike—meaning that you always have to be on the lookout for new wrinkles—I was surprised by the eerie precision with which some past examples seemed to repeat themselves. An even bigger surprise was that the application of these principles is a constant process; there is almost no downtime. What follows are the highlights from two years of real-time weather-based investing.

The Summer of 1992: The Search for Losers

The summer of 1992 confirmed that the weather doesn't have to be an outright disaster for the stock market to feel its effects. In a way, it's lucky that I developed most of my weather strategies just before 1992 rolled around—if I hadn't had weather on the brain, I might not have been steered away from some stocks that turned out to be big losers.

Common sense suggests that losers are most likely to be spawned by seasons that don't fulfill their usual promise, as in a warm winter that ruins the ski business or a cool summer that ruins the beach resort business. But does anyone remember the cold summer of 1992? Probably not. Yet the summer's effects were national, they were multi-industry in character, and they hit the stock market in dozens of ways—most of them bad.

How cold was it? As *The Wall Street Journal* reported in early August, when violinist Itzhak Perlman arrived for an outdoor concert in Chicago, space heaters had to be brought out to keep his fingers warm. The mean temperature in Chicago for the month of July was a mere 69 degrees, one of the coldest on record. The summer was also wet. If you had to concoct a summer that was the opposite of the 1988 drought, 1992 was the one. Figuring out what companies were particularly vulnerable became the name of the game.

Admittedly, it is hard to make money just by avoiding stocks, but it always helps to know that some otherwise good companies are about to run into a head wind—after all, these are stocks you may already own. And for those who thrive on action rather than avoidance, there is always the hope that some short-sale candidates will emerge.

We will focus on two specific effects of the cold, wet weather. The first effect was that people used less air-conditioning, and the second was that people didn't need to quench their thirst as often. With those simple truths as a starting point, a whole lot of stock market losers turned up.

AIR-CONDITIONING.   We have seen before that when a company's earnings decline from one year to the next, its stock seldom reacts favorably. With that in mind, the cool weather of 1992 made electric utility stocks no place to be.

From the standpoint of an electric utility analyst, weather was more important in 1992 than it ever had been, because many of the industry's headline issues had basically gone away. The nuclear controversy was a thing of the past, new plant construction was all but dead, and applications for rate increases were few and far between. Weather therefore became an unusually potent swing factor for utilities' earnings because of its effect on consumer demand.

That summer, cooling degree days (utility talk for the level of air-conditioning use) were far below normal. As a result, industry earnings were down as much as 10 to 15 percent for the summer quarter alone. Iowa-Illinois Gas & Electric, to pick on one, saw its annual earnings fall from $1.86 per share in 1991 to $1.45 per share in 1992, and the company attributed $0.17 of the decline to the weather—a huge number for a utility company.

Utilities such as Northern States Power and Baltimore Gas & Electric were also hit hard because of their concentration on residential business, but those names might as well have been drawn from a hat. The cool weather also affected American Electric Power, Philadelphia Electric, Potomac Electric, and countless others, all the way down to the Carolinas and even as far west as Texas.

This does not mean that investors lost their shirts, because utility stocks are yield-oriented investments; as long as dividends aren't threatened, small fluctuations in earnings tend not to rock utility stocks. In fact, American Electric Power, Northern States Power, Centerior Energy, and many others continued their high dividend payouts even though weather-related losses temporarily put the payout ratio near or even above 100 percent. In other words, for that particular year, these utilities paid out in dividends as much as or more than they earned. These sustained payouts kept the stock prices up, and most utility stock charts were flat as a pancake for the year.

However, you couldn't take stability for granted. When Nevada-based Sierra Pacific Resources cut its dividend in July, the company specifically cited weather as a factor. Analysts were stunned. The basic assumption on Wall Street had been that the companies would grin and bear it until conditions improved, rather than capitulate in the face of one difficult year. Following the cut, Sierra Pacific shares quickly tumbled 33 percent.

Another story of haplessness within the utility sector in 1992 was Pacificorp. Located in Portland, Oregon, Pacificorp owns both Pacific Gas & Electric and Utah Power and Light. That year, the company faced at least a double whammy. Not only was air-conditioning demand down, but the company was also hurt by the ongoing difficulties in the hydro business (even though the main culprit, the longstanding drought in the region, ended that year).

Even diversification efforts went sour that summer. Pacificorp had made a huge investment in NERCO—a bunch of oil and gas properties —only to see natural gas prices plummet because the cool summer reduced air-conditioning demand. Although Pacificorp later announced the divestiture of NERCO, the anticipated reduction in the asset base caused by the sale (they had overpaid in the first place) prompted the company to cut its dividend by 30 percent in early 1993. The stock, which had traded above $25 in early 1992, was down to $17 a year later—a decline of 32 percent.

Even bigger casualties of the air-conditioning fallout could be found outside the utility industry. One was an obscure company named L. E. Myers, an Illinois-based company that does contracting work for electric utilities. The company started out 1992 full of optimism, having posted strong earnings numbers for 1991 and having just inked a couple of sizable contracts. As 1992 began, the stock doubled in two months, flying from $12½ to $25. It seemed too good to be true. It was.

Even before the summer began, Myers was hurt by 1992's mild winter. Ordinarily, winter storms create a good deal of business because they bring down power lines—and Myers gets to put the lines back up. In a storm-free year, though, the lines stay put without My-

MYERS L E CO GROUP (MYR)

Expectations high

Until cold summer

Fig. 7 L. E. MYERS CHART (Courtesy of Securities Research Co.)

ers's help, and that's what happened in early 1992. The lower-than-expected revenues pushed the stock down from $25 to under $20 by midsummer.

At that point, I was tempted to view Myers as a second-leg rebound candidate, the likes of which we examined during the 1988 drought. However, the cold summer made a rebound next to impossible, because the difficult earnings environment for utilities made the entire industry cut back on its capital spending plans, which translated into lost business for L. E. Myers. Whereas earnings estimates for Myers had run as high as $1.50 per share early in the year, actual earnings came in at $1.37. The stock finished the year at $18 per share, down more than 40 percent from its February high. Moral: When an industry struggles, its suppliers may struggle even more.

A more familiar name that had a lousy 1992 was Fedders. If it seems self-evident that a manufacturer of room air conditioners would be one of the biggest casualties of the cool summer, good, you've made progress. Before this chapter started, you might have thought that the stock market wouldn't care about one lousy summer, and now you know it does. Better still, there was money to be made as Fedders shares plummeted 50 percent between June and September, because the stock fit our short-sale model perfectly.

If you remember the Toro snowthrower story, you can see that history truly does repeat itself (which is precisely why these anecdotes from the past are so valuable). As with Toro, Fedders had been coming off a period of exceedingly favorable weather. The summers of 1988 and 1989 had been blistering hot, and the company's sales jumped from $128 million in 1987 to $367 million in 1989. Meanwhile, the stock quadrupled. As weather-savvy investors, we are officially skeptical.

The hidden problem was that the extra capacity that Fedders had acquired to meet the higher demand, including the purchase of competitor Emerson Quiet Kool, was a questionable move despite its early success. Not only was the industry shifting increasingly from room air conditioners toward central air-conditioning, but Fedders was now more than ever at the mercy of the weather.

In 1990, there was a foreshadowing of sorts. Sales dropped to $240 million—a 33 percent decline in one year—and profits vanished altogether. The stock declined from a peak of $17 all the way down to $5 as the recession hit later in the year. The sales decline continued in 1991 despite a warm summer—another warning sign. (Advantageous weather, success, excess capacity, disadvantageous weather. Sound familiar?) The stock had inched back up to $10 by early 1992, making it more vulnerable than ever.

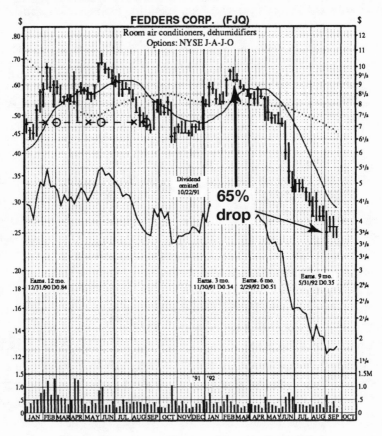

Fig. 8 FEDDERS CHART (Courtesy of Securities Research Co.)

There are no mysteries to the rest of the story. Once the cool weather hit, it was clear that things would get worse before they got better—the perfect environment for the short seller. In response to the unfortunate summer, Fedders closed two of the facilities obtained in the Emerson acquisition, and also sold its Rotorex compressor subsidiary. These were important indications that management was intent on streamlining, but the damage had already been done. The stock, which had been around $7 in June, dropped to a low of $3½ by September and remained stuck in a limited trading range for the next two years.

BEVERAGES.   Going from air-conditioning to beverages is more logical than it might seem, and I'm happy to report that I'm not the only one to make the connection. My favorite connection between the two industries took place midway through the summer of 1992, at UBS Securities in New York. There, the firm's utility analyst was on the "squawk box" (an in-house communication to salespeople), and she mentioned for the umpteenth time that season how weather was affecting her industry. As she talked, the firm's beverage analyst came to an inevitable conclusion: Sales estimates for Gatorade (a subsidiary of Quaker Oats) would have to come down.

It was true. That year, Gatorade, which had been one of Quaker's prime growth properties, struggled to match the sales levels of the year before. Its problems were shared by the entire beverage industry. Focusing on the summer alone, soft-drink consumption declined to the tune of about 4 percent. For the full year, consumption was up, but by only 1 percent, compared with consistent growth in the 3 percent range in previous years. That's a big, big difference.

Inevitably, not all companies were affected equally, but all you needed were a few simple details to help you isolate the real losers. Coke and Pepsi were cushioned by their exposure to international markets and to other businesses. Which did better? Consider that the soft-drink business accounts for just 35 percent of Pepsi's net income, compared to 96 percent at Coke. Wall Street isn't above simple logic: While PepsiCo shares rose 20 percent for the year, shares of Coca-Cola gained just 4 percent.

Location played a crucial role in determining which beverage stocks to be wary of—as usual, the less geographically diversified the company, the greater the risks. Root beer leader A&W Brands, whose primary market is the Midwest, was hurt disproportionately by the cool weather there, and its stock dropped 18 percent for the year.

Beer makers also had a geographical problem. For companies such as Anheuser-Busch and Adolph Coors, the United States market is virtually their entire market. Busch in particular had been chided by

Wall Street for many years for its timidity about entering the international marketplace, and in 1992 this weakness showed. The company was already being squeezed by cheaper brands such as Heileman and Stroh's, and the price wars were only made worse by the lower volumes resulting from the cool temperatures. Busch shares started the year north of $60 but were pushed down to the $52 level by the combination of these effects.

Bottling companies were another casualty in 1992. Shares of Whitman, the country's largest Pepsi-Cola bottler, managed a 10 percent gain that year, but only because of diversification (half of Whitman's earnings come from Midas Muffler and Hussman Corporation, which had up years in 1992). Contrast that with Coca-Cola Enterprises, a pure play in bottling, whose shares fell 20 percent for the year.

And when soft drinks aren't selling, the demand for fructose syrup isn't as great (struggling industry, struggling suppliers—a familiar pattern). Archer Daniels Midland, the premier company in the fructose market, saw its stock underperform throughout the summer. Likewise for American Fructose, whose shares declined from $25 in March to under $20 by September, at which time its parent company, American Maize Products, stopped the slide by announcing it would buy out the shares of the company it did not already own.

All this is bad, but the biggest casualty among beverage companies fared much, much worse. The company: Clearly Canadian Beverages of Vancouver, British Columbia, whose shares declined 70 percent between March and December of 1992. Following a pattern that we've now seen many times, Clearly Canadian's difficulties in 1992 were in large part tied to the company's phenomenal success in prior years.

Between 1987 and 1991, Clearly Canadian's revenues exploded, growing from just $5 million to $127 million. The company was the leader in the "New Age" soft-drink category, as distinguished from conventional sodas. The combination of a clear drink, pathbreaking fruit flavors, and attractive packaging enabled the company to charge a decidedly premium price.

Business was booming right up until the summer of 1992. Revenues for the first quarter were $40 million, compared to just $13 million in 1991; second-quarter revenues were $61 million versus $26 million. The stock was at $25 per share, up eightfold from its levels of early 1991. However, when the cool nonsummer reared its ugly head, all of these numbers would reverse their field. A short sale was brewing in the Toro and Fedders tradition.

What investors had to understand was that in 1991, Clearly Canadian's only problem was a lack of production capacity. The company responded by adding capacity—and by making sure that the company's distributors were heavily loaded up on inventory as the 1992 summer season began. The move seemed to make sense at the time, but they hadn't counted on the lousy weather.

Like A&W and Anheuser-Busch, Clearly Canadian was at the mercy of the pitifully weak North American market in 1992. As the nonsummer progressed and sales stalled, the stock steadily lost ground, falling from $25 to $14 by September.

At that point, it would have been tempting to apply the second-leg rebound theory and buy the stock—on the grounds that the summer was over and, therefore, so was the bad news. But other clues suggested that the downside was only beginning.

One vital accounting detail was that the company booked its revenues at the point of the sale to the distributor, not the consumer. The slowdown in demand during the seasonally strongest months meant that distributors would still be working off their own inventories well after summer was over, resulting in negligible new revenues for Clearly Canadian. And so it was: With reorders far below normal, third-quarter revenues declined from $47 million in 1991 to $38 million in 1992. The fourth quarter was even worse, as revenues dropped from $41 million to just $16 million. The stock was under $8 by the end of the year.

Just to complete the story, let me say that weather wasn't the only problem. On top of the seasonality issues, investor psychology concerning Clearly Canadian had turned negative because competition was on its way. Crystal Pepsi and Tab Clear, for all their faults, came first; then came the announcement of Coca-Cola's Nordic Mist line, a blatant knockoff of Clearly Canadian. These alternative products revealed Clearly Canadian's fatal flaw: Their products cost too damn much. Even if the brand name retained its cachet, consumers had plenty of lower-priced alternatives—a good reason to leave the stock alone. By early 1995, Clearly Canadian was trading for under $2 per share.

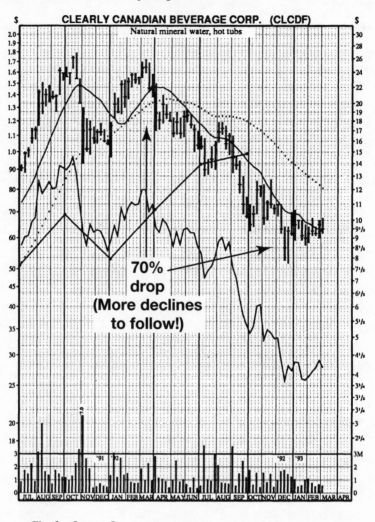

Fig. 9 CLEARLY CANADIAN CHART (Courtesy of Securities Research Co.)

Cranberries

In the fall of 1992, an investor would have been well advised to scour the stocks that had fallen that summer in search of rebound candidates —in other words, second-leg winners. Already, we've ruled out Clearly Canadian. But what about Anheuser-Busch, Sierra Pacific Resources, or Pacificorp? Well, there was a much better story than any of those. It was a Wisconsin-based outfit called Northland Cranberries.

It was a bit surprising to find any downtrodden stocks from the agriculture sector in 1992, because the damp conditions made virtually everything grow in abundance. The cranberry was an exception. It seems that cranberries, with their long gestation period, require plenty of sunlight to reach their proper size. They didn't get nearly enough sun in 1992, and the crop stunk.

Otherwise the Northland investment story looked great. In 1992, the company was in the process of splitting off from the vaunted Ocean Spray cooperative, which dominates cranberries the way OPEC dominates crude oil. The motivations behind the split were several-fold. First of all, as part of the cooperative, Northland never knew what its earnings for a given year would be until Ocean Spray's results were known, a process that could keep everyone guessing for months; as a freestanding supplier with contracts to several independent juice makers, Northland's earnings visibility was destined to improve. Furthermore, earnings themselves were destined to improve, given the prevailing world cranberry shortage (it was news to me, too). Specifically, by entering the private-label market for fresh cranberries, Northland could realize much higher prices for its crops than ever before.

However, not only was Wisconsin wet and cold that summer, but the state also experienced a series of hailstorms in the fall, during the critical "sizing" period for cranberries. Many berries were knocked off their bushes and couldn't be harvested. The bottom line was a crop more than 20 percent below expectations. As investors became aware of this disappointment, the stock dropped from $13 to $10. So do you bail out or do you buy more?

You buy more, of course, on the grounds that things couldn't get worse. Sure enough, by early 1993, the shares were back above the $13 level, which is all you can really ask of a near-term rebound.

As it happened, Northland shares proceeded on a prolonged roller-coaster ride, with weather often to blame for short-term disappointments. The cold, wet weather of 1992—and 1993, which wasn't all that much better—not only affected the crops of those years, it also lengthened the maturing process for much of Northland's new planting, meaning that the company's crop yields were affected through 1994. And although initial investor enthusiasm for the 1994 crop pushed the stock north of $20, those gains came back when a September heat wave caused berries earmarked for the fresh fruit market to ripen prematurely, meaning that an above-average portion of the crop spoiled during the cold storage period that ordinarily keeps berries fresh and ready for the prime Thanksgiving buying season.

Suffice it to say that this stock has caused me both joy and aggravation over the years. The moral: You should be wary about paying up for a stock with this much weather sensitivity. But in Northland's case, the saving grace is that when (if) that banner crop finally arrives, the earnings should get a very favorable reception from Wall Street.

Hurricane Andrew

Hurricane Andrew, history's most devastating storm, arrived in late August 1992, and you could have filled a whole portfolio with its effects. As we've come to expect, the first-leg winners included companies that experienced increased demand following the Andrew disaster.

If it makes you uncomfortable to view the Andrew tragedy with an eye toward making money, at least there was an ethically sound midpoint. One of the items most in demand was housing, and you could hardly begrudge the housing industry its gains. With the storm's homeless total somewhere in five figures, companies with a sales presence in the affected areas, including Clayton Homes and Oakwood Homes, were the biggest beneficiaries. Clayton shares rose from $16 to $25 between September 1992 and March 1993; Oakwood rose from $13 to $23. An even bigger beneficiary was Nobility Homes, a long-standing laggard that moved from $2 all the way up to $8. Nobility was the prime beneficiary of the well-publicized distress of the Homestead area.

Even Lennar, a homebuilder that was the center of a class action suit because of the ease with which Andrew pried the roofs off its homes, wasn't as villainous as first believed. The stock market, fearful of a multimillion-dollar liability, ratcheted Lennar shares down from $30 to $20 immediately following the storm. However, given that some 90 percent of power lines were also down in South Dade—lines that were governed by even stricter building standards—the case

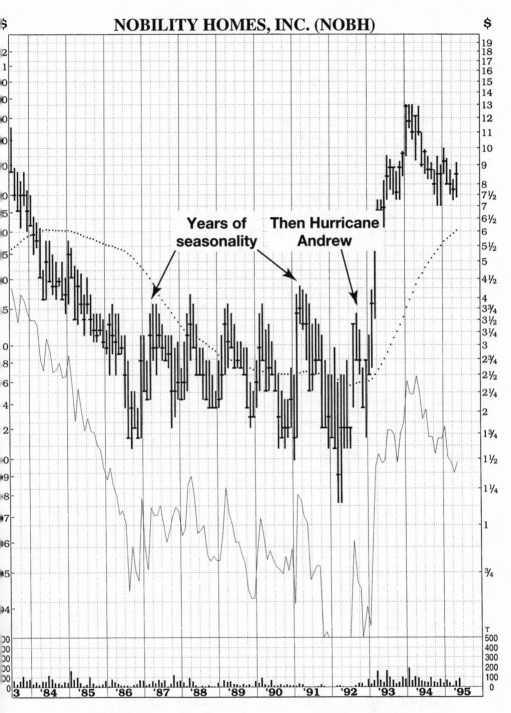

NOBILITY HOMES, INC. (NOBH)

Years of seasonality

Then Hurricane Andrew

Fig. 10 NOBILITY HOMES CHART (Courtesy of Securities Research Co.)

against Lennar was hardly clear-cut. Not only that, the insurers came through with flying colors, paying 100 percent of replacement value for those who lost their homes. Lennar shares quickly rebounded once the entire picture was better known, and were back at $30 by early 1993.

But what about the insurers themselves? Personally, I found myself caught in a "crying wolf" position. The argument for investing in insurance stocks—that insurers would raise rates because of storm-related losses—was the same argument that had failed at the time of Hurricane Hugo. It sounded extremely stale to me, so I wasn't at all quick to react, and almost missed the entire move.

The difference was that Andrew wasn't just any old storm. The estimates for insured damages, which started out at an already staggering $7 billion, got higher and higher in the months after the storm, not stopping until actual insured damage turned out to exceed $15 billion. (Remember, Hugo, at $4.2 billion, was the prior record.) Insurance stocks rallied sharply during this time, posting an average gain of over 20 percent in just four months.

Fig. 11 HURRICANE ANDREW AND INSURANCE STOCKS

Date	Damage Estimate (in billions)	S&P Property/ Casualty Stock Index
September 1	$ 7.3	412.7
September 30	$10.2	452.4
December 31	$15.5	480.4

The table looks reversed, but it's not. As damage estimates for Hurricane Andrew ran higher, investors concluded that insurers would have to raise their rates. This favorable expectation pushed the stocks higher as well.

Despite these share-price gains, I insisted on being a skeptic. The underlying logic about catastrophe losses triggering higher policy pricing seemed faulty for many insurance companies. Although State Farm and Allstate got hit especially hard ($3.5 billion and $2.5 billion in losses, respectively), Aetna was hit with only $80 million in damages. And more to the point, the industry's all-important surplus position—representing the amounts available for future claims—ended the year essentially unscathed, the result of outstanding returns from the bond market. As a general rule, insurers aren't truly compelled to raise rates unless their surplus positions are threatened.

However, one place where Andrew made an immediate and undeniable imprint was among *reinsurance* stocks. Reinsurance is basically insurance for insurance companies; by buying reinsurance, the primary carriers are better able to manage their own risks. When primary insurers sought increased property coverage following Andrew, the heavy demand meant that reinsurance rates had nowhere to go but up.

The effect wasn't necessarily immediate, because price increases kick in at the time of policy renewals, not at the time of the storm. However, investors correctly foresaw big hikes in reinsurance deductibles and premiums for the January 1993 renewal period, and the stocks wasted no time in getting going. General Re, the nation's largest reinsurer, was a bit of a laggard, but stocks like National Re, NAC Re, Phoenix Re (now PXRE), and Trenwick Group were up an average of 80 percent in the six months following the storm. (The "Re" in these names looks a little odd, but it is simply shorthand for "reinsurance," and is pronounced with a long "e.")

I finally woke up when Phoenix Re hit $20 per share, the stock having been in single digits pre-Andrew. Even though I felt like a dope for missing the initial move, I had chanced upon a report that noted how reinsurance rates remained strong for six years following Hurricane Betsy in 1965. By that reckoning, there was still time, and, sure enough, Phoenix kept rising. It didn't peak out until the summer of 1993, when a rash of new money came in to the reinsurance market, creating the possibility that the high rates would be short-lived. But by that time, the stock had hit $38. A near double in six months is enough to make you forget how late you were in the first place.

The Winter of 1993

The extremely harsh weather in the winter of 1993 briefly slowed down the housing rally started by Andrew, but it also led to some new opportunities. In particular, the severe winter provided me with a milestone that only an analyst would get excited about: my first weather play in the ground transportation sector.

Do you know how maddening the transportation industry is to the meteorologically inclined? Take the railroads in particular. Are cold winters good? It seems that way. Demand for coal is greater during cold weather, and that translates into more coal carriage for companies like Burlington Northern, Union Pacific, Norfolk Southern, and CSX. Yet cold periods frequently require railroad companies to shorten the length of their trains, because air brake pressure cannot be sustained on a long train in frigid weather. In addition, the rail itself contracts during extreme cold, and that can cause derailments and route closings. The net result is that extreme weather doesn't necessarily create opportunities in rail stocks.

However, just when I was about to write off the entire transportation sector, along came the storms of January 1993. A classic second-leg winner emerged in the form of trucking company Swift Transportation out of Phoenix, Arizona.

Swift had built a reputation as a well-managed company, but the first quarter of 1993 was a disaster. The heavier-than-usual snow and rainfall in the western states lowered the overall level of business activity, and with it the need for freight carriage. To make matters worse, whereas the company would normally "balance" an L.A.-to-Phoenix haul of retail merchandise with a Phoenix-to-L.A. load of cotton, the unusually poor Arizona cotton crop made for a lot of unprofitable return trips. Because these western routes accounted for 85 percent of Swift's operating income, it was far more exposed than the average trucker (location, location, location). The stock, which had been trading at $19 at the beginning of the year, was down to $14 by mid-March. Meanwhile, other, more geographically diversified trucking companies, such as Werner Enterprises, Heartland Express, and J. B. Hunt, were still trading near their yearly highs.

On the usual grounds that Swift's problems were temporary, the stock seemed worth a shot, and the near-term reward was a rebound to $21 by January of 1994. I should emphasize that confidence in the company's fundamentals was a key part of catching that rebound, because the essence of the rebound theory is that, *all other things being equal,* the stock market will forget about the one negative weather episode and give the company a more generous valuation. With weaker companies you run the risk of the rebound being temporary or not occurring at all (because other things *aren't* equal—e.g., Clearly Canadian). Swift was different. I'll spare you the rest of the story, but if you were lucky enough to forget to sell after the rebound was attained, you could have ridden the stock all the way to over $40 per share by the summer of 1994.

March 1993: The Storm of the Century

There was a much bigger event that winter, namely, the "storm of the century," which dumped a couple of feet of snow on the entire eastern seaboard on a mid-March weekend. On the bright side, it was the biggest weekend in the history of Blockbuster Video and a significant boon to Morton International's road salt business. As usual, however, the near-term losers outnumbered the winners.

The biggest casualties (or rebound opportunities, if you've already put your rose-colored glasses on) came from the retail sector. Same-store sales figures for March were simply horrendous, as you'd expect when an entire Saturday produced a goose egg. Pick a retailer, any retailer, and odds-on its stock was down for the month. Wal-Mart managed a 3 percent same-store sales gain, but that was well below the double-digit growth that investors had come to expect. And April wasn't much better. When Wal-Mart projected that same-store sales growth for the year would be on the order of 7 percent, its stock continued a slide that would amount to just about 30 percent: $34 down to $24.

An even bigger casualty was Filene's Basement, the off-price re-tailer that we met earlier in this chapter. The company had already been struggling in its effort to make a national concept out of its stunningly successful downtown Boston operation (New England in-stitutions don't necessarily travel well). In fact, analysts thought of Filene's Basement as essentially two companies: the flagship Boston store and "everything else." So when weather closed down the flagship store, and when March same-store sales growth came in at *negative* 7 percent, the stock dropped in short order from $16 to $10 and didn't trough out until a few months later, at $7 per share. Just a year earlier, when the company's geographic expansion had seemed more promising, the stock had traded at $36.

Of course, there's no rule that says a stock has to go back up to a certain level just because it's been there before. But the stock did seem oversold, on the by now familiar grounds that bad weather was providing the bad numbers to make an already risky situation seem even worse. It was back up to $11 by year-end—not a great rebound, but there was still money to be made for those with good timing.

Playing the storm rebound by buying just Filene's Basement stock would have been far too risky, so I looked for other Boston-area companies affected by the snow. Out popped Staples, the office supply company, whose stock I had been following closely for a couple of years.

Staples was supposed to be an extremely fast grower, so when it reported zero progress in same-store sales for March, shareholders lost faith. Staples dropped from the mid-30s to the mid-20s between February and April. As we have seen before, though, the weather's role was in providing the lousy numbers that made investors wrongly believe that the company had fallen apart. Within a matter of months, clearer heads prevailed, and the stock rebounded more than 50 percent. If you had invested right after the bad weather, you could have come out ahead.

As spring gave way to summer, it made sense to consider soft-drink shares, because a favorable year-to-year comparison was coming up. (Remember, 1992 had been a lousy year because of the cold summer.) The stocks surpassed my wildest expectations. The biggest gainers turned out to be the bottling companies, because their high operational leverage makes earnings extremely sensitive to changes in soft-drink volumes. Coca-Cola Enterprises, the nation's largest Coke bottler, had declined 20 percent in 1992, but was up by a like amount in 1993. Coca-Cola Bottling, the second-largest Coke bottler in the United States, leapt up precisely 100 percent in 1993 after being on a downtrend for six years. That type of gain was extraordinary, but it confirms that favorable year-to-year comparisons can provide a powerful tailwind.

The Midwestern Flood

The great midwestern flood of 1993 provided another great reason to invest. Although the weather pattern was a world apart from the drought of five summers earlier, one investment conclusion remained the same: The higher commodity prices meant that, amid the horror stories, a lot of farmers were doing well.

In fact, farmers lucky enough to be on the fringe of the wet weather had good crops and sharply reduced irrigation expenses. Enough farmers were doing well that sales of row crop tractors rose from 15,936 in 1992 to 18,442 in 1993. On the strength of these improved numbers, John Deere stock, which had climbed 50 percent in the first half of 1993, added another 50 percent by early 1994.

Not everyone escaped, though. In the last week of June, shares of irrigation equipment makers Valmont Industries and Lindsay Manufacturing—two of our first-leg winners during the drought—each slipped 10 percent. Shares of Younkers, the department-store chain based in Des Moines, dropped more than 20 percent during the first week of July when flooding forced the closure of the company's downtown stores.

By mid-July, or thereabouts, you should have been asking yourself which if any of these stocks were apt to rebound. As it turned out, Valmont and Lindsay quickly returned to prior levels. But Younkers did not. Why?

As is so often true, the answer could have been found by paying attention to location. Investors had to understand that the flooding was *not* occurring in Valmont and Lindsay's main markets of Nebraska and Kansas. Furthermore, the summer was quite dry in Texas, which was becoming an increasingly important market for these companies. The stock market's knee-jerk dismissal of irrigation stocks was, therefore, misplaced, and both stocks came back within a few short months.

Younkers wasn't as lucky, because even after the water had receded enough for stores to be reopened, these stores were still located in Des Moines, and people in that area had much more important things on their minds than shopping for clothes. Younkers management also had to deal with digestion pains in the company's freshly acquired Wisconsin operation, and the rest of the year became a struggle. The coup de grâce was severe weather during the Christmas season, which caused a number of stores to close early and miss the all-important holiday traffic. By the summer of 1994, the stock was at just $12—off more than 50 percent from its 1993 high.

Actually, I had considered setting up another section in this chapter to talk about 1994, but enough is enough. (I don't want you to get sick of this stuff before you've had a chance to use it yourself!) Suffice it to say, many of the same names reappeared, and the results were mostly according to form.

For example, although I had missed Coca-Cola Bottling on the upside in 1993, I put it on my "avoid" list in early 1994, in part because of the unsustainability of weather-aided results. I was soon "rewarded" when the stock dropped from $39 to $25. On the buy side, I recommended Younkers that July at $13 per share as the anniversary of the flood approached and better sales comparisons loomed. The timing proved propitious. Several Wall Street analysts raised their estimates that month and the stock hit $17 by August, for a near-term gain of 30 percent—even before Carson Pirie Scott announced a takeover bid for the company. These successes *do* happen.

As 1994 came to an end, practically every retailing stock on the planet got trampled by a balmy December that ruined the Christmas season. Many proclaimed the retail group dead, but I had to wonder whether a rebound might be in store for 1995 and beyond. We'll see.

I hope that this real-life discussion has brought out the richness of weather-based investing, because it is a subject that truly goes on and on. Each situation has its own individual wrinkles, but, as we've seen, we can get extraordinary mileage just by knowing the simple principles of location, year-to-year change, and corporate mistakes. With any luck, other investors will continue to overlook the patterns laid out in this chapter. That way, we can make money from the weather for many years to come.

2 ❏ An Undervalued Investment Screen: Television

What follows is a defense for the TV generation, the generation that I happen to belong to. Practically since birth, our parents have been asking the question, "What will television do to our kids?" Now we have our answer: Properly watched, TV can make us a lot of money.

This chapter will be divided into three sections. The first—and longest—plucks out nine actual television schedules from the past forty years. For each of these schedules, we will divine powerful investment ideas purely by the nature of the programming (you heard me). One benefit of this long-term approach is that our knowledge builds over time, making it clear how mastering one example could have helped you profit from the next. To maintain this continuity, each example contains "subplots" that can be applied in the future. The second section looks at investment-worthy products and trends that got a major boost from television (for good measure, we'll throw movies into the mix). Finally, the third section closes the chapter with some actual TV episodes involving the stock market; the between-the-lines advice they manage to give might surprise you.

TELEVISION SCHEDULES THAT MADE INVESTMENT HISTORY

1955: Too Many Words from the Sponsor

A glance at the 1955–56 network television schedule reveals a world much different than today's. Two major differences stand out.

One is that during television's early years it was commonplace for companies to sponsor entire programs, as opposed to merely buying ad time on the shows of their choice. Anyone watching TV during the fifties would have had little difficulty connecting shows with their sponsors: *You Asked for It*—Skippy peanut butter; *Your Hit Parade*—Lucky Strike; *Studio One*—Westinghouse. Some companies went so far as to put their names right on the program. There were eighteen such shows in the 1955–56 season, including *General Electric Theater, Texaco Star Theater,* and *The Voice of Firestone.* (These shows have slanted lines through them on the schedule.)

In and of itself, show sponsorship was nothing for investors to get excited about; the share price of U.S. Steel was tied to the price of steel, not to the ratings for *The U.S. Steel Hour,* and similarly for most of the program sponsors of that era. So to find the best stock play in television for 1955, we have to introduce another element: the primetime quiz show. Fourteen quiz and game shows (the shaded ones) were part of the 1955 schedule.

Where is all this going? Well, combining game shows with corporate sponsorship would have led you to one of the great investment stories of the entire decade. The company in question was a small cosmetics firm called Revlon. Revlon's show, airing at 10:00 on Tuesday nights, was *The $64,000 Question.*

An investor's first responsibility was to see that the show was the hottest thing going, but that wasn't a difficult task. At the risk of stating the obvious, $64,000 was a lot of money back in 1955, and the drama of the big-money quiz shows captivated the nation. Just how big was *Question?* Big enough to knock *I Love Lucy* from the number-one slot in the Nielsens. Big enough, at its peak, to capture an unheard-of 82 *percent* of the viewing public. Said Sonny Fox, onetime host of the follow-up show *The $64,000 Challenge,* "On Tuesday nights, you could walk down the streets and not hear a thing, because everybody was in front of their TV sets watching [that] show."

PRIME TIME SCHEDULE: 1955

Day	Net	7:00 PM	7:30	8:00	8:30	9:00	9:30	10:00	10:30	11:00
SUNDAY	A	You Asked for It		Famous Film Festival		Chance of a Lifetime	Original Amateur Hour	Life Begins at Eighty		
	C	Lassie	Jack Benny Show/ Private Secretary	Ed Sullivan Show		G.E. Theater	Alfred Hitchcock Presents	Appointment with Adventure	What's My Line	
	N	It's a Great Life	Frontier	Colgate Variety Hour		Goodyear TV Playhouse/ Alcoa Hour		Loretta Young Show	Justice	
MONDAY	A	Kukla, Fran & Ollie	News	Topper	TV Reader's Digest	Voice of Firestone	Dotty Mack Show	Medical Horizons	Big Picture	
	C		News	Adventures of Robin Hood	George Burns and Gracie Allen Show	Arthur Godfrey's Talent Scouts	I Love Lucy	December Bride	Studio One	
	N		Tony Martin Show	News	Caesar's Hour		Medic	Robert Montgomery Presents		
TUESDAY	A	Kukla, Fran & Ollie	News	Warner Brothers Presents		Life and Legend of Wyatt Earp	Make Room for Daddy	DuPont Cavalcade Theater	Talent Varieties	
	C		News	Name That Tune	Navy Log	You'll Never Get Rich	Meet Millie	Red Skelton Show	$64,000 Question	My Favorite Husband
	N		Dinah Shore Show	News	Martha Raye Show/ Milton Berle Show/ Chevy Show		Fireside Theater	Armstrong Circle Theatre/ Pontiac Presents Playwrights 56		Big Town
WEDNESDAY	A	Kukla, Fran & Ollie	News	Disneyland		MGM Parade	Masquerade Party	Break the Bank	Wednesday Night Fights	
	C		News	Brave Eagle	Arthur Godfrey & His Friends		The Millionaire	I've Got a Secret	20th Century-Fox Hour/ U.S. Steel Hour	
	N		Coke Time	News	Screen Director's Playhouse	Father Knows Best	Kraft Television Theatre		This is Your Life	Midwestern Hayride
THURSDAY	A	Kukla, Fran & Ollie	News	Lone Ranger	Life is Worth Living	Stop the Music	Star Tonight	Down You Go	Outside U.S.A.	
	C		News	Sgt. Preston of the Yukon	Bob Cummings Show	Climax		Four Star Playhouse	Johnny Carson Show	Wanted
	N		Dinah Shore Show	News	You Bet Your Life	People's Choice	Dragnet	Ford Theatre	Lux Video Theatre	
FRIDAY	A	Kukla, Fran & Ollie	News	Adventures of Rin Tin Tin	Adventures of Ozzie & Harriet	Crossroads	Dollar a Second	The Vise	Ethel & Albert	
	C		News	Adventures of Champion	Mama	Our Miss Brooks	The Crusader	Schlitz Playhouse of Stars	The Lineup	Person to Person
	N		Coke Time	News	Truth or Consequences	Life of Riley	Big Story	Star Stage	Gillette Cavalcade of Sports		Red Barber's Corner
SATURDAY	A			Ozark Jubilee		Lawrence Welk Show		Tomorrow's Careers		
	C	Gene Autry Show	Beat the Clock	Stage Show	The Honeymooners	Two for the Money	It's Always Jan	Gunsmoke	Damon Runyon Theatre	
	N		Big Surprise	Perry Como Show		People Are Funny	Texaco Star Theater Starring Jimmy Durante	George Gobel Show	Your Hit Parade	

Fig. 12 1955 TV SCHEDULE

Surprisingly, Revlon's Charles Revson had reservations about the show—at least initially—because Revlon's print advertising had always stressed *colors*, something that the new medium of television wasn't ready to provide. Luckily, he got over it. Said brother Martin Revson, "I don't know where we would have been without that show."

The $64,000 Question turned out to be the perfect vehicle for a company that wanted to promote glamour. (To think that Lewyt Vacuum Cleaners was one of the early candidates for sponsorship!) The show amounted to a nonstop advertisement. Revlon signs hovered over emcee Hal March and over the "isolation booths" where contestants heard their questions. Barbara Britton, the stunning model/spokeswoman, touted lipstick, nail polish, you name it, on the commercial breaks. ("If it's the best of its kind, it's by Revlon.") The ads themselves were to ordinary commercials what the Orange Bowl halftime show is to an ordinary sports intermission. They sometimes stretched for as long as three minutes, in blatant defiance of the rules; but what was CBS going to do about it? *The $64,000 Question* was a major event in America's week.

And the ads worked! Wednesday mornings produced a run on Revlon products at department stores everywhere, especially those products featured the night before. Revlon's sales in 1955 were up over 50 percent from the pre-*Question* levels of 1954. The central point is that *The $64,000 Question* made the company what it was, not vice versa.

At first, there was no way for an investor to participate in the action, because Revlon was privately held. The public was finally let in on the action in December 1955, when Revlon sold 338,000 shares at $12 each in its initial public offering (IPO).

The Revlon share offering might have looked like the sort of red-hot IPO that everyone tells you to avoid. After all, the company had earned only $0.49 per share in 1954, so the stock appeared to be valued at a hefty twenty-five times earnings ($25 \times \$0.49 = \$12.25$, approximately the offering price). But those were *trailing* earnings, which told you nothing about the company's potential. The fact was, *Question* made 1954 ancient history. Not only was Revlon's sales growth phenomenal, its profit margins were still widening, meaning that earnings growth was even greater. Earnings for 1955 came in at $1.37 per share, almost three times the prior standard. By 1959, Revlon earned

$4.19 per share. Between 1955 and 1959, the stock moved from the offering price of $6 (adjusted for a subsequent 2-for-1 split) to over $60 per share, a tenfold gain. All this from watching television.

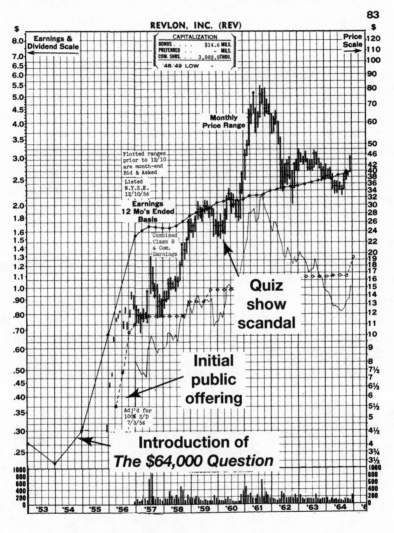

Fig. 13 Revlon chart (Courtesy of Securities Research Co.)

The bad news is that in 1959, the Revlon story took a brief turn for the worse (note the dip in the stock chart during the second half of that year). The good news is that the clue to the reversal could again be found simply by consulting your local listings.

A look at the network schedule for 1959 reveals that the quiz shows were gone. Some of the classics remained, including *What's My Line?*, *The Price Is Right*, and *I've Got a Secret*, but those were *game* shows. The big-money quiz shows had all been taken off the air the previous year amid allegations that they were rigged—this was the scandal that the movie *Quiz Show* revisited thirty-five years later. In the near term, the cancellation of *The $64,000 Question* seemed to be a frightful sign for Revlon shares: If Revlon was built from TV show sponsorship, then perhaps it would crumble without it.

This logic was a trifle panicky but not without basis. Sales of Geritol, the sponsor of the tainted game show *Twenty-One*, dropped 12 percent the year the show was canceled, having risen 30 percent the previous year. What was a Revlon investor to do? To get to the answer, we'll have to wade through some details of the scandal that weren't covered in *Quiz Show*. (The story is a personal favorite of mine, so please forgive the drawn-out approach.)

The roots of the quiz show scandal were in the control that sponsors had over television programming. At first glance, this control was constructive. Said Joyce Hall of the Hallmark Card Company, sponsor of *The Hallmark Hall of Fame*, "[Other companies] have told me they never watch the junk they sponsor. For the life of me I can't understand such lack of pride in anything identified with a company."

But pride can go too far. One *Hallmark Hall of Fame* broadcast, a production of George Bernard Shaw's *Man and Superman*, produced strenuous objections from the company's advertising agency, which succeeded in altering a segment that portrayed mothers unfavorably; after all, Mother's Day was (and is) very important to the greeting card business. Similarly, Westinghouse's sponsorship of *Studio One* made itself felt when the show broadcast a rendition of Rudyard Kipling's *The Light That Failed*. A Westinghouse light, failing? Unthinkable. The name was changed to "The Gathering Night."

Where quiz shows were concerned, sponsors saw the contestants themselves as corporate image bearers. Eventually, sponsors began pressuring the shows' producers to prolong the exposure of those contestants with the greatest telegenic appeal, and the fix was on. The late Merton Koplin, producer of *The $64,000 Question*, cited enormous

PRIME TIME SCHEDULE: 1959

Day	Net	7:00 PM	7:30	8:00	8:30	9:00	9:30	10:00	10:30	11:00
SUNDAY	A	Colt .45	Maverick		The Lawman	The Rebel	The Alaskans		Dick Clark's World of Talent	
SUNDAY	C	Lassie	Dennis the Menace	Ed Sullivan Show		G.E. Theater	Alfred Hitchcock Presents	Jack Benny Show/George Gobel Show	What's My Line	
SUNDAY	N	Riverboat		Sunday Showcase		Dinah Shore Chevy Show		Loretta Young Show		
MONDAY	A		Cheyenne			Bourbon Street Beat		Adventures in Paradise		Man with a Camera
MONDAY	C	News	Masquerade Party	The Texan	Father Knows Best	Danny Thomas Show	Ann Sothern Show	Hennesey	DuPont Show with June Allyson	
MONDAY	N		Richard Diamond, Private Detective	Love & Marriage	Tales of Wells Fargo	Peter Gunn	Alcoa/Goodyear TV Playhouse	Steve Allen Plymouth Show		
TUESDAY	A		Sugarfoot/Bronco		Life and Legend of Wyatt Earp	The Rifleman	Philip Marlowe	Alcoa Presents	Keep Talking	
TUESDAY	C	News		Dennis O'Keefe Show	Many Loves of Dobie Gillis	Tightrope	Red Skelton Show	Garry Moore Show		
TUESDAY	N		Laramie		Fibber McGee & Molly	Arthur Murray Party	Startime			
WEDNESDAY	A		Court of Last Resort	Hobby Lobby Show	Adventures of Ozzie & Harriet	Hawaiian Eye		Wednesday Night Fights		
WEDNESDAY	C	News	The Lineup		Men into Space	The Millionaire	I've Got a Secret	Armstrong Circle Theatre/U.S. Steel Hour		
WEDNESDAY	N		Wagon Train		Price is Right	Perry Como's Kraft Music Hall		This is Your Life	Wichita Town	
THURSDAY	A		Gale Storm Show	Donna Reed Show	Real McCoys	Pat Boone—Chevy Showroom	The Untouchables		Take a Good Look	
THURSDAY	C	News	To Tell the Truth	Betty Hutton Show	Johnny Ringo	Dick Powell's Zane Grey Theatre	Playhouse 90/Big Party			
THURSDAY	N		Law of the Plainsman	Bat Masterson	Staccato	Bachelor Father	Ford Show Starring Tennessee Ernie Ford	You Bet Your Life	The Lawless Years	
FRIDAY	A		Walt Disney Presents		Man from Blackhawk	77 Sunset Strip		Robert Taylor: The Detectives	Black Saddle	
FRIDAY	C	News	Rawhide		Hotel de Paree	Desilu Playhouse		Twilight Zone	Person to Person	
FRIDAY	N		People are Funny	The Troubleshooters	Bell Telephone Hour		M Squad	Gillette Cavalcade of Sports		Phillies Jackpot Bowling
SATURDAY	A		Dick Clark Show	High Road	Leave it to Beaver	Lawrence Welk Show		Jubilee U.S.A.		
SATURDAY	C		Perry Mason		Wanted: Dead or Alive	Mr. Lucky	Have Gun, Will Travel	Gunsmoke	Markham	
SATURDAY	N		Bonanza		Man & the Challenge	The Deputy	Five Fingers		It Could Be You	

Fig. 14 1959 TV SCHEDULE

pressure from the Revsons to "stiff" a woman contestant who apparently didn't represent what cosmetics were all about. Her name was Dr. Joyce Brothers.

Dr. Brothers won anyway, without help. But many contestants needed all the help they could get. Shows in which the contestants were the stars were simply not good television if the stars didn't know the answers. So the producers supplied the answers in advance.

The charade worked for a while, but in the fall of 1958, a disgruntled contestant from the short-lived show *Dotto* decided to let the authorities know what was going on. Other potential scandals began to emerge and the networks were quick to respond. *Twenty-One, The $64,000 Question,* and many others were abruptly pulled off the air. Investors, start your engines.

One curious aspect of the story was that no one really wanted to believe the fix, the stock market included. Hundreds of contestants went before the New York grand jury to protest their innocence. Charles Van Doren, the popular champion on *Twenty-One,* denied any wrongdoing and remained a commentator on NBC's *Today Show*—one of the many trophies of his newfound fame. Only when the congressional investigation into the scandal began on November 2, 1959—at which time Revlon stock remained within a whisker of its high—was the denial game over. It was time to sell.

Van Doren came out of hiding to testify, "I have been involved, deeply involved, in a deception." Charles Revson also took the stand, though he never admitted any guilt. Under all this scrutiny, Revlon shares dropped from $60 to $47 within the month.

It was fair to ask whether this stigma would last. For Van Doren, alas, the answer was yes. As for Revlon, if *The $64,000 Question* had been called *Revlon Quiz Time* instead, perhaps the company's good name would have been besmirched forever. But it wasn't. Although Revlon won't talk about its quiz show involvement to this day, the end of *Question* sponsorship didn't undo the franchise it had created. Earnings continued to hit record levels, and the stock made up all its lost ground by 1960.

As a footnote to the issue of sponsorship, check the television schedule for 1965. Only two shows—*The Bell Telephone Hour* (Sunday, 7:00 P.M.) and *Bob Hope Presents the Chrysler Theater* (Wednesday, 9:00 P.M.)—bore a sponsor's name.

PRIME TIME SCHEDULE: 1965

		7:00 PM	7:30	8:00	8:30	9:00	9:30	10:00	10:30	11:00
SUNDAY	A	Voyage to the Bottom of the Sea		The F.B.I.		ABC Sunday Night Movie				
	C	Lassie	My Favorite Martian	Ed Sullivan Show		Perry Mason		Candid Camera	What's My Line	
	N	Bell Telephone Hour/Actuality Specials	Walt Disney's Wonderful World of Color		Branded	Bonanza		Wackiest Ship in the Army		
MONDAY	A		Twelve O'Clock High			Legend of Jesse James	Man Called Shenandoah	Farmer's Daughter	Ben Casey	
	C		To Tell the Truth	I've Got a Secret	Lucy Show	Andy Griffith Show	Hazel	Steve Lawrence Show		
	N		Hullabaloo	John Forsythe Show	Dr. Kildare	Andy Williams Show		Run for Your Life		
TUESDAY	A		Combat		McHale's Navy	F Troop	Peyton Place	The Fugitive		
	C		Rawhide		Red Skelton Hour		Petticoat Junction	CBS Reports/News Hour		
	N		My Mother the Car	Please Don't Eat the Daisies	Dr. Kildare	NBC Tuesday Night Movie				
WEDNESDAY	A		Adventures of Ozzie & Harriet	Patty Duke Show	Gidget	Big Valley		Amos Burke— Secret Agent		
	C		Lost in Space		Beverly Hillbillies	Green Acres	Dick Van Dyke Show	Danny Kaye Show		
	N		The Virginian			Bob Hope Presents the Chrysler Theatre		I Spy		
THURSDAY	A		Shindig	Donna Reed Show	O.K. Crackerby	Bewitched	Peyton Place	Long, Hot Summer		
	C		The Munsters	Gilligan's Island	My Three Sons	CBS Thursday Night Movie				
	N		Daniel Boone		Laredo		Mona McCluskey	Dean Martin Show		
FRIDAY	A		The Flintstones	Tammy	Addams Family	Honey West	Peyton Place	Jimmy Dean Show		
	C		Wild Wild West		Hogan's Heroes	Gomer Pyle U.S.M.C.	Smothers Brothers Show	Slattery's People		
	N		Camp Runamuck	Hank	Convoy		Mr. Roberts	The Man from U.N.C.L.E.		
SATURDAY	A		Shindig	King Family Show	Lawrence Welk Show		Hollywood Palace		ABC Scope	
	C		Jackie Gleason Show		Trials of O'Brien		The Loner	Gunsmoke		
	N		Flipper	I Dream of Jeannie	Get Smart	NBC Saturday Night Movie				

Fig. 15 1965 TV SCHEDULE

SUBPLOTS

- Not all hot IPOs work out poorly. In particular, a high price relative to trailing earnings needn't be a deterrent.
- Sometimes the market gives you time to sell on bad news. In this case, many months elapsed between the initial quiz show allegations and the congressional hearings.
- True franchises are hard to destroy. If you're willing to hold through the difficult times, you can have the last laugh.

1959, 1965: A Couple of Hokey Indicators

Not every year produces a great investment play like Revlon, and sometimes the television-related inferences are far less direct. As long as we have the 1959 and 1965 schedules at our fingertips, we might as well look at a couple of these fringy examples.

The idea behind these indirect stock picks is that a television schedule serves as a barometer of its time. For example, the 1959 schedule, in addition to revealing the end of the quiz show mania, also displayed an unusually high number of suburban sitcoms: *The Donna Reed Show, The Adventures of Ozzie and Harriet, Leave It to Beaver, Dennis the Menace,* and *Father Knows Best.*

These programs were of tremendous investment significance because they symbolized the suburban migration of the fifties. Investing in the beneficiaries of that migration—for example, appliance makers such as Westinghouse, Maytag, and Whirlpool, or household products companies such as Procter & Gamble and Colgate-Palmolive—made a lot of sense.

There were, of course, many ways to identify the demographic trends that made these companies worthy investments; I'm merely suggesting that television was as good as any. Leaping from *Dennis the Menace* to an investment in Maytag isn't everybody's idea of fiduciary responsibility, but the underpinnings were quite solid—and so were the results. Appliance stocks (particularly Maytag) did quite well in the late fifties. Household products stocks did even better, moving up almost 300 percent as a group between 1957 and 1961, compared to a 50 percent gain for the Dow Jones Industrial Average.

Fast-forwarding to 1965, we get an example of indirect investing that truly pushes the edge of reason. Would you believe that the TV schedule of that year—and for several years thereafter—suggested high valuations for defense stocks?

It's all there in black and white, because those were the spy show years. In 1965, *The Man from U.N.C.L.E.* was in its second season on NBC, joining *I Spy, Get Smart,* and *Amos Burke—Secret Agent,* which was a remake of *Burke's Law* to fit the times. (These four shows are highlighted on our schedule.) Not even making the schedule because of a brief hiatus was *Secret Agent,* starring Patrick McGoohan, and *The Avengers,* with Patrick MacNee and Diana Rigg, which would arrive the very next year.

What the presence of all these shows suggested was that the Cold War was very much part of the national scene. This by itself didn't tell you much about defense projects that could affect individual companies. But if global tensions were powerful enough to make the television screen, you wouldn't expect defense budgets to be ratcheted downward. And many defense stocks traded at premiums to the overall market during that time.

Before you reject this connection as *completely* absurd, consider that today, with the Cold War a thing of the past, about the only spy shows you can find on television are *Get Smart* reruns—and the stock market doesn't pay nearly as much as it used to for the earnings of defense companies. To be sure, by the early nineties stocks such as General Dynamics and McDonnell Douglas had gotten so cheap that they became terrific value investments; in fact, I recommended the group in early 1991 and haven't regretted it one bit. But the point is that these and other defense stocks peaked in popularity during the sixties and were terrible long-term investments if you bought during that time.

I couldn't let a section on hokey indicators end without bringing up a trend that encompassed both the 1959 and 1965 schedules: the western. As we'll see in the advertising section of this book, the infiltration of the American cowboy into the popular media was a tremendous—albeit indirect—boon for Philip Morris and its Marlboro Man, a campaign that was initiated in 1955.

Conveniently, the surge of television westerns began that same year with the debut of *Gunsmoke.* By 1959, there were no fewer than thirty-one westerns on TV. Because of midseason shifting, not all of them made it onto our single-snapshot schedule, but *Rawhide, Bat Masterson, Cheyenne,* and many others were there to be seen. By 1965, even though the mania had subsided, the TV westerns still included such ratings smashes as *Bonanza, Gunsmoke, The Virginian,* and even *The Wild, Wild West,* which was sort of a spy show set in the 1800s. All in all, the western was the single most visible programming category throughout this period.

To see why this is of investment significance, put yourself in the shoes of the chairman of RJ Reynolds, Philip Morris's chief competitor. Wouldn't you be upset that your archrival was receiving a constant flow of free publicity? Wouldn't you want the allure of the cowboy to accrue to your product, not theirs?

Philip Morris saw the connection. The company was an early sponsor of *Bonanza.* And the theme music for their ads—taken from *The Magnificent Seven* with James Coburn, Yul Brynner, and Eli Wallach—further strengthened the tie to the cowboy.

I don't mean to take anything away from the folks at Leo Burnett, the advertising agency that dreamed up the Marlboro Man, but television surely played a role in Marlboro's relentless market-share growth. For the record, shares of Philip Morris more than doubled between 1959 and 1961.

SUBPLOTS

- TV programming can be indicative of the times.
- Hokey indicators don't by themselves make stocks go up, but they can tip you off to sound investments. Sometimes you have to fight through your embarrassment and buy.

1971: Where Did All the Programs Go?

Even a quick glance at the television schedule of 1971 suggested a fundamental shift in the television business. By way of perspective, the 1959 schedule contained 114 separate show slots per week for the three major networks. Most shows lasted a half hour, some were just fifteen minutes, and some were aired more than once. As the medium matured, though, the number of shows steadily decreased. By 1965, they numbered 89—already a meaningful decline. That number remained fairly stable until 1971, when only 66 show slots appeared on the schedule. That one simple fact could have led you to literally dozens of investment ideas.

The first step was to understand *why* the number of shows was declining, and there turned out to be several reasons. One was that more shows were a full hour in length. Another was that more movies were being shown. But the single most important reason for the smaller number of shows was that prime time itself had shrunk. The cause was the much-heralded prime-time access rule (PTAR) handed down by the FCC, which mandated that prime time be cut from three and a half hours per night down to three.

The trade referred to the prime-time access rule as the "Westinghouse rule" because it emanated from that company's powerful Group W broadcasting division. The ostensible idea behind the rule was to improve the quality of programming by giving the stations more freedom and incentive to air original work. From 7:30 to 8:00 P.M., stations would be liberated from the networks and their small cadre of standard-fare Hollywood suppliers. In that trailblazing spirit, the rule also prevented affiliated stations in the nation's top fifty markets from filling their extra time by simply rerunning network shows.

A daily reduction of thirty minutes of prime time may not seem like much, but it was the equivalent of eliminating fifteen programs from the airwaves each week—plenty enough to cause tumult in the media world. As experienced investors know, any legislation of this sort sends the financial press scurrying to find the winners and the losers within the affected industry: The assorted reactions to PTAR will shed light on just how useful all that scurrying is.

In this case, the "obvious" winners were the station owners, because advertising revenues brought in during the extra half hour would flow directly to the station—as opposed to the small percentage of advertising revenues a network-affiliated station would get for carrying that network's programming (typically, a network might account for 90 percent of an affiliate's prime-time airings). I placed "obvious" in quotes because stations initially opposed the new legislation, fearful that they wouldn't be able to come up with enough new programming

PRIME TIME SCHEDULE: 1971

		7:00 PM	7:30	8:00	8:30	9:00	9:30	10:00	10:30	11:00
SUNDAY	A			The F.B.I.		ABC Sunday Night Movie				
	C		CBS Sunday Night Movie			Cade's County				
	N		Wonderful World of Disney		Jimmy Stewart Show	Bonanza		Bold Ones: The New Doctors/The Lawyers		
MONDAY	A			Nanny & Professor		ABC Monday Night Football				
	C			Gunsmoke		Here's Lucy	Doris Day Show	My Three Sons	Arnie	
	N			Rowan & Martin's Laugh-In		NBC Monday Night Movie				
TUESDAY	A		Mod Squad		Movie of the Week			Marcus Welby, M.D.		
	C		Glenn Campbell Goodtime Hour		Hawaii Five-O		Cannon			
	N		Ironside		Sarge		The Funny Side			
WEDNESDAY	A			Bewitched	Courtship of Eddie's Father	Smith Family	Shirley's World	Man and the City		
	C			Carol Burnett Show		Medical Center		Mannix		
	N			Adam 12		NBC Mystery Movie: Columbo/McCloud/McMillan and Wife		Night Gallery		
THURSDAY	A			Alias Smith & Jones		Longstreet		Owen Marshall		
	C			Bearcats		CBS Thursday Night Movie				
	N			Flip Wilson Show		Nichols		Dean Martin Show		
FRIDAY	A			Brady Bunch	Partridge Family	Room 222	Odd Couple	Love, American Style		
	C			Chicago Teddy Bears	O'Hara, U.S. Treasury		New CBS Friday Night Movie			
	N			The D.A.	NBC World Premiere Movie					
SATURDAY	A			Getting Together	ABC Movie of the Weekend			The Persuaders		
	C			All in the Family	Funny Face	New Dick Van Dyke Show	Mary Tyler Moore Show	Mission: Impossible		
	N			The Partners	The Good Life	NBC Saturday Night Movie				

Fig. 16   1971 TV SCHEDULE

to fill their slates. However, when it became clear that the economics of the new system would work in their favor, those objections disappeared.

An investor therefore did well to scout out public companies that owned blocs of stations, including Cox Communications, Metromedia, Taft Broadcasting, Storer Communications, Cap Cities, and, lest we forget, Westinghouse. Westinghouse had a specific initiative for PTAR in the form of *Evening* (or *P.M.*) *Magazine,* which soon became a fixture in the 7:30 time slot. This slot, called "access" time, also provided the launching pad for *The Muppet Show.* Hopes for other innovative and profitable programming ideas boosted valuations throughout the broadcasting group: By the end of 1971, the average broadcasting stock was up more than 100 percent from the summer of 1970.

As for losers, one unfortunate aspect of PTAR was that it squeezed many independent studios out of prime time as the networks reshuffled their fall lineups. *Green Acres* and *The Beverly Hillbillies,* both produced by Filmways Productions, were eliminated by CBS as part of a more general purge of rural comedies; Filmways shares, which had traded at $10 in February 1971, dropped below $5 in November. Similarly, Chuck Barris Productions lost *The Newlywed Game* and *Let's Make a Deal* from prime time and saw its stock drop from $5¾ in March to just $2⅜ by November. These declines illustrate the important point that regulations such as PTAR don't always lead to the intended results. Squeezing independent producers was presumably not what the FCC had in mind.

Whether you made money with television station stocks or lost money with production companies, the ripple effects of PTAR were far from over. It is not unusual for the early predictions of winners and losers, whether of PTAR or any major legislation, to be woefully incomplete, and that's where the methods in this chapter come in handy. By piecing together some simple bits of information—and by reverting back to the 1971 television schedule—it would have been possible to identify a surprise winner: ABC.

I say surprise winner because, remember, PTAR was supposed to be a victory for the stations at the networks' expense. To the networks, the rule meant that they lost the equivalent of one night per week at a time when prime time was decidedly profitable. Not only that, the all-important companion legislation to PTAR—the infamous "fin-syn" regulations—forbade the networks from owning a financial stake in the programs they ran, meaning that syndication profits were off-limits.

The idea of investing in ABC in 1971 was more controversial than it might appear. Today, of course, the company is Capital Cities/ABC, which as this book went to press was the number one network and was also in the process of merging with the Walt Disney Company to form the world's largest media/entertainment firm. And the ABC network has had innumerable programming successes since 1971, some of which we'll encounter later on. Back then, however, ABC carried no respect whatsoever. In the words of *Variety,* the network was "running fourth-place in a three network race."

Because ABC's programming had never generated the ratings success of either of its rivals, ABC affiliates were far more likely not to carry the full network programming slate. This lower degree of sponsorship meant that program distribution was smaller, which in turn meant that fewer households were being reached. In the words of Les Brown, former television editor of *Variety,* "Such was the spiral: ABC ventured a new show, too few stations carried it, advertisers buying the circulation therefore paid too little for it, the show failed in the ratings, and ABC was forced to cancel it and offer a new program in its place, which in turn would be passed over by the stations. Thus failure perpetuated failure."

It doesn't sound so great, does it? But the clue to investors that ABC might turn itself around was as straightforward as you could possibly want: NBC and CBS opposed the prime-time access rule vigorously, while ABC approved of it.

ABC knew what it was doing. As convoluted as it sounds, the prime-time access rule helped ABC's cost structure because it cut down on the number of wasted shows! Investors noticed the improvement. Between May 1970 (when PTAR obtained initial passage) and the end of 1971 (when it had been in effect for three months), shares of ABC had risen from $7 to $27, almost a quadrupling.

If you are thinking that there were factors other than cost cutting that led to this dramatic price move, you'd be right. But in keeping with our approach, these extra factors could also have been gleaned directly from the television schedule.

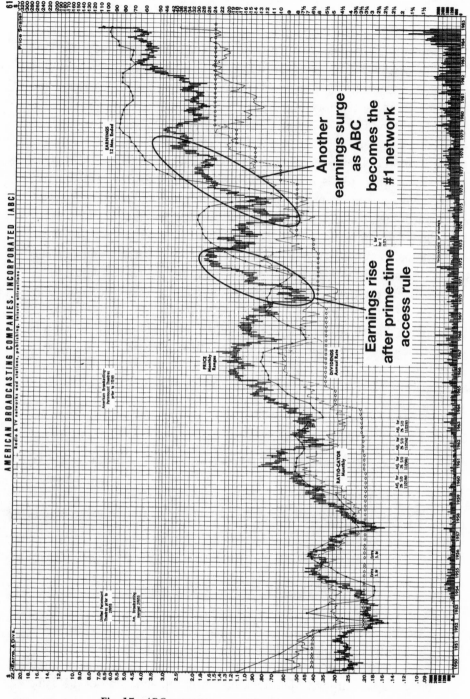

Fig. 17 ABC CHART (Courtesy of Securities Research Co.)

ABC's Monday Night Football was new to the schedule in 1971. Today, it is an institution, but back then it was considered a big risk— so big that the other two networks both said no to the proposal. But ABC's very weakness as the number-three player made it receptive to the gamble, which paid off handsomely for the network and its shareholders. (History was on ABC's side: The network's first hit, the fifties show *Disneyland,* was also acquired on a "no one else wanted it" basis.)

Another bright spot on the 1971 calendar was *Marcus Welby, M.D.* —incredibly, ABC's *first* number-one show for a full season in the network's then thirty-year history. In 1970, *Welby* benefited from its scheduling, being slotted opposite *CBS News Hour* and *The NBC Tuesday Night Movie.* The three-hour restriction of 1971 gave the show another boost: Because of the way the networks gerrymandered their lineups, *Marcus Welby* went unopposed in its second half hour!

Well, those were your three clues to the impending turnaround at ABC. That's as much as the stock market ever gives you, and all three sprang directly from the layout of prime-time programming. As for the prime-time access rule, suffice it to say that we haven't heard the last of it.

SUBPLOTS

- Minor-looking shifts can in fact be tumultuous.
- Many regulations produce results contrary to their original purpose, and the investment winners and losers aren't always easy to predict.
- The previous subplot notwithstanding, companies usually know whether a new regulation helps them or hurts them. For an investor, it pays to know their stances.

1976: ABC Makes Another Move

Unfortunately, if you kept holding ABC shares (or almost anything else) throughout the seventies, you'd have been disappointed. The 1973–74 bear market was perhaps the meanest one in history, and before it was through ABC stock had given up almost all of the gains we worked so painstakingly for in the previous section. However, there was one more opportunity to make some big money in ABC shares before the decade was through, and it came in 1976.

In this case, I've decided to bypass the schedule and go straight to the ratings, because they provide the telling numbers. In 1974, ABC's highest-rated show was *S.W.A.T.*, which checked in at number sixteen. Among the top twenty-five shows, ABC accounted for only three: *S.W.A.T.*, *The Rookies*, and *The Streets of San Francisco*.

A mere two years later, however, ABC was at the top, led by nonpareil programmer Fred Silverman. The network's redoubtable Tuesday night combo of *Happy Days* and *Laverne & Shirley* came in at numbers one and two in the ratings, and *Charlie's Angels* wasn't far behind. By the 1978–79 season, with the addition of *Three's Company*, *Mork & Mindy*, and *Angie*, ABC would have each of the top five series under its wing.

I'm not going to suggest that you could have seen this coming. Even the country's most talented programmers don't know for sure which series will succeed and which will fail, so we investors shouldn't even try. What we *can* do, however, is to understand the tremendous advantages of being number one, and to understand that it can take several years for a ratings leader to be displaced. With that in mind, it follows that you had plenty of time to commit your money to ABC.

And that's the way it was. As 1976 began, ABC traded at $12; by year-end, with earnings up fourfold from the down year in 1975, the stock had doubled. But even if you had missed that initial move, it wasn't too late. Starting with the $24 level of late 1976, the stock didn't top out until late 1979, at $45 per share. Only then, following the ascension of *Dallas* on CBS, did ABC's ratings advantage disappear.

To complete the story, ABC shares didn't perk up again until the bull market began in 1982. The biggest spurt of all occurred in 1986, when ABC merged with Cap Cities. Analyzing that particular merger is, as they say, beyond the scope of this book. Besides, why get greedy? By that time, you could have already had two outstanding opportunities in ABC without ever taking your eyes off *TV Guide*.

SUBPLOTS

- When investing in an industry that feeds off advertising revenues, ratings matter.

- The daffiness of the shows that top the ratings does not matter.
- Leadership in ratings, once attained, can last for several years.

1984: Syndication Hopes Boost Lorimar

Ratings leadership doesn't always directly translate into stock market gains. In the mid-eighties, as the ratings game shifted again, NBC (which had been occupying ABC's traditional third-place spot) climbed from the cellar all the way to the top—the by-product of successful new launches such as *Cheers* (1982), *The A-Team* (1983), and *The Cosby Show* (1984). In ratings terms, *Cheers* was actually a slow starter, but the other two were immediate hits, and by the 1985–86 season NBC was the number-one network. It was the first time that NBC had led the ratings since the near-prehistoric season of 1950–51.

Such success was nice if you happened to be Grant Tinker (then president of NBC), but it didn't automatically extend to the investing public. First of all, you couldn't buy NBC directly; you had to buy shares of then-parent RCA. Second, although NBC clearly was the profit center for RCA during this time, the main investment gains came because RCA was bought out by GE in 1986.

Did the NBC ratings turnaround make RCA worth more? I suppose. Did this extra value make itself felt in the takeover negotiations? Presumably it did. Yet there's a fair amount of work between seeing NBC's higher ratings and capitalizing on the GE buyout—far too much work to put in a couch potato section such as this. More to the point, I can't in good faith suggest that a peek at the 1984 schedule would have enabled you to see the GE buyout coming.

The main schedule-related investment play from this period came from a studio, not a network. The studio was Lorimar, producers of *Dallas* (introduced in 1978), *Knots Landing* (1979), and *Falcon Crest* (1981). These shows, all on CBS, are the shaded entries in our 1984 schedule. Three hours doesn't look like much relative to the full programming slate, but three prime-time hours is an awful lot for a single studio, and three *highly rated* prime-time hours is nothing short of a bonanza. At least, that's how it looked for Lorimar in 1984.

Even if Lorimar wasn't a household name, there was no secret to the company's association with its three shows. The production credits

PRIME TIME SCHEDULE: 1984

		7:00 PM	7:30	8:00	8:30	9:00	9:30	10:00	10:30	11:00
SUNDAY	A	Ripley's Believe it or Not		Hardcastle & McCormick		ABC Sunday Night Movie				
	C	60 Minutes		Murder, She Wrote		The Jeffersons	Alice	Trapper John, M.D.		
	N	Silver Spoons	Punky Brewster	Knight Rider		NBC Sunday Movie				
MONDAY	A			Call to Glory		Monday Night Football				
	C			Scarecrow & Mrs. King		Kate & Allie	Newhart	Cagney & Lacey		
	N			TV's Bloopers & Practical Jokes		NBC Monday Movie				
TUESDAY	A			Foul-Ups, Bleeps & Blunders	Three's a Crowd	Paper Dolls		Jessie		
	C			AfterMASH	E/R	CBS Tuesday Movie				
	N			The A-Team		Riptide		Remington Steele		
WEDNESDAY	A			Fall Guy		Dynasty		Hotel		
	C			Charles in Charge	Dreams	CBS Wednesday Movie				
	N			Highway to Heaven		Facts of Life	It's Your Move	St. Elsewhere		
THURSDAY	A			People Do the Craziest Things	Who's the Boss	Glitter		20/20		
	C			Magnum, P.I.		Simon & Simon		Knots Landing		
	N			Cosby Show	Family Ties	Cheers	Night Court	Hill Street Blues		
FRIDAY	A			Benson	Webster	Hawaiian Heat		Matt Houston		
	C			Dukes of Hazzard		Dallas		Falcon Crest		
	N			V		Hunter		Miami Vice		
SATURDAY	A			T.J. Hooker		Love Boat		Finder of Lost Loves		
	C			Airwolf		Mickey Spillane's Mike Hammer		Cover Up		
	N			Diff'rent Strokes	Gimme a Break	Partners in Crime		Hot Pursuit		

Fig. 18 1984 TV SCHEDULE

came reliably at the end of each episode—an important time to be watching these serials, because that's when they'd preview the next episode. Even if you didn't catch on to the trend until *Falcon Crest's* debut year of 1981, you would have been well rewarded: Lorimar stock moved from under $10 per share in 1981 to over $25 by mid-1984.

As is so often the case, though, these investment stories come in several stages. Personally, mid-1984 was the beginning of my investment experience with Lorimar, because that's when the company's management came to Boston in connection with an offering of convertible bonds. (These are securities that pay out a fixed rate of interest, like any other bond, but which can be converted to common stock over time. The conversion feature enables the issuing company to raise money at a lower interest rate than it would pay with straight bonds, though it may have to issue more shares of common stock in the future.) This was my first look at the company, and the visit posed the usual question of "Is it a buy or not?" Let's see if you would have done better than I did.

Frankly, the only reason I attended the Lorimar lunch was in the hope that either J.R. or Sue Ellen would show up. They didn't, but not all was lost. My table was heavily stocked with local fund managers clamoring to talk with the insiders. (It was Lorimar president Lee Rich's table, not mine. I just happened to be sitting at it.) Syndication was what had brought everybody there. Here was Lorimar with not one but three hit shows to be released for syndication in successive years.

The lunch amounted to a crash course in the finances of a hit show. Studios, it turned out, don't make money during the early years of a series. Instead, they are locked into contracts, typically for four years, during which time they are compensated by the networks at a level well below their actual production costs. This deficit financing is tolerable to the studios because of the ever-present dream of hitting it big in the syndication market (recall that the prime-time access ruling of 1970–71 included a stipulation that barred the networks from syndication profits).

Lorimar's share-price rise after 1981 was tied to the increasing likelihood of a successful syndication, first with *Dallas,* then with the other shows. It was vital to understand that because of the industry's quirky accounting, the mere likelihood of a successful syndication was enough to make Lorimar's earnings go up. That's because the expenses of show production are essentially matched against revenues: If it looks as though revenues will be high in the future—that is, because of syndication—then a studio can postpone some of these costs, meaning that they will be recognized on the income statement on that later date when syndication revenues finally arrive. This accounting practice has the benefit of smoothing out a studio's bumpy revenue stream. Of course, it also enables owners of a hot property to report an early profit even though the initial network payments do not cover actual production costs, and even though the syndication dollars may not have kicked in yet. (Remember that part.)

Anyway, if all went well with the syndication sales for *Dallas* and its kin, Lorimar would lock in a giant annuity. Despite the stock's strength pre-1984, everyone at the luncheon seemed to understand that a top-dollar syndication sale was likely to push it even higher.

And that's where I blundered. I asked Lee Rich whether the average viewer really wanted to see reruns of *Dallas*. After all, *Dallas* was a serial. In order to understand any particular episode, you had to have seen the one before. That's okay on the first run, but summer reruns were taxing enough, and reruns of old shows (with the real version still on the air!) just didn't make any sense. Lee Rich was not pleased by my observation. Moral: If you're a twenty-eight-year-old securities analyst with limited experience in the media field, do not—repeat, do not—take issue with a studio president about the value of his television properties. Given the public setting, his understated brush-off was actually quite generous.

I bought the bonds anyway, and actually made some money fairly quickly: In the near term, Lorimar stock was far more likely to go up than down, given the momentum created by the company's exciting story. In fact, between 1984 and 1986, the stock *tripled,* and the convertible bonds followed suit—at least until the company called them, which, in the vernacular of convertible bonds, essentially gave investors the choice of selling the bonds or converting them to common stock. Not wanting to push my luck, I sold.

Little did I know that my lunchtime suspicion was about to be vindicated. Once the smoke had cleared and Lorimar had collected its $50 million-plus for first-year syndication rights for *Dallas,* it became evident that the viewing public did *not* want to watch reruns of a serial. Not only did *Dallas* reruns lose out to such programs as *Wheel of Fortune* and *Jeopardy!* (more about these later), in some markets they lost out to such space fillers as *The Munsters, Divorce Court,* and even *Romper Room.*

In fact, the entire syndication market for hour-length shows soon began to wane. *Magnum, P.I.* was perhaps the most successful of the hour-long dramas, netting $1.6 million per episode in syndication fees in 1986. *Knots Landing* also made a reasonable debut. But by the time *Falcon Crest* had enough episodes for syndication, the market was no longer strong enough to match Lorimar's annuity hype of a couple of years before. Sitcoms were in, dramas were out.

To make matters worse, the syndication shortfall meant that past earnings—you know, the ones that had been based on top-dollar syndication—would one day have to be restated. The day of reconciliation came when Lorimar merged with Telepictures in 1986; the merger forced the books to be straightened, and the ensuing write-downs created losses for the combined company that totaled $160 million between 1986 and 1988. Against that negative backdrop, Lorimar-Telepictures stock started falling from its high of $32 in 1986 (a couple of months after the merger) and hit just $8 per share following the 1987 crash, a decline of 75 percent.

The Lorimar swoon wasn't the only fallout from the changing syndication market. Orion Pictures' television subsidiary (which we earlier met as Filmways) found *Cagney & Lacey* to be a much less valuable property than once thought, creating write-downs and deficits that eventually forced the company into bankruptcy. And, on a different note, there were changes in the television schedules themselves, which, following the syndicators' lead, began to include more and more half-hour shows. This trend continued for the remainder of the decade.

SUBPLOTS

- In the stock market, you can be right in the near term even when your hypothesis is dead wrong, and vice versa. To the TV aficionado who

doubted *Dallas*'s syndication potential all along, congratulations. Just don't get upset about the money that some people made while betting the "wrong" way.
- Questionable accounting can stay alive for many years, and the stock market is fully capable of bidding a stock up on bogus earnings.
- Justice always prevails . . . eventually.

1986: What Happened to the Three Major Networks?

It did not take a genius to look at the television listings for 1986 and see that cable television had changed the media world. This process did not begin in 1986, to be sure, but even if you didn't see the inroads of cable TV until 1986, you'd have to conclude that future investment opportunities might be found away from the networks. (Good thing: By that time, GE had bought RCA/NBC, Cap Cities had bought ABC, and CBS had been trailed for months by Ted Turner before finding a white knight in the form of Loew's Corporation's Larry Tisch.)

It is more than a mite simplistic to suggest that you should have invested in cable stocks on the basis of this schedule alone. Cable stocks were just plain different, and not for everybody's tastes. The massive initial investment in setting up a cable system meant that the cable companies by and large lacked that vital quantity called current earnings, which in turn meant that they had to be valued by means to which Wall Street was unaccustomed.

I won't bore you with a lengthy examination of the complexity of the cable market and Wall Street's reaction. Instead, I'm going to concentrate on an even better investment idea emanating from the 1986 network schedule. The stock in question is called King World Productions. King World's claim to fame is that they are the syndicators who brought you *Wheel of Fortune* and *Jeopardy!* If you knew that—and, again, they identified themselves at the end of each program—you were off to a great head start.

The differences between King World and Lorimar (our first exposure to the syndication business) are fundamental and worth a little bit of our time. Despite its name, King World Productions has made its fame by *distributing* television shows, not producing them. The com-

Sample Cable Schedule 1986

	8:00 PM	8:30 PM	9:00 PM
2	Nova: "Father of the H-Bomb"		Frontline
4	No Secrets		Hunter
5	Who's the Boss	Perfect Strangers	Moonlighting
7	Morningstar/Eveningstar		Mary
25	Movie: *Invasion of the Body Snatchers*		
27	Movie: *Love's Dark Ride*		Movie: *Kate Bliss and the Ticker Tape Kid*
38	Movie: *The Producers*		
44	MacNeil/Lehrer	Te Maori	
56	NBA Basketball: Celtics at Cavaliers		
64	Movie: *Great Guy*		
A & E	Woman in White		Stage: *The Misanthrope*
BRV	Movie: *The Company of Wolves*		
DIS	Movie: *Beau Brummel*		Movie: *Something Wicked This Way Comes*
ESPN	Wrestling		Roller Derby
HBO	Movie: *Police Academy 2*		
MAX	Movie: *The Woman in Red*		
MC	Movie: *Stick*		
NESN	Auto Racing		
SHO	Movie: *The Jerk*		
SC	NHL Hockey: Sabres at Whalers		
USA	Movie: *What's Up, Tiger Lily?*		
WOR	News	Family Feud	Movie: *The New Centurions*
WPIX	Movie: *Dummy*		
WTBS	Movie: *Captain Newman, M.D.*		

	9:30 PM	10:00 PM	10:30 PM
2		News	Business Report
4		Stingray	
5		Spenser: For Hire	
7	Foley Square	The Equalizer	
25		Matt Houston	
27			
38		The Odd Couple	
44	Great Decisions	News	Business Report
56		News	
64		Jimmy Swaggart	Express
A & E			
BRV		Andre LaPlante	
DIS			DTV
ESPN		Demolition Derby	
HBO	Ray Bradbury Theater	Movie: *The Breakfast Club*	
MAX		Movie: *Revenge of the Nerds*	
MC		Movie: *Richard III*	
NESN		Boxing	
SHO		Movie: *The Lonely Guy*	
SC			Postgame
USA		Dick Cavett	
WOR			
WPIX		ITN News	News
WTBS			Movie: *Band of Angels*

Fig. 19 SAMPLE CABLE LISTINGS FROM 1986

PRIME TIME SCHEDULE: 1986

		7:00 PM	7:30	8:00	8:30	9:00	9:30	10:00	10:30	11:00
SUNDAY	A	Disney Sunday Movie				ABC Sunday Movie				
	C	60 Minutes		Murder, She Wrote		CBS Sunday Movie				
	N	Our House		Easy Street	Valerie	NBC Sunday Movie				
MONDAY	A	Wheel of Fortune	Jeopardy	MacGyver		Monday Night Football				
	C			Kate & Allie	My Sister Sam	Newhart	Designing Women	Cagney & Lacey		
	N			Alf	Amazing Stories	NBC Monday Movie				
TUESDAY	A	Wheel of Fortune	Jeopardy	Who's the Boss	Growing Pains	Moonlighting		Jack and Mike		
	C			The Wizard		CBS Tuesday Movie				
	N			Matlock		Crime Story		1986		
WEDNESDAY	A	Wheel of Fortune	Jeopardy	Perfect Strangers	Head of the Class	Dynasty		Hotel		
	C			Together We Stand	Better Days	Magnum, P.I.		The Equalizer		
	N			Highway to Heaven		Gimme a Break	You Again	St. Elsewhere		
THURSDAY	A	Wheel of Fortune	Jeopardy	Our World		The Colbys		20/20		
	C			Simon & Simon		Knots Landing		Kay O'Brien		
	N			Cosby Show	Family Ties	Cheers	Night Court	Hill Street Blues		
FRIDAY	A	Wheel of Fortune	Jeopardy	Webster	Mr. Belvedere	Sidekicks	Sledge Hammer	Starman		
	C			Scarecrow & Mrs. King		Dallas		Falcon Crest		
	N			The A-Team		Miami Vice		L.A. Law		
SATURDAY	A			Life with Lucy	Ellen Burstyn Show	Heart of the City		Spenser: For Hire		
	C			Downtown		New Mike Hammer		Twilight Zone		
	N			Facts of Life	227	Golden Girls	Amen	Hunter		

Fig. 20   1986 TV SCHEDULE

pany earns a fee for distributing television programs from the stations that air them. The fee is a percentage of the license fees (which the stations pay the producers for the right to broadcast their programs) plus the amounts paid by national advertisers for barter advertising time (time that is retained by King World and sold in connection with its programs).

Basically, what this means is that King World is the production company's agent in its dealings with the stations. King World's incentives are straightforward: The more stations it can line up, and the higher the license fees the programs can command, the more money the company makes. (Note: On our schedule, *Wheel* and *Jeopardy!* are on ABC; of the three major networks, King World's ties with ABC are the strongest.)

Actually, the King World story was in many ways a play on our old friend PTAR, the prime-time access rule of 1971. When King World picked up the distribution rights for *Wheel of Fortune* in 1982, it was a cautious time for the syndication market; many of King World's competitors were worried that PTAR was about to be struck down by the FCC and were thus reluctant to bid on properties whose time slots might be repossessed by the networks. As it happened, both PTAR and the fin-syn rules remained intact after a close brush with oblivion (playing a key role in maintaining the status quo was a former actor named Ronald Reagan).

Curiously, Dean Burch, chairman of the FCC in 1971, had voted against PTAR, on the grounds that stations would resort to frivolous programs such as game shows to fill the 7:30 time slot. Twelve years later, his fears were coming true, and a new investment play was just beginning—another reason quick predictions of the winners and losers from regulations such as PTAR inevitably don't tell the full story.

King World went public in late 1984, approximately one year after introducing *Wheel of Fortune* to evening viewers (it had been on daytime TV since 1975). By that time, they had also introduced *Jeopardy!*, which in eastern markets aired at 7:30, right after *Wheel* at 7:00. It would prove to be the biggest one-two punch in game show history.

Ironically, part of the problem in recognizing the investment potential of a company such as King World is that we the viewers tend to take the process for granted. When we see Pat Sajak and Vanna White do their shtick, we overlook what an accomplishment it was to get them on the air in the first place. By definition, though, if you are in a major market and watching these shows, you are already witnessing something significant.

When King World first bid on *Wheel,* the show aired in about 40 percent of the country, but before long you'd have been hard pressed to find a market without it. The *Jeopardy!* success story was much the same. Increased "market clearance" in these two shows propelled King World's total revenues from $29 million in 1984 to $81 million in 1985. By January 1986, the stock was up 500 percent from its initial offering price.

I'm picking up the story in 1986 because it still wasn't too late to buy. As is so often the case, the King World story had a rich-get-richer aspect that made additional success more likely than not. After all, if you were someone with a syndicatable TV property back in 1986, King World's success with *Wheel* and *Jeopardy!* would surely have caught your eye. You might have said, "These guys must be doing something right. Maybe they should be selling *my* show." One blossoming television personality did just that. Her name was Oprah Winfrey.

For King World, *Oprah* started where *Wheel* and *Jeopardy!* left off. The contribution of *The Oprah Winfrey Show* was the single biggest reason for King World's continued revenue growth over the next five years. In 1987, King World's distribution fees from *Oprah* amounted to only $31 million. By 1992, that figure had risen to $171 million— representing a compound annual growth rate of 40 percent. Between 1987 and 1992, King World's (split-adjusted) earnings advanced from $0.74 per share to $2.43. Not surprisingly, the stock followed suit, moving from $9 per share in early 1987 to $25 in mid-1992.

The epilogue of the story is that there was still a good reason to buy King World shares in mid-1992, even though the high-growth periods of *Wheel, Jeopardy!,* and even *Oprah* were now clearly behind the company. In fact, in June 1992, I recommended King World, then trading at $25 per share. This time, the reasoning was somewhat different.

I wrote the recommendation within a more general article featuring stocks whose price/earnings ratios were lower than the market as a

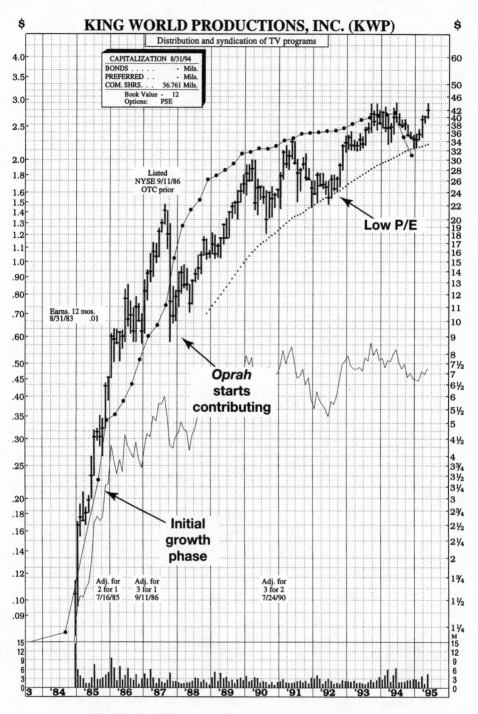

KING WORLD PRODUCTIONS, INC. (KWP)

Distribution and syndication of TV programs

CAPITALIZATION 8/31/94
BONDS . . . . .   - Mils.
PREFERRED . .   - Mils.
COM. SHRS. . . .   36.761 Mils.
Book Value -   12
Options: PSE

Listed
NYSE 9/11/86
OTC prior

Low P/E

Earns. 12 mos.
8/31/83   .01

Oprah
**starts
contributing**

**Initial
growth
phase**

Adj. for   Adj. for
2 for 1   3 for 1
7/16/85   9/11/86

Adj. for
3 for 2
7/24/90

Fig. 21 KING WORLD CHART (Courtesy of Research Securities Co.)

whole. King World certainly qualified, because at $25 per share it was trading at only eleven times expected earnings, while the S&P 500 was trading somewhere in the neighborhood of twenty times earnings.

The stock was cheap because investors were starting to become concerned about King World. Revenue growth was down to only about 6 percent per year. And there were new worries. What if the ratings for *Wheel* and *Jeopardy!* started to go down? What if the FCC repealed the PTAR or fin-syn regulations?

The low P/E is the market's way of expressing its concern about such issues. This does not mean that a stock with a low P/E is impervious to bad news: If any one of those unwanted events did come to pass, King World stock would almost surely go down. However, when confronted with a low P/E, it often makes sense to take a more positive attitude. In this case, you had to ask yourself, What if *Wheel* and *Jeopardy!* were renewed for several years at attractive prices? (That's what happened.) What if the FCC does *not* take any immediate action adverse to King World's interests? (It did not.) Finally, what if some *new* show takes off? (Alas, that didn't happen either, but with several new offerings in the works, it was at least a possibility.)

When a stock is kept low because of concerns that don't come to pass, the market eventually loses its concern—and that's what happened to King World. By the fall of 1993, the stock had reached $40 per share, a 60 percent gain from its level of mid-1992. That's an epilogue worth participating in.

SUBPLOTS

- Over the years, the same stock can be attractive at different times for completely different reasons.
- The high-growth phase and the value phase of an individual stock are likely to be many years apart.

1990: A Digression to the New Kid on the Block

Most investment books don't spend much time on dead ends. Instead, they concentrate on situations where you could have made a lot of money (the "dos") or lost a lot of money (the "don'ts"). By and large, they don't acknowledge that real life in the stock market often involves spending hours on a potential investment only to conclude that one isn't there.

I'm not here to quibble with this black-and-white approach. Stories without punch lines make for lousy entertainment, even if they do happen to be realistic. To make a TV analogy, if the real lives of most of us were made into a soap opera, there would be no J. R. Ewings and no Erica Kanes. And there would be no viewers.

However, I'm going to tempt fate in this section and provide some stock market realism. When the Fox network was launched with a limited schedule in 1987 (it moved to five nights per week in 1990), investors had to decide what to do about it. Today, I can tell you that if you had bought shares of Rupert Murdoch's News Corporation—the parent company of 20th Century–Fox and Fox Television—you would have made an awful lot of money. But making that call on the basis of the schedule would have been very tough indeed.

The Fox network was guaranteed to be a big money loser in the near term by the very nature of the business. But even in its early days, Fox showed that no institution, however ingrained, is invulnerable to competition. In competing with the three major networks, Fox exposed a serious weakness: The networks, by trying to appeal to everybody, often appealed to nobody. The way to exploit that weakness was with targeted programming. If Fox had been just another set of programs, however well done, the network never would have lasted. Instead, Fox gave itself a chance by targeting the youth market.

Beverly Hills 90210, In Living Color, The Simpsons, even *Married with Children*—Fox was one youth hit after another. The other networks could argue that they didn't even want youth demographics (advertisers prefer more mature audiences), but it was hard not to admire what Fox had accomplished. Fox certainly made Rupert Murdoch look like a visionary, and he got points from investors well before his network turned any sort of profit.

Speaking of business developments without apparent investment significance, the discussion of Fox closes a longstanding loop. One of the fallouts of the prime-time access rule and fin-syn regulations of the early seventies was the tremendous growth in independent television stations, which quickly tripled in number so as to absorb the considerable material that the networks and their affiliates suddenly faced re-

PRIME TIME SCHEDULE: 1990

		7:00 PM	7:30	8:00	8:30	9:00	9:30	10:00	10:30	11:00
SUNDAY	A	Life Goes On		America's Funniest Home Videos	America's Funniest People	ABC Sunday Movie				
	C	60 Minutes		Murder, She Wrote		CBS Sunday Movie				
	F	True Colors	Parker Lewis Can't Lose	In Living Color	Get a Life	Married with Children	Good Grief	Against the Law		
	N	Hull High		Lifestories		NBC Sunday Movie				
MONDAY	A			MacGyver		Monday Night Football				
	C			Uncle Buck	Major Dad	Murphy Brown	Designing Women	Trials of Rosie O'Neill		
	F			Fox Night at the Movies						
	N			Fresh Prince of Bel Air	Ferris Bueller	NBC Monday Movie				
TUESDAY	A			Who's the Boss	Head of the Class	Roseanne	Coach	Thirtysomething		
	C			Rescue 911		CBS Tuesday Movie				
	N			Matlock		In the Heat of the Night		Law & Order		
WEDNESDAY	A			Wonder Years	Growing Pains	Doogie Howser, M.D.	Married People	Cop Rock		
	C			Lenny	Doctor, Doctor	Jake and the Fatman		WIOU		
	N			Unsolved Mysteries		Fanelli Boys	Dear John	Hunter		
THURSDAY	A			Father Dowling Mysteries		Gabriel's Fire		Primetime Live		
	C			Top Cops	The Flash		Doctor, Doctor	Knots Landing		
	F			The Simpsons	Babes	Beverly Hills 90210				
	N			Cosby Show	A Different World	Cheers	Grand	L. A. Law		
FRIDAY	A			Full House	Family Matters	Perfect Strangers	Going Places	20/20		
	C			Evening Shade	Bagdad Cafe	Over My Dead Body		Dallas		
	F			America's Most Wanted		D.E.A.				
	N			Quantum Leap		Night Court	Wings	Midnight Caller		
SATURDAY	A			Young Riders		China Beach		Twin Peaks		
	C			Family Man	Hogan Family	E.A.R.T.H. Force		48 Hours		
	F			Totally Hidden Video	Haywire	Cops	American Chronicles			
	N			Parenthood	Working It Out	Golden Girls	Empty Nest	Carol & Company	American Dreamer	

Fig. 22 1990 TV SCHEDULE

strictions on. Well, guess what? By the late eighties, many independent stations had gotten weary of having to constantly acquire or produce programming. A network affiliation carried tremendous appeal, not only because programming needs could be satisfied at the push of a button, but also because the value of the station was likely to increase. The point is that Fox would have never gotten off the ground if it hadn't had a base of independent stations eager and willing to sign up.

Because News Corp was really a publishing operation first and an entertainment operation second, investors had to accept the fact that Fox would never be the driving force behind the company's stock. But even if the network's emergence did nothing more than establish the connection between Fox and News Corp, investors were well served by a different development.

In late 1990—by which time the recession (and the company's indebtedness) had pushed News Corp stock down to just $6 per share —20th Century–Fox came out with *Home Alone,* one of the most successful movies of our time.

Me? I saw the previews for *Home Alone* and thought they had given away the whole plot. It didn't dawn on me that kids don't care! *Home Alone* grossed a stunning $285 million, placing it at that time third, behind *E.T.* and *Star Wars,* on the all-time list. News Corp shares rallied from $6 to $15 within a few months. By 1993, buoyed by events on the publishing front that were outside the TV- (and movie-) watcher's grasp, the shares hit $60—a tenfold gain in just three years.

No, the television schedule didn't tell you everything. But maybe our digression to the Fox network wasn't such a dead end after all.

SUBPLOTS

- It's okay to start analyzing the right stock for the wrong reason.
- Roundabout routes to success are a way of life on the stock market.

1992: What Happened to NBC? Plus, The Tyranny of the Newsmagazines

In 1992, NBC faced one disappointment after another. *The Cosby Show,* perhaps the single biggest symbol of that network's mid-eighties rejuvenation, was leaving the air after a long, successful run. *The Golden Girls* was headed for a similar fate. A couple of other series were perhaps pulled too soon: *Matlock* was axed by NBC and then picked up by ABC, while *In the Heat of the Night* moved over to CBS. (These "missing" NBC time slots are shaded on the accompanying schedule.) Now for the usual question: What should an investor have done about these scheduling shifts?

In the summer of 1992, I recommended buying shares of CBS, then trading around $170. An important part of the thesis, as simple as it sounds, was that CBS stood to benefit from NBC's troubles. The investment worked out better than I could ever have imagined.

Some of the benefits were already taking shape. Around that time, CBS was in the process of regaining the ratings lead, keyed by such entries as *Murphy Brown,* which combined high ratings and great demographics (not only that, it aired on Mondays, a night with consistently high viewership). And Dan Quayle helped make Murphy Brown even more of a household name by questioning her family values. Knowing our TV history, it was quite likely that the ratings shifts CBS was achieving could last for years, creating the potential for a long-term turnaround.

There was more to the CBS turnaround story, of course. Operating expenses were being trimmed. Interest costs were coming down as debt was refinanced. And the losses in sports programming were coming to an end; specifically, the company had taken a $322 pretax charge in the third quarter of 1991 to cover the shortfall of advertising income relative to the high-priced contracts for major-league baseball and other sporting events. The losses from baseball obscured CBS's gains at other points of the programming spectrum. So if NBC started having its own troubles in 1992, you could say it was about time.

I should mention that recommending CBS at $170 didn't exactly make me Johnny-on-the-spot. The stock had fallen as low as $130 in late 1991, when some investors got rattled by the sports write-off and the ensuing loss for the year (CBS's first as a public company). Rather

PRIME TIME SCHEDULE: 1992

		7:00 PM	7:30	8:00	8:30	9:00	9:30	10:00	10:30	11:00
SUNDAY	A	Life Goes On		America's Funniest Home Videos	America's Funniest People	ABC Sunday Movie				
	C	60 Minutes		Murder, She Wrote		CBS Sunday Movie				
	F	True Colors	Parker Lewis Can't Lose	In Living Color	ROC	Married with Children	Herman's Head	Sunday Comics		
	N	Adventures of Mark and Brian	Eerie, Indiana	Man of the People	Pacific Station	NBC Sunday Movie				
MONDAY	A			MacGyver				Monday Night Football		
	C			Evening Shade	Major Dad	Murphy Brown	Designing Women	Northern Exposure		
	F			Fox Night at the Movies						
	N			Fresh Prince of Bel Air	Blossom	NBC Monday Movie				
TUESDAY	A			Full House	Home Improvement	Roseanne	Coach	Homefront		
	C			Rescue 911		CBS Tuesday Movie				
	N			I'll Fly Away				Dateline NBC		
WEDNESDAY	A			Dinosaurs	Wonder Years	Doogie Howser, M.D.	Sibs	Anything But Love	Good & Evil	
	C			Royal Family	Teech	Jake and the Fatman		48 Hours		
	N			Unsolved Mysteries		Night Court	Seinfeld	Quantum Leap		
THURSDAY	A			Pros and Cons		FBI: The Untold Stories	American Detective	Primetime Live		
	C			Top Cops		Trials of Rosie O'Neill		Knots Landing		
	F			The Simpsons	Drexell's Class	Beverly Hills 90210				
	N				A Different World	Cheers	Wings	L. A. Law		
FRIDAY	A			Family Matters	Step by Step	Perfect Strangers	Baby Talk	20/20		
	C			Princesses	Brooklyn Bridge	Carol Burnett Show		Palace Guard		
	F			America's Most Wanted		Ultimate Challenge				
	N				Exposé	Dear John	Flesh 'N' Blood	Reasonable Doubts		
SATURDAY	A			Who's the Boss	Growing Pains	Young Riders		The Commish		
	C			CBS Saturday Movie				P.S.I. Luv U		
	F			Cops		Totally Hidden Video	Best of the Worst			
	N				The Torkelsons	Empty Nest	Nurses	Sisters		

Fig. 23 1992 TV SCHEDULE

than lamenting the $40 opportunity cost, however, a simple check of the price/earnings multiple indicated that the stock still had room to run: Using a conservative earnings estimate of $15 per share for 1993, CBS shares were priced at only eleven times expected earnings—far less than the overall market (whose P/E was somewhere in the high teens, depending on whose earnings estimate you were using). This low P/E meant that CBS was a cheap stock, even though its dollar price of $170 was one of the highest on the New York Stock Exchange.

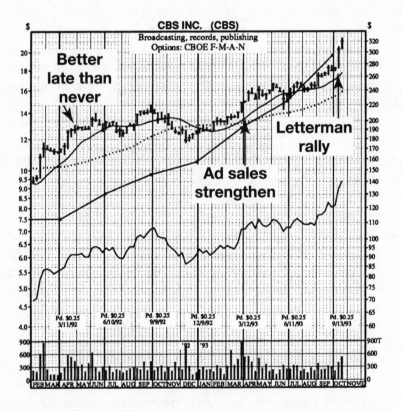

Fig. 24 CBS CHART (Courtesy of Securities Research Co.)

Low P/E stocks with the capacity for positive earnings surprises are always worth looking for, and, in this case, the whole story was coming together nicely. The ratings gains translated into superior performance in the upfront advertising market—that rite of spring wherein advertisers place their bets for the upcoming fall season. Selling ads at higher prices flows directly to the bottom line because fixed costs are, well, fixed. This operating leverage is precisely why network people fuss about a few ratings points here and there. Investors shouldn't fret in quite the same way, but they should appreciate the value of a favorable trend once it is established. CBS shares were up to $250 by the middle of 1993.

When CBS wrestled David Letterman away from NBC in 1993 in the ultimate off-camera soap opera, the network had yet another victory. Letterman's enormous price tag ($16 million a year) got all the attention, but the ratings numbers justified the apparent largesse. So even if you had waited until after Dave's debut (Monday, August 30) to consider CBS, it still wasn't too late. That Wednesday, CBS was up 19 points, to a record $266 per share, and it wasn't through by a long shot. CBS was on its way to earning $20 per share in 1993, 33 percent above my conservative estimate of the year before. In the media-stock frenzy of the fall of 1993, CBS shares vaulted to $325, making for a gain of 90 percent in just fifteen months. And by the time Westinghouse bid for CBS in the summer of 1995, the shares were at a split-adjusted level of $400, 135 percent above where it stood in 1992.

Another noteworthy feature of the 1992 television schedule was the preponderance of newsmagazines: old reliable *60 Minutes* on CBS, *PrimeTime Live* and *20/20* on ABC, and the new kid on the block, NBC's *Dateline* with Stone Phillips and Jane Pauley. These shows are attractive to many parties because, like game shows, they are much cheaper to produce than dramas. (Note that the news shows accounted for a sizable chunk of the hour-length programming on the schedule.)

The reason that investors should have cared about the newsmagazines was that the competition between them was fierce and they began trying to outdo one another in the headline-grabbing game of corporation bashing. Before the 1992–93 TV season was half through, three particular companies would see their stock prices fall prey— rightly or wrongly—to what the networks had to say. For those with a trading mentality, it was a field day. Here goes:

Food Lion

This was the one that started it all and the one to which I'll devote the most attention. The date was Thursday, November 5, 1992, and the show was ABC's *PrimeTime Live*. The appointed victim was Food Lion, a highly successful grocery chain headquartered in North Carolina and with stores across the entire Southeast.

Stated simply, Food Lion's meat department was caught by the camera's seemingly unerring eye serving reground, reconstituted, rotten, smelly meat. Voice-overs mentioned putting bleach on ham to hide the odor. Expiration dates on chicken appeared to be disregarded or even covered over by employees. The whole thing was so nauseating it made you want to set up a poison center in Raleigh-Durham.

In the interest of equal opportunity, I should mention that viewers never saw what was left on the cutting room floor. The unedited tapes apparently included footage of meat being thrown away *after* it was identified as spoiled—as opposed to being put back on the shelves, as viewers were left to assume. But this is not the place to assess the relative guilt of Food Lion and ABC (the matter went to litigation). What we *can* do is to suggest how a Food Lion investor might have responded to the crisis.

First of all, we need some context as to why you might have owned the stock in the first place. Once a struggling operation, Food Lion resuscitated itself back in the 1970s when it introduced an everyday low pricing policy à la Wal-Mart. Their LFPINC strategy (lowest food prices in North Carolina) didn't exactly trip off the tongue, but it worked. Because the stores and distribution centers were truly cookie-cutter operations, and because of the expertise of the company's buyers, Food Lion's SG&A (selling, general, and administrative expenses) amounted to only 13 percent of sales, more than 5 percentage points lower than the supermarket industry average. Even though low pricing kept gross margins low (around 20 percent), Food Lion's profit margins were among the industry's highest.

The other investment allure was the chain's constant expansion. In 1984, Food Lion's store base numbered two hundred and fifty; by 1992, it was over a thousand. In virtually all the company's targeted expansion areas, customers proved receptive to the combination of low prices and convenient location. Because of these attributes, Food

Lion stock had for years been one of the most expensive of its peer group, trading at thirty times earnings or even higher. (Good news if you happened to own it before it got so expensive.)

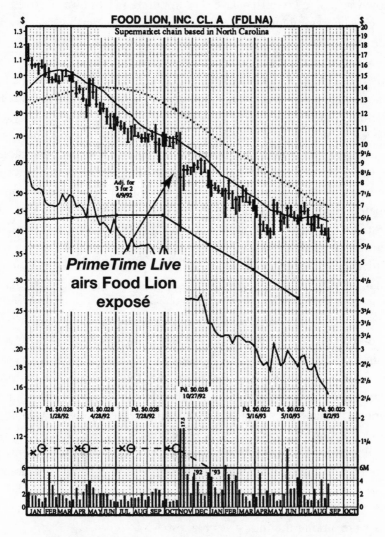

Fig. 25 FOOD LION CHART (Courtesy of Securities Research Co.)

But the supermarket industry was slowing down even before the fateful broadcast, and Food Lion could not escape the trend. Same-store sales growth, which was 8.6 percent in 1989, dropped to 4.5 in 1990 and 2.7 in 1991. In 1992, the monthly figures were ranging mostly between 1 percent and −1 percent, a reflection of difficult economic times and price competition among the supermarkets.

For Food Lion, difficulties emerged in 1992 with the company's operations in Texas, where Albertson's met them head on. The increasingly competitive environment, coupled with the absence of food price inflation (which can *help* supermarkets), caused the stock to drop from its early 1992 peak of $18. As the chart shows, the stock had been dropping well before *PrimeTime Live* entered the scene. But the worst was yet to come.

If you already owned Food Lion shares at the time of the broadcast, there was not much to do in the very short term: The stock dropped 13 percent the day after the broadcast, from $10 to $8⅝. Now the all-important question: Hold, sell, or buy more?

The trap was in thinking that the price decline made it too late to sell. If you objectively assessed the program's fallout, three negative outcomes seemed especially likely:

GROSS MARGINS WOULD DECLINE. The company would almost certainly be forced into a higher-than-normal level of promotional activity to make sure that customers came back to the stores.

EXPENSES WOULD RISE. If Food Lion had an image problem—and it did—the company would have to fix it. Post–*PrimeTime Live* focus groups conducted by Food Lion complained about worker uniforms, lighting, product displays, you name it. Fixing these problems automatically created a higher level of expenses in the near term.

EXPANSION WOULD SLOW DOWN. This took a little more time to map out. In North Carolina and West Virginia, where Food Lion was a well-established name, prospects for customers returning were good. A typical reaction might be, "Hey, I've bought meat there for ten years and I've never gotten sick." (The fact that North Carolina wasn't rife with food poisoning was a suspicious part of the *PrimeTime Live* story.)

In expansion areas such as Texas, however, the results were disastrous. Stores that were doing $150,000 per week in sales a year before were now doing $80,000, well below the break-even level. Consumer reaction from that area was more like, "So *that's* why Food Lion can sell for less." Whether true or not, Food Lion stood to suffer from the perception.

When the broadcast aired, an investor had to realize that things could get even worse, and they did. For November 1992, Food Lion's same-store sales were down 9.5 percent. Same-store sales on the order of −5 percent followed for much of the next six months. But even at $8 per share, the stock was still trading at twenty-five times expected 1993 earnings. It doesn't take much of a comparison shopper to realize that paying twenty-five times earnings for a company with a massive public relations problem is not what you'd call a bargain. By the end of 1993, Food Lion shares were languishing around the $5 level.

Those that failed to sell because "the damage had been done" suffered the most. The stock's immediate decline from $10 to $8⅝ (13 percent) ended up being dwarfed by the subsequent decline from $8⅝ to $5¼ (40 percent). Phoning in your Food Lion sell order the day after the show might have seemed like panic selling at the time, but it turned out to be the best long-term move.

GM

Buy shares of General Motors? In November 1992, the idea seemed preposterous, for several reasons.

The most recent stain on the once-proud GM record came from *Dateline NBC,* the network's new entry in the newsmagazine derby. On November 17, the show revealed horrifying pictures of a GM pickup truck bursting into flames after a collision from the side.

It was a monumental case of insult being added to injury. Just weeks earlier, GM had reported a $753 million loss for the third quarter. On October 26, chairman Robert Stempel was forced to step down from his post, which he had held for only two years.

There were other, more chronic negatives to the GM investment picture. The company's labor costs exceeded $2,360 per car, $500 more than Chrysler's and $800 more than Ford. Market share was dropping. As the presidential election was winding down, Ross Perot was swimming in the headlines with claims that GM never faced up to its problems. A major story in *Time* magazine (November 9) suggested "if the financial squeeze grows too tight, GM might even file for bankruptcy protection."

Wall Street was scared stiff. General Motors shares were trading hands at just $30 per share, which was arguably the combined value of such subsidiaries as GMAC, EDS, and Hughes Aircraft. In other words, the market was according *no value at all* to GM's core North American automobile operations, a rare situation indeed. The attack on pickup trucks was the last straw. Pickups were an extremely profitable portion of GM's otherwise-besieged automobile lines.

The case against GM pickup trucks was not without merit. The roots of the problem actually dated back to 1973. Prior to that time, the gas tanks in GM trucks (and those of Ford and Chrysler) were mounted inside the cab, behind the seats. Federal regulations then forced the companies to relocate the gas tanks. Ford and Chrysler both elected to place the tank underneath the chassis, protecting it with a steel frame. GM trucks, on the other hand (at least, those made between 1973 and 1987), had their tanks mounted outside the frame, like a saddlebag. In the eyes of many, this placement made GM trucks more vulnerable in the event of a side-impact collision.

The vehicles consistently passed federal safety standards, but some of GM's own internal memoranda suggested conflicts about the safety of the sidesaddle tanks. Engineers worried about fuel leaks, fires, and, ultimately, liability. According to the Center for Auto Safety, since 1973 more than three hundred people had been killed in collisions involving burning gas tanks in GM pickups. Then *Dateline NBC* decided to bring the whole matter into the public domain by burning one itself.

As a rule, it pays to buy at times like these, assuming that you can find some comfort amid the uncertainties. Regarding *Time*'s suggestion of possible bankruptcy, similar rumors had encircled Ford (not to mention Chrysler) some twelve years earlier, in what turned out to be a major buying opportunity. These precedents triggered some investor bottom fishing that helped GM move off its $30 trough, and the shares hit $40 by January. You'd be forgiven for missing a speculative move like that, but another one was coming.

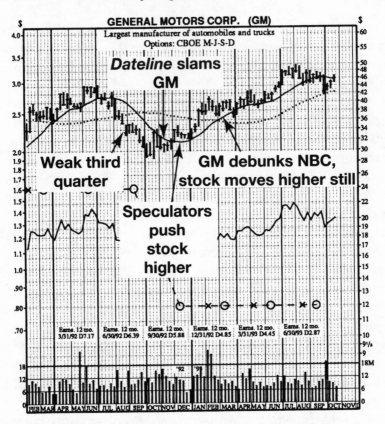

Fig. 26 GM CHART (Courtesy of Securities Research Co.)

In early February, a resurfacing of the pickup issue brought the uptrend to a temporary halt. A jury in Atlanta awarded $105.2 million to the parents of a teenager killed in a crash of a GM truck in 1989. Of this amount, $101 million was in the form of punitive damages. With more than twenty-five similar cases outstanding, GM again looked on the defensive, and the stock backtracked a bit, to $38. One point in GM's favor was that such punitive awards are generally vastly reduced upon appeal. But the ultimate buy signal for GM shares occurred just a few days later.

On February 9, 1993, GM held a press conference in Detroit, broadcast to securities analysts across the country. In this now-famous exposé, GM turned the tables on NBC's investigation. The fire that viewers saw, it turns out, was started by an "incendiary device" that

Dateline had attached to the vehicle. And that wasn't all. The speed of the incoming car that "caused" the explosion had been greatly understated by NBC. And the fuel cap had been fitted improperly, further advancing the likelihood of an explosion.

For the first time in years, public opinion was swinging the way of General Motors. Securities analysts came away from the presentation with a fresh regard for GM's new management and a fresh distrust for the integrity of the newsmagazines. Out of the woodwork came the stories of past newsmagazine gaffes—notably, *20/20*'s 1990 interview with the alleged "Buckwheat," of *Little Rascals* fame (alas, the real Buckwheat had died ten years earlier).

The pickup saga wasn't over, but the chances for a favorable result for GM looked better than ever. As a case in point, in July GM settled thirty-six class action suits by providing all registered owners of 1973– 86 C/K model pickup trucks (and their successors, the 1987–92 R/V models) with certificates good for a $1,000 discount on the purchase of a new GM truck.

There were many other favorable events for GM in 1993. In April, the company reduced its head count of hourly workers by 16,500 via a special onetime agreement with the UAW. For the second quarter, GM's North American automobile operations reduced their losses to $98 million, down from a $761 million loss in the same period of 1992. The stock still moved in fits and starts, but the general direction was favorable: In August, it hit a yearly high of $49 per share. But the point is that you didn't need an iron stomach to participate: Even if you had waited until after GM's debunking of *Dateline* to buy shares, you would have been up 27 percent—in just six months.

Wal-Mart

The Wal-Mart story completes the TV newsmagazine circle. With Food Lion, the victim was a nonhousehold name that had been doing pretty well; with GM, it was a household name that was doing terribly. Wal-Mart was both a household name and a company that didn't seem to know about bad news. On December 22, 1992, that changed.

Again, the instigator was *Dateline NBC*. In its segment on Wal-Mart on the Tuesday before Christmas, the show alleged that contrary to the "Buy American" campaign started by the late Sam Walton in 1985, Wal-Mart was in fact sourcing garments from Bangladesh. Not only that, they were using child labor.

This time around, an investor had to see it coming to take the proper action. Remember, the GM incendiary device embarrassment hadn't happened yet, so the newsmagazines were riding high. *Dateline*'s intention to chip away at Wal-Mart was advertised well in advance, and it wouldn't have been a bad strategy to sell in anticipation: Not only were Wal-Mart shares trading near an all-time high, they were commanding a hefty premium of thirty times expected earnings for 1993, a level that left little room for disappointment. Sure enough, on the two trading sessions before *Dateline* (Monday the 21st and Tuesday the 22nd), Wal-Mart shares dropped a total of $2\frac{3}{8}$ points, from $65\frac{5}{8}$ to $63\frac{1}{4}$.

In this case, it seemed easy to shrug off the news. Yes, Wal-Mart appeared to be caught absolutely red-handed. But discount retailing is not like food retailing. Wal-Mart customers didn't have the same incentive to avoid the stores that Food Lion customers had. That argued for a rebound, and the shares complied by advancing $1\frac{3}{8}$ on Wednesday, the first trading session after the report. The moral: The effect of newsmagazine exposés on trading activity can be limited to the very short term.

As a postscript, though, I should point out that those who stayed out of the stock had the last laugh. The *Dateline* report, though by no means the cause of Wal-Mart's troubles, turned out to come at a watershed time for the company and its perception on Wall Street. Wal-Mart continued to excel by the standards of the average retailer, but it no longer matched up well with its own exalted standards. Same-store sales growth was about 8 percent at the beginning of 1993, a far cry from the double-digit advances the company had posted for years. The Sam's wholesale clubs were a particular weak spot. The stock, which split 2-for-1 in March, traded down as far as $24 per share in June, a 25 percent decline from its level after the *Dateline* broadcast. It was serendipitous, but *Dateline* turned out to have taken the first chip out of Wal-Mart's halo, and the stock hasn't been the same since.

- Newsmagazines can create short-term turning points in share prices, but you need to use your own judgment to see whether the effect will endure.
- The next time the newsmagazines assail some corporate no-goodnik, I'm betting they get their story right.

MEDIA-INSPIRED PRODUCTS AND TRENDS

It's time to change our tack. There is general agreement that the television shows and movies of any given period must say something about society as a whole. What isn't as well known is that the pursuit of investment indicators from these media offerings has already developed into something of a cottage industry. In this section, I'd like to make some additions to the cottage. First, though, I should give you a sampling of what's already out there.

When the movie *Darkman* was released in August 1990, Bob Prechter (founder of *The Elliott Wave Theorist* newsletter) suggested a correlation between the movie and the recession that began that summer. Prechter's theory was that the very salability of something "dark" reflected the national mood, which was decidedly somber in the second half of 1990. Prechter noted that gangster films such as *Goodfellas* were also popular at the time, just as they had been in the depression-bound thirties. If you went so far as to be out of the stock market in late 1990 (Prechter was bearish throughout), you would have escaped a big decline.

Score one for *Elliott Wave*—with an asterisk. I am not here to say that Prechter won't be right again, but *Darkman*-type inferences inevitably have a selective component. Other movies released in 1990 include *My Blue Heaven*, *The Freshman*, and *The Jungle Book*: Anything sinister about those? Indicators that purport to predict the entire market are great when they're right, but they put a bit too much on the line for my tastes.

An even bigger worry about such media-based inferences is the lag time between conception and release. For example, the movie *Wall Street* was conceived in the heyday of the corporate raider, but it didn't come out until December 1987, two months after the worst day ever on the real Wall Street. What sort of indicator is that? In a similar vein, the movie version of *Other People's Money,* starring Danny DeVito as corporate raider Lawrence Garfield, came out in the fall of 1991, by which time corporate raiders were a vanished breed. If anything, these films were useful to investors as *negative* indicators, in that they suggested an end to the very eras they depicted.

Negative indicators can also apply to individual companies. For example, Brunswick was one of the great stocks of the late fifties, buoyed by the nationwide explosion of pool halls and bowling alleys. However, when pool finally made it onto the big screen in 1960 with *The Hustler,* starring Paul Newman, it was a reflection of what *had* happened, not what was going to happen. If you had stopped investing in pool and bowling in 1960, your timing would have been outstanding, because Brunswick, having risen fiftyfold between 1956 and 1960, proceeded to completely fall apart. The stock didn't push through its 1960 high until 1985.

I'd like to concentrate on something much more basic and investigate those cases where the movie or television show actually *created* the public's tastes. Ever since Clark Gable bared his chest in 1934's *It Happened One Night*—sending undershirt sales plummeting—the media have had this power. They create useful indicators for specific industries and stocks, not for the overall market.

Examples of the media's clout aren't hard to find. *The Adventures of Davy Crockett* made coonskin caps a national craze in 1955. A few years later, Mary Tyler Moore made capri pants the rage by insisting (it was in her contract) that her character Laura Petrie wear them on *The Dick Van Dyke Show.* Speaking of Mary, her former boss Lou Grant started a rush in journalism school applications after moving to the *Los Angeles Tribune,* just as the movie *The Paper Chase* stimulated law school applications. Finally, *On Golden Pond* caused a stunning rise in property values along the shores of New Hampshire's Squam Lake, the actual site of the film.

Not surprisingly, our focus will be on situations where the media's impact carried over into the stock market. These impacts can be very different, so it helps to lump them into categories according to their level of seriousness. For investment purposes, media-inspired stock plays fall into three types: vague, closer, and bull's-eyes.

Vague Indicators

The release date of the movie *The China Syndrome* was March 16, 1979. The date of the Three Mile Island nuclear accident was March 28, 1979. It's safe to say that the movie did not cause the accident, but investors who saw the film may nonetheless have had an edge.

If you happened to own shares of General Public Utilities, coadministrators of the TMI-1 and TMI-2 nuclear plants, 1979 was a very rough year. The stock dropped from $18 in January to under $11 by April as the market sorted out what the Three Mile Island disaster meant to the company. Everyone knew the plant had to be shut down following the accident, but questions remained as to how long the shutdown would last, how much the cleanup would cost, and whether the interim financial drain would imperil the all-important dividend. Buy, sell, or hold? It was a tough call.

At that point, whether you owned the stock or not, it made sense to be conservative, and that's where *The China Syndrome* comes in. The movie, after all, was about fear; its very title referred to the prospect of nuclear debris burning a hole in the earth that went all the way to China. The movie was responsible for bringing the term "meltdown" into the national lexicon. Three Mile Island would have made the investment community—and society as a whole—queasy under any conditions. But *The China Syndrome* surely helped crystallize the fears that were already there. As if the connection between the film and the accident wasn't clear enough, the film coincidentally chose the phrase "an area the size of Pennsylvania" to describe what a meltdown could wipe out.

If you appreciated the atmosphere of fear, you would have sold the stock even after the initial decline. Fear alone made it very unlikely that the Three Mile Island plants would quickly return to service, suggesting a prolonged distress for both the company and its shares. And that's exactly what happened. From its postaccident level of $11 per share, GPU stock dropped to a low of less than $4 per share in 1980, shortly after the company omitted its quarterly dividend.

For those who like to think optimistically, you could have made the exact opposite argument—namely, that the initial emotions to Three Mile Island would eventually wear off and normal operations would one day return. But the key word is "eventually." With the advantage of many years of hindsight, the strategy of buying GPU shares at *any time* during the crisis makes a lot of sense, because the stock hit $40 by the end of the decade. However, putting yourself in the decision-making moment, it was also clear that you didn't have to rush back in at $11 per share. It's tough to hold on stoically during a swoon from $11 to $4 (the eventual $40 price was then but a pipe dream), and by holding off you could have saved both your psyche and your pocketbook during that eventful year of 1979.

A different sort of vague indicator came from 1982's *E.T.*, whose $400 million in gross receipts made it then the biggest box office hit of all time. As a generation of young Americans could tell you, E.T. followed a trail of Hershey's Reese's Pieces (not M&M's, the first choice of MCA, the movie's producer; after being rebuffed by M&M/ Mars, MCA shot the Reese's Pieces sequence and *then* went to Hershey for approval).

Now, *E.T.* did not by itself make Hershey a successful investment during that time. The great bull market was just beginning, and its early years were kind to all leading consumer companies. But *E.T.*'s display of Reese's Pieces pushed sales of the fledgling brand up 50 percent, to over $25 million in annual sales. Conveniently, this was the level required for a new brand to survive in the vast Hershey empire. And the success of Reese's Pieces had a spillover effect into the flagship Reese's peanut butter cups, Hershey's single biggest seller. Measuring these factors into the stock price movement cannot be done with any accuracy, but surely the effect was positive.

Another unquantifiable case was the second incarnation of Brunswick. Recall that *The Hustler* had come out *after* the 1950s pool boom and, therefore, after a gigantic run-up in the stock of this pool-equipment manufacturer. But when Paul Newman returned to the role of a pool hustler in *The Color of Money* (1986), the movie reawakened interest in the game. The new billiard parlors were upscale (i.e., yuppie) and charged up to $20 per hour for a table. Brunswick was by that time a diversified leisure company, with most of its earnings coming from its marine division, but it still stood to benefit from anything that pushed up sales of pool tables and equipment. Earnings for 1987 were up strongly, and the movie's November 1986 release date turned out to be a wonderful time to buy the stock—in the short term. Brunswick shares doubled by August of 1987 but then lost those gains and more in the crash of that October. There are some things movies can't help with.

Closer

In our search for the strongest possible media indicators, we would like something a wee bit more specific than what we have just seen. Here are a few movies that could have pushed investors further in the right direction.

Crocodile Dundee, the 1986 mythologizing of a character from the Australian outback, did its part by creating a surge of interest in Australia as a vacation destination. Said *The New York Times,* "*Crocodile Dundee* successfully creates the impression that there is something approaching a smogless, classless, American heaven on earth, though it's called Australia."

This time, the effect could be quantified. In 1984, when *Dundee* star Paul Hogan began doing tourism spots, 160,000 Americans traveled to Australia; within two years, that figure had nearly doubled. The influx of tourism was indicative of an extremely healthy economy, and it showed. Between 1985 and 1988, a period that included a global market crash, Australian stocks rose 125 percent.

A movie that gets us even closer to the stock market action was *Desperately Seeking Susan.* Released in March 1985, *Desperately* was Madonna's first big splash on the big screen and a wonderful vehicle for her vagabond chic persona. In particular, one of Madonna's trademarks was costume jewelry. To the extent that teenage mall-hopping girls chose to emulate her, the potential beneficiary was Claire's Stores, a fast-growing chain of mall-based costume jewelry shops.

For a while after the movie's release, Claire's stock behaved just as you'd like. From just under $10 in March of 1985, it surged to $16 per share by June, a 60 percent gain in three months. Same-store sales were up a stunning 28 percent for the first quarter of the year. In the second quarter, the advance was 31 percent. Considering that Wal-Mart was for years the envy of the retail industry with "only" 10 percent same-store sales gains, you get an idea of just how good business was at Claire's Stores.

Basically, the movie added an extra kick to a company that Wall Street already liked. In the mid-eighties, Claire's was in the middle of an aggressive expansion phase: The company had 195 stores in 1983 and would have a thousand by the end of the decade. As an extra plus, unlike other expanding chains, Claire's new stores were profitable almost immediately. This was a consequence of the extraordinary gross margins in the costume jewelry business (make it for a quarter, sell it for a dollar).

Now the bad news. All of these factors were woven into the price of the stock. At $16 per share, Claire's was trading at precisely fifty times its 1984 earnings of $0.32 per share. This wouldn't have been so bad if same-store sales continued their torrid pace. However, *Desperately* created an extra risk factor: If the movie was responsible for some of the sales gains, surely those gains were destined to wear off. And if the stock was trading on the new level of expectations, it just had to be on thin ice.

They did and it was. Same-store sales, which were up 28 percent for all of 1985, dropped to only a 5 percent gain for 1986, including a 10 percent *decline* for the fourth quarter of that year. Against this negative backdrop, the stock fell from its peak of $16 to just $5 by late 1986—a decline of almost 70 percent.

In retrospect, Claire's stock was pretty richly valued even before *Desperately Seeking Susan* was released, having already appreciated almost fiftyfold from its 1983 low. What this example shows is that even high P/E stocks can go much higher if short-term conditions are right. But investors have to be very wary about paying big multiples if there is any question about the sustainability of the company's growth. The more 70 percent declines we can avoid, the better off we'll be.

Bull's-eyes

Finally, we have reached the ultimate level within our spectrum of media power. What follows are four stocks that were given a valuable boost by the vast reach of television, not because they were hyped by

Dan Dorfman on CNBC but because the companies' products were displayed in an interesting and unintentional fashion. These opportunities don't occur every day, but, as we will discover, you can't afford to assume they *won't* happen. To profit in the future, you have to know what's possible. So here goes:

Remington Rand: 1954

As the chart shows, 1954 witnessed a dramatic price rise for the shares of Remington Rand (later, Sperry Rand, and now part of Unisys). What the chart doesn't say is that the price rise had its foundation in perhaps the greatest PR move of the still-young television era. It began as follows:

"Good evening, everyone. This is Walter Cronkite speaking to you from CBS television election headquarters here in New York City. The big election night, 1952 . . ."

It was Eisenhower versus Stevenson for all the marbles, a race that, to hear the preelection polls, was going to be neck and neck. Back then, projecting the winner on the basis of early returns was an infant science. And Remington Rand decided to baptize the infant on national TV.

CRONKITE:	"And now, let's turn to that miracle of the modern age, the electronic brain UNIVAC, and Charles Collingwood."
COLLINGWOOD:	"UNIVAC is a fabulous electronic machine which we have borrowed to help us predict this election from the basis of the early returns as they come in. UNIVAC is going to try to predict the winner for us just as early as we can possibly get the returns in. . . . This is not a joke or a trick, it's an experiment. We think it's going to work. We don't know, we hope it will work."

As Collingwood's trepidation suggests, the public wasn't completely ready for the computer era. The investment history of the new innovation was then quite spotty.

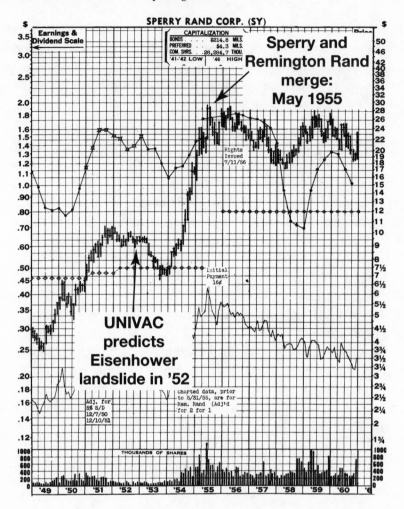

Fig. 27 SPERRY (REMINGTON) RAND CHART (Courtesy of Securities Research Co.)

Until 1950, the American computing industry essentially lay in the hands of pioneer inventors John Mauchly and J. Presper Eckert. The early motivation for computing power had come from World War II, with the first commercial contract being signed in 1946. Unfortunately, the vacuum tube technology was notoriously unreliable and production costs extremely high, the result of which being that the Eckert-Mauchly company fell seriously into debt. After a couple of abortive bailouts, the company was sold to Remington Rand on February 1, 1950. For a few years, Remington Rand—then best known for razors and typewriters—had the fledgling computer market essentially to itself.

The earnings gains the company posted in 1951 came from established lines of business, not the UNIVAC (which stood for Universal Automatic Computer). In fact, there were still only a handful of UNIVACs on order on election night of 1952. That's the night when UNIVAC made its way into the American consciousness.

At first, the PR move had the makings of a big mistake. "Can you say something, UNIVAC?" asked Collingwood. Obviously, UNIVAC couldn't talk, but it was supposed to type out a prediction when asked. Instead it did nothing.

Collingwood persisted. "Can you tell us what your prediction is now on the basis of the returns that we have so far? Have you got a prediction, UNIVAC?" Still nothing.

What the American public (and Collingwood himself) didn't know was that just before CBS's election night coverage had begun, UNIVAC had boldly predicted that Eisenhower would beat Stevenson by a landslide. But no one at CBS believed it. *They* were the ones that silenced UNIVAC.

After midnight—at which point Eisenhower's record landslide victory had taken shape—the network confessed to the public what had happened. Said one CBS executive, "As more votes came in, the odds came back and it was obviously evident that we should have had nerve enough to believe the machine in the first place. It was right. We were wrong. Next year we'll believe it."

As it happened, an investor didn't have to act right away to capitalize on UNIVAC's extraordinary accomplishment. Just as UNIVAC had to wait a bit before redemption, Remington Rand shares sat around for a while because the market was still waiting for the publicity to translate into orders. In late 1953, a year after the election, the stock had actually dropped some 25 percent, from just under $10 per share to the $7 level.

But if investors were worried about the future of computers, their fears were soon allayed. Starting from such a low base, practically every new UNIVAC order added materially to the company's growth rate. In May 1955, Remington Rand merged with Sperry Corporation in an effort to get the critical mass to dominate the industry, and Wall

Street approved. By the time the merger was consummated, Remington Rand's share price has risen to $28, almost three times its level when Eisenhower beat Stevenson. And the entire election-viewing public had a chance to capitalize.

As we know, though, despite the UNIVAC's early lead, Sperry Rand did *not* become the number-one force in computing, so the story deserves an epilogue.

Unfortunately for Sperry Rand, IBM founder Thomas Watson, to whom computers meant very little, stepped down in 1953 in favor of his son, who realized that computers meant everything. As a result, IBM moved aggressively to manufacture and market its flagship 650 model. All other things being equal, being first in any marketing battle can create a prohibitive advantage—but here not all things were equal. IBM's vaunted sales force proved decisive in the battle, and the late fifties turned out to be a period of tremendous growth for the company.

For investors, the best strategy would have been to invest in both companies rather than decide in advance who would win the battle for computer supremacy. As we saw, Sperry Rand got the early jump, and IBM shareholders had every reason to grouse. But they got redemption. Between 1955 and 1961, IBM shares went up eightfold while shares of Sperry Rand made no net progress whatsoever.

Milton Bradley: 1966

Back in 1966, Johnny Carson had only been with *The Tonight Show* for four-plus years, but already he was developing his place in TV history. A year before, his show had aired the infamous Ed Ames tomahawk throw (if you didn't see it, I'm surprised you're reading this section). Now came an opportunity of a different sort. Johnny's guest one fateful night was Eva Gabor of *Green Acres* fame. Johnny eyed her low-cut gown and decided to bring out a new game from Milton Bradley, a game called Twister.

What made Twister different was that it was the first game to use the human body as a playing piece: right hand on red, left foot on yellow, et cetera. It didn't take long for Carson and Gabor to be literally falling all over each other on the game's plastic mat, and the rest is history. In the year that followed, *three million* Twister games were sold. Even if Twister didn't have quite the impact on civilization that the computer did, an investor has to be on the lookout for all the possibilities, because the impact on Milton Bradley's bottom line was immediate.

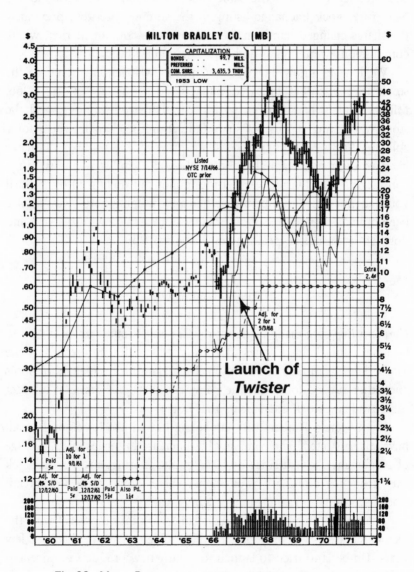

Fig. 28 MILTON BRADLEY CHART (Courtesy of Securities Research Co.)

Here's why. First of all, Twister was unusually cheap to manufacture: a plastic mat and a little spinner to tell you where to place the
parts of your body. Although high advertising expenses often cut into
the profitability of a new game, in this case Milton Bradley was getting
national advertising for free: The game would not have sold as quickly
without *Tonight Show* exposure. Conveniently, the stock's exposure
was broadened around the same time, as Milton Bradley obtained a
New York Stock Exchange listing in the summer of 1966; previously
the shares changed hands in the tiny over-the-counter market, where
commissions were higher and liquidity much lower.

We'll never know exactly how much Twister contributed to the
stock-price rise that followed, but consider this: As of late 1966,
Milton Bradley had under two million shares outstanding, and the
stock was selling at $18 per share (adjusting the chart for the 2-for-1
split in 1968). Multiplying the share price by the number of shares
gives you a market capitalization of about $35 million—pretty puny,
considering that Twister was netting millions of dollars all by itself. If
you had put these numbers together and bought shares, you'd have
been quickly rewarded. Milton Bradley stock tripled within a year and
doubled again before peaking sometime in 1968.

Timberland: 1991

Northern Exposure made its debut on CBS in the summer of 1990 and
became a full-fledged series in April of the following year. For the
Timberland Company of Hampton, New Hampshire, makers of boots
and other rugged footwear, the show couldn't have come at a better
time. And the stock chart bears that out.

If you were a Timberland shareholder in mid-1991, you might well
have felt frustrated. The company had increased its sales by an average
of 20 percent per year since its 1987 public offering, and yet the stock
was struggling along at about $8 per share, down some 40 percent
from its original offering price of $14.

The poor timing of the initial offering—just four months before the
October crash—was only part of the problem. During the next few
years, Timberland tried to launch too many new products at once and
before long encountered problems satisfying retailers' delivery sched-

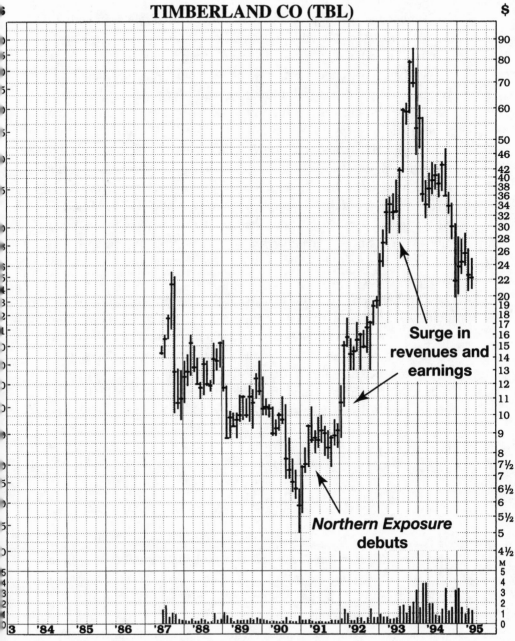

Fig. 29 TIMBERLAND CHART (Courtesy of Securities Research Co.)

ules. By the 1990–91 period, these internal difficulties had given competitors some extra business and had caused Timberland's profit margins to decline.

Timberland would probably have come back nicely even without *Northern Exposure*. And it's not as if Joel (Rob Morrow) or Maggie (Janine Turner) visibly promoted Timberland boots. But the series' special flair did wonders not only for promoting Alaska, where tourism picked up noticeably, but more generally for promoting the great outdoors. Any business with an outdoor orientation benefited, from Timberland to Jeep to Eddie Bauer.

Perhaps the short-lived *Twin Peaks* (1990–91) deserves credit for an assist in the Timberland story: *Northern Exposure* was actually filmed in Bellevue and Roslyn, Washington, not far from Twin Peaks territory. But you didn't have to live in Cicely, Alaska, or Twin Peaks to be interested. Timberland boots became status symbols in the inner city as well. Sneaker manufacturers such as Nike and Reebok lost significant business to the bootmakers and began planning more rugged lines of their own.

The numbers were the final test, and Timberland didn't disappoint. The company's revenues increased 29 percent in 1992, from $226 million to $291 million. For 1993, sales were up almost 40 percent. Earnings per share more than kept pace with sales growth, rising 166 percent during the 1991–93 period. *Northern Exposure* gathered in the Emmys, and Timberland shareholders finally had the profits they had sought since 1987. The stock hit $20 per share by the end of 1992, and in 1993 moved to over $80, a 900 percent increase in just two years.

Snapple: 1992

Thus far we've seen three great moneymaking opportunities arise from television shows, but the process has taken us forty years! I suppose I should feel sheepish about the time lapses between these bonanzas but I don't—for two reasons.

One is that this book was designed to give you multiple salvos with which to attack the market: No single one of them appears frequently, but together they appear almost constantly. The second, even more compelling reason is that you never know when the media will strike again. If you missed Timberland, you only had to wait one year before you got another chance. The stock in question is Snapple, which went public in December 1992 at a split-adjusted price of $5 per share.

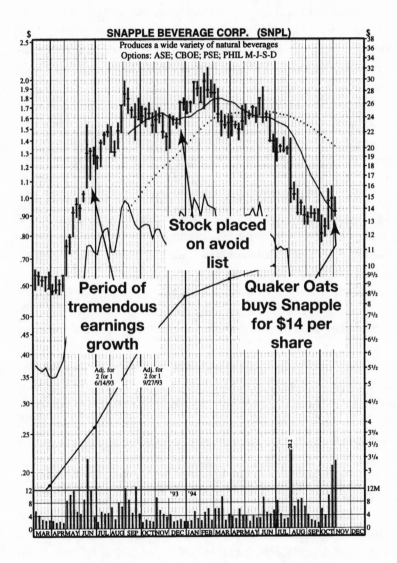

Fig. 30 Snapple chart (Courtesy of Securities Research Co.)

Did I say Snapple?! To many, the very name conjures up everything you *don't* want in a stock: overhype, overvaluation, unsustainable earnings growth. And I should admit that eventually I joined the
pessimistic fold. In late 1993, with Snapple trading at $25—over
thirty times the prevailing earnings estimates for 1994—I put the
stock on the avoid list I ran for *Worth* magazine; to me, the stock's high
P/E looked like nothing but trouble if the company couldn't live up to
what appeared to be inflated expectations. In fact, although the stock
reached $30 per share in early 1994, Snapple's earnings were soon
undone by a wave of price competition in the iced tea and fruit drink
categories; that fall, when the company agreed to be bought by Quaker
Oats, it fetched just $14 per share.

But let's take a step back. Just how do you think a stock gets to be
overhyped and overvalued? By going up a lot, that's how. As you may
have noticed, that's exactly what Snapple did in 1993. Within a year of
its initial offering, its share price had quintupled.

In this case the credit for the investment clue goes to Jerry Seinfeld
—with honorable mention to noted Snapple-sipper Howard Stern
(perhaps his first such mention). As any fan of *Seinfeld* can tell you,
Jerry makes a point of keeping Snapple in his refrigerator. The whole
cast drinks it. That, in a nutshell, was your clue. The hottest TV show
in America featuring the hottest beverage in America. By now, you
should feel no shame in viewing that clue as a serious buy signal.

Yes, Snapple might have looked overvalued when it first went public in December 1992, because the company only earned a couple of
pennies per share that year. But as we found out in the Revlon example earlier in this chapter, *trailing* earnings are useless when analyzing
fast-growing companies.

In Snapple's case, earnings for 1993 came in at $0.49 per share.
Relative to the $5 offering price, the P/E was now only 10, which made
it a bargain. Of course, the stock wasn't at $5 anymore. It was at $25.
That's what great earnings will do for you.

I should mention that many investors resent these gains or even
dismiss them. They think that the only way to make money is to buy a
stock when it's cold and sell it when it's gotten warm. I have no
problem with that strategy, and I wouldn't suggest that people invest
in stocks that make them uncomfortable. But if I may stretch the
thermometer metaphor to its fullest, it's possible to make money from

any increase in temperature. Cold to warm is nice, but so is warm to hot—or, in Snapple's case, from hot to scalding. Rejecting Snapple because of its "overvalued" label was akin to Yogi Berra's famous rejection of a popular night spot: "No one goes there. It's too crowded."

I'm not done with the hot to hottest analogy. Wasn't Jerry Seinfeld a hot comedian even before he got his own TV show? The answer is yes: That's why he got the show. And wasn't Howard Stern hot even before hitting the cover of *Time* and releasing his book, *Private Parts*? The answer is also yes. But the extra media exposure catapulted each of them to an entirely different level of fame. And that's exactly what happened to Snapple. Its fast-growth phase didn't last forever, but nothing can take away those glory years of 1992 and 1993. If you had bought shares at the initial offering and not sold until the day the Quaker Oats deal was announced, you still would have almost tripled your money in less than two years.

STRANGE LESSONS FROM TV PLOTS

So far, the investment signals we have divined from television have come about inadvertently, in that the medium wasn't trying to help us out. When television *tries* to incorporate the stock market into its plot lines, the results are quite different.

In general, television is a terrible source of investment role models. Making money in the market isn't considered good entertainment, and whoever writes the plots makes sure, for our amusement, that TV's stock market practitioners always lose their shirts. Remember, Blake Carrington made his killing well before *Dynasty* ever started; likewise, John Beresford Tipton, the millionaire on the fifties show by the same name. And although Jed Clampett quietly increased his fortune from $25 million to $95 million during the *Beverly Hillbillies'* nine-year run, we were left in the dark as to *how*. Not a single episode was devoted to the financial shrewdness of Clampett's banker/adviser, Milburn Drysdale.

Even the assorted single-episode market successes have been fraught with peril. Baby Tabitha on *Bewitched* once plucked some great stocks from the newspaper, but the Kravitzes next door were almost bankrupted when her streak ran out. The story was similar for *Car 54's*

Gunther Toody. Toody, as police precinct treasurer, invested all of the precinct's savings in a company called International Sulphur, then displayed his anxiety by repeatedly taking his buddies to visit the chairman's office—in uniform. The constant sightings of policemen created rumors of wrongdoing that made the stock plunge, day after day, until someone figured out the vicious circle. The chairman eventually bought Toody's shares at a substantial premium just to get rid of him, thereby displaying the merits of "greenmail" two decades before it got popular. Another accidental victory.

For all of my digging, I could find only three classic episodes from TV land that deserve more of our attention. As we will see, in addition to always depicting the market as dangerous, TV does an astoundingly good job of getting its investment facts wrong. However, underneath the foibles of both character and plot line, these three episodes will leave us with some surprisingly sage advice as we set out to create our own portfolios.

Fibber McGee and Molly

This show is better known as one of radio's all-time classics, but it also aired on NBC during the 1959–60 television season, with Bob Sweeney as Fibber and Cathy Lewis as Molly. One of the episodes in this limited run centered on Fibber's equally limited run as a financier.

The plot developed as follows: Molly didn't want Fibber's ugly fishing trophy on the living room mantel, so the two of them decided to add a den to their modest but comfortable dwelling at 79 Wistful Vista. The addition would be financed by selling some stock they conveniently happened to own. McGee was dispatched downtown to sell the stock and to come home with a check to cover the renovations.

Already TV has tinkered with the facts. When you sell shares of stock, for God's sake don't expect a check that afternoon. Stock sales involve a trading date and a settlement date, generally several days apart, and you don't get your money until the latter. That's why you can't sell for year-end tax-loss purposes on New Year's Eve. Anyway, this was television in the fifties, and anything was possible. Gracie Allen got a painter to arrive in three hours on *Burns and Allen*. We didn't quibble then, so we won't quibble now.

Back to the show. When Fibber strolled into the neighborhood brokerage to conduct his transaction, he ran into a little bit of peer pressure. His good friend Mayor La Trivia was surveying the board with great interest (always comforting to have the mayor spending his day watching the ticker tape). La Trivia and the friendly broker Roger Duncan conveyed a bullishness that made McGee a mite embarrassed to be on the sell side. "I like Canfield Mines at $48," Duncan gushed. "International Metals at $58," countered La Trivia.

Poor Fibber. Caught up in the fray, he quickly scoured the board and exclaimed, "I like U.S. Miscellaneous at $1 a share."

Needless to say, the broker cautioned Fibber against such a risky investment. Also needless to say, he took Fibber's impulsive buy order. Fibber had intended to buy only twenty-five shares, but the broker took that to mean twenty-five hundred shares instead (the old decimal point gag). So instead of walking out with the $2,654 from his earlier sale, McGee found that his cash proceeds, after commissions, amounted to precisely $4.

Upon getting to the front door at 79 Wistful Vista, Fibber explains his plight to Teeny, the neighbor's daughter. "I bought some stock for $1 a share . . . U.S. Miscellaneous," Fibber says proudly. "They make missiles?" asks Teeny. "No," Fibber laughs, "they make . . . hmmm . . . what do they make?" No matter. "When it goes up, you make a lot of money," he rationalizes.

"Does it always go up?" Teeny asks. Fibber assures her that there is no risk in the market, because you get advice from stockbrokers. "If they're so smart, how come they're broke?" (Pause for laugh track.) "No," Fibber explains. "The stockbroker sells you the stock. He doesn't go broke, you do."

Those were the fumbling moments that a guy nicknamed Fibber was obliged to provide. The exchange with Teeny at least warmed him up to come clean with Molly upon stepping inside, even if it left him feeling a little sheepish. "All of it?" Molly asked incredulously. Fibber must have known how Jack felt before the beanstalk grew.

His personal beanstalk didn't take long. Mayor La Trivia arrived at the McGee homestead that very afternoon, enraged. "Why didn't you let me in on that stock you bought?" he cried. Apparently, U.S. Miscellaneous had gone up a full dollar, thereby doubling in price within a single day.

Now for the Solomonic investment wisdom we were waiting for. Though Molly is unable to wipe the smug grin off her husband's face, she is able to convince him to sell off half of his holding in U.S. Miscellaneous. That way, she reasons, they'll have the money for the den and he still gets to be a big shot.

Actually, USM still has a little life left in it. When Fibber next appears at the brokerage, he is told that his stock has gone up another point—presumably, putting it somewhere in the $3 to $4 range.

Inevitably, though, the stock falls apart. The next time Roger Duncan calls, he asks Fibber what he wants to do now that the stock is at seventeen. "Seventeen dollars?" exclaims Fibber. "No, seventeen cents," says Duncan. (Note: the decimal point gag used twice in one show.) Now, Fibber McGee may be cheap, but he's not that cheap. Right then and there, he decides to write the whole thing off. Molly comes to his side, the music starts playing, and the episode comes to an end.

Believe it or not, this thirty minutes of confectionary fifties schmaltz leads to an important investment discussion. Remember when Molly saved the day by suggesting that they sell an amount equal to the original investment? People do that all the time. The idea behind the strategy is that the remaining investment is *free*.

There are precisely two schools of thought on this strategy—and they violently disagree. On the one hand, as McGee discovered in the extreme, taking out the original investment does nothing to lessen the risk of what's still there. McGee apparently forgot that the idea of investing is still to make money, not to lose your risk capital. Selling part of a holding can make sense if the holding has become too big or the risk/reward picture has taken a slightly unfavorable turn. But selling what you put in just because that's what you put in? From a dollars-and-cents standpoint, it makes no sense whatsoever. If the stock is truly that risky, it's best to sell it all.

However, as we saw with the McGees, what makes investment sense and what makes emotional sense are often quite far apart: They ended up happy! The moral is that anyone who manages his or her own money has to take both performance and emotions into account and, most important of all, recognize that they can work at cross purposes.

Leave It to Beaver

Like Fibber McGee, Theodore Cleaver's first brush with high finance was influenced by peer pressure. Beaver's experiences started quite innocently, as you might expect. Ward Cleaver had convinced his two sons to put up $25 apiece from their savings—which he would then match—to invest in the market. Now, even in 1961 a $50 portfolio didn't allow for more than a single holding, and Ward put the boys into Mayfield Power and Electric, that unbearably quaint but nonetheless venerable purveyor of light to 211 Pine Street and environs.

But such a stodgy holding didn't sit well with the boys' self-appointed financial adviser, a Mr. Edward Haskell. Eddie sang the praises of a "swingin' " stock called Jet Electro, a low-priced beaut involved in "space-age junk." Wally and Beav didn't bite at first, but when Jet Electro flew from $2 to $2.50 (with Mayfield P&E lagging badly) the disgruntled pair railroaded their father into making a switch. In at $2½, the brothers Cleaver were bursting with joy when Jet Electro hit $3 per share on its presumed path to $300.

Which it never did quite reach. The company soon lost a vital government contract—vital enough to send its stock plummeting to just $0.75 cents a share. The result: a 75 percent overnight loss and two crestfallen Cleavers.

But wait. Ward had not sat idly watching his sons' speculations. Eddie (described to a tee by *Time*'s Richard Stengel as "smarmy to his elders and sneering to his peers") never did gain Ward and June's trust. His newfound research capabilities seemed typically suspect, so Ward had arranged with the local broker to sell Jet Electro if it returned to the original purchase price of $2.50 per share (and to put the proceeds back into Mayfield Power and Electric, naturally). In market parlance, he had placed a stop-loss order on Jet Electro, and all was well.

Except for one teensy-weensy problem, lost in the sitcom surrealism: Stop-loss orders don't work that way. The market's behavior may not allow you to get out of a stock exactly when you want to—especially, as in the case of Jet Electro, if a company's key revenue source is lost. Any such calamity can produce an immediate "gap" in the stock price. If the news is announced *after* the market close, trading activity is apt to resume the next day at a much lower level.

In the simplified stock pages of *The Mayfield Times,* Jet Electro trading might have looked something like this:

JET ELECTRO STOCK

Day	High	Low	Close
Tuesday	3	$2\frac{7}{8}$	3
Wednesday	$\frac{3}{4}$	$\frac{5}{8}$	$\frac{3}{4}$

The price commanded through a stop loss is the *best available bid* after the stock has traded at the "strike price" (in this case, the strike price was set at $2½, or $2.50). Unfortunately, the stock's dramatic drop made the best available bid just $¾, not $2½, and that's where the sale would have been made. Stop loss? Not even close.

But all this was lost on Wally and Beav. They had their profit preserved and a reinstated position (albeit still a minority one) in a utility stock whose stability was starting to look pretty darn attractive. Ward had pulled a miracle with the stock switch, and even he was humbled come episode end. As he confided to June, "When your sons think you're smarter than their friends, you've really got it made."

There is no telling what became of Mayfield Power and Electric. As for the stock market itself, it began a serious downturn in the spring of 1962, declining 30 percent in just three months. It didn't forge to a new high until September 1963, the fateful month when *Leave It to Beaver* aired its final episode.

For that matter, it is a little-known fact that the Dow Jones Industrial Average dropped 2 percent immediately following the launch of *Beaver* on October 4, 1957. But, again, we should know enough not to blame the Beav. That very day, the Soviet Union made a launching of its own. It was called Sputnik.

Upstairs, Downstairs

It's one thing for a couple of wholesome fifties sitcoms to tinker with the realities of Wall Street. We'd expect more from *Masterpiece Theatre* and its renowned *Upstairs, Downstairs* series from the seventies. But snafus still abounded, and for the sake of stock market history it's time to set things straight.

For those who didn't catch the series the first time around, it was basically a soap opera involving the lives of a well-heeled British family (the Bellamys) and the lives of their servants. As the title implies, each group was vital to the show's chemistry.

In this case, the stock market setting was real. It is 1929—in fact, the fall of 1929. James Bellamy, the bon vivant son, has just returned from America and reports that massive sums are being made by speculators on Wall Street. By the sound of it, he has garnered some tidy profits himself.

One of the listeners to his tales of high finance is a maid named Rose, played by Jean Marsh. Her curiosity comes out when fellow maid Daisy has a conversation with Hudson, the butler. The setting is the kitchen—downstairs.

DAISY: "How do you make money on the stock exchange, Mr. Hudson?"

HUDSON: "You buy shares in certain commodities and when the shares rise in value you sell them and keep the profits, that's the principle."

DAISY: "Sounds easy."

HUDSON: "Oh, the shares can also lose their value, and then you lose your money. It's a matter of great expertise judging which to buy and which to leave alone."

ROSE: "Oh, you'd have to have people advise you, wouldn't you? People that knew about it."

HUDSON: "You can also have people advising you on horse racing, Rose, jockeys and stable lads, and look where that can lead you."

DAISY: "Yeah, but that's not the same."

HUDSON: "It's very much the same, Daisy; it's called speculating, which is another word for gambling, if you look in the dictionary."

Upstairs

Never mind that the preceding conversation sounds a whole lot like *Fibber McGee*. When Rose finally develops the courage to take her curiosity to James, she gets a very different picture of Wall Street.

ROSE: "I don't know if you remember, sir, but Sergeant Wilmott left me some money and . . . it's on deposit in the bank, and I was wondering if I should invest some of it."

JAMES: "Yes?"

ROSE: "It's just a little . . . a small amount."

JAMES: "Yes. Well, that sounds like a very good idea, Rose."

ROSE: "Oh, do you think so, sir? Only Hudson seems a bit doubtful."

JAMES: "Really, why?"

ROSE: "Well, he says it's like gambling on the horses."

JAMES: "Oh, no it isn't, Rose. It is speculating—now, there's a world of difference. Your money will go to make new factories and new jobs for thousands of people." [Nice spin.]

ROSE: "Will it, sir? I hadn't thought of it like that."

JAMES: "It's very simple. Now, how much do you want to invest?"

ROSE: "Oh, I don't know. I've got twelve hundred and seventy-five pounds altogether."

JAMES: "Oh, now, that's very good, Rose. Now, how much shall we say —it's your money; you must decide."

ROSE: "I'll leave it to you, sir."

JAMES: "Right. Well, then, what we'll do—we'll put your money through an investment trust, and that means that expert people will be handling it, do you understand? (She nods.) Right. Now, where is this bank of yours?"

ROSE: "Do it now, sir?"

JAMES: "Well, there's no time like the present, Rose, come on!"

Meanwhile, we the viewing audience are squirming as if James and Rose have just boarded the Titanic (the device by which James's mother was written out of the script some episodes earlier.) If only they'd waited, we think to ourselves. But then, of course, there'd be no plot.

Downstairs

Just days later (it doesn't take long for our TV investors to lose money, does it?), the bad news is out. Hudson is reading the bold headlines of the newspaper as a group gathers in the kitchen.

HUDSON:	"Terrible news, terrible. The slide has begun in earnest, I'm afraid."
MRS. BRIDGES:	"What slide, Mr. Hudson?"
HUDSON:	"The economic slide in America, Mrs. Bridges, on Wall Street. The bottom has fallen out of the stock market . . . . There have been signs of it for several days now. Rumors circulating that shares have lost their value. Investors panicking and trying to sell, causing the shares to drop even further in value. They're finally not worth the paper they're written on. Thousands are ruined!"
EDWARD:	"I don't understand that, Mr. Hudson. I mean, how can money be there one minute and disappear the next?"
HUDSON:	"It's the mysteries of high finance, Edward. It would take too long to explain the details."

Rose, who has been listening quietly all the while, finally leaves.

Upstairs, Drawing Room

Eventually, the camera finds its way to James, who is full of excuses as some of the ladies of the household commiserate.

GEORGINA:	"Put us out of our misery, James."
VIRGINIA:	"How badly has it hit?"
JAMES:	"Well, if Darner had only sent a cable I could have . . . I could have saved something. As it is, I've been hit pretty hard, yes."
GEORGINA:	"Wiped out?"
JAMES:	"I don't know . . . yes."
RICHARD:	"Couldn't your London brokers have warned you?"

JAMES: "No, no, it was too late. See, the first hint of any trouble was last Thursday. Then the bankers stepped in and checked it, so, yesterday, when the news was bad again, everyone thought they'd do the same. They didn't. Even Goldman, Sachs was buying its own stock, deliberately swindling itself trying to get confidence back, but it was . . . it was too late over here. Over there, too, the damn ticker tape was lagging. Lack of proper information . . . snowballing . . . panic."

Downstairs

James has given Rose the bad news, and the next scene finds her crying in the kitchen.

ROSE: "I only wanted to do a little, but he said there was no risk, and it was safe, and now it's all gone."

MRS. BRIDGES: "How could he do it, Mr. Hudson? How could he take money from a servant like that?"

HUDSON: "Oh, the major's always had a rash streak in his nature. But this takes the biscuit, I must say."

News of James's dealings with Rose has by now reached the entire household, and in a later scene James's father reprimands him severely for meddling in the servants' monetary affairs. James protests that Rose approached him, but the discussion degenerates into a heated argument and James decides to leave. In the meantime, Rose disappears for hours and has everyone worried sick. Eventually, she returns, but James doesn't fare as well. In the end, the police come to the Bellamy residence to advise that James has taken a revolver to his head and ended his life.

Under the circumstances, it feels somewhat churlish to take issue with James's explanations, but—on the grounds that his was a fictional death—what in the world was he talking about? Bankers stepping in and making sure everything was all right? People thinking they'd do the same? Bad news? What bad news was there, except for the fact that stocks were down (not rumored to be going down, as Hudson had said)?

The crash has been exaggerated by history, not only by *Masterpiece Theatre*. Contrary to modern-day depictions, the crash of Tuesday, October 29, 1929, wasn't even a headline event: Unless you were invested heavily on margin (i.e., with borrowed money), you couldn't have been wiped out on the so-called Black Tuesday because the Dow Jones Industrial Average fell only 11.7 percent. It had actually fallen 12.8 percent the previous day and 15.3 percent from the monthly high achieved on October 10 (plenty of time for James to have gotten a cable).

The reason for the legacy of the crash is that, unlike 1987, the stock market's worst days were yet to come. On Black Tuesday, the Dow finished the day at 230.07: It didn't bottom out until July 8, 1932, when it closed at 41.22—a decline of 82 percent *after* the alleged crash. The silver lining to James's untimely demise is that he never had to experience that decline.

The part about Goldman, Sachs buying its own shares truly takes the biscuit. First of all, Wall Street investment houses aren't known for deliberately sabotaging themselves. Their efforts at propping up their own stock might fail, but that's different than intentionally throwing money away. Worst of all, though, Goldman, Sachs has never been a public company. As a partnership, they didn't have any shares to buy back.

I suppose I could go on, but only so far. These shows aren't to be denied their poetic license, and if a single reader thinks poorly of *Leave It to Beaver* as a result of these ramblings, I've done a great disservice.

But there is a message here. Whether it be the case of Fibber McGee, Theodore Cleaver, or Rose the maid, none of the investment catastrophes we saw was made alone. That fact incorporates one of the least-understood pitfalls in all of investing, one worth stating as a rule: *Two people can often conspire to invest in something that neither one would have invested in by themselves.*

Because our relationships with brokers or investment advisers are almost necessarily two-person affairs, the rule is worth keeping in mind at all times. In the investment business, IQs are not cumulative.

There is more. When it comes to stocks gone awry, we almost always point our fingers at the sell side of the transaction—McGee's greedy broker, Eddie Haskell, or the ne'er-do-well James Bellamy.

Often, though, the stimulus comes from the other side. Consider this imaginary conversation between portfolio manager and client:

CLIENT: "I'm calling to get your opinion on Plasma-Lube Corporation."

MANAGER: (*Our research department doesn't cover this one. I'm sure it's gonna be a lot more trouble than it's worth.*) "Plasma-Lube? I don't know. It looks awfully risky to me. Not much of a track record, high P/E. Pretty risky, I'd say."

The portfolio manager has long since learned that it's better to state some opinion rather than none, because clients expect their manager to know about every stock they mention. It's silly, but after all they're paying the freight.

CLIENT: (*feeling a trifle put down*) "Gee, that's too bad. I thought their story looked real interesting."

MANAGER: (*Damn. The last time I said no to somebody on a speculation like this one, the stock went up fourfold and the client hasn't shut up about it. I'll try looking on the bright side.*) "Well, the company's earnings aren't great, but they went from three cents per share last year to five cents per share this year. Maybe they're on to something."

CLIENT: (*delighted to hear something positive*) "Great. Why don't we buy 1,000 shares?"

MANAGER: (*Hey, it's his money.*) "Fine."

CLIENT: (*At least I got my manager's approval before buying shares on my own.*) "So long. Speak to you later."

MANAGER: (*At least, if it goes down, I can say that it wasn't my idea.*) "So long."

There you have it. The stock gets bought and each person can safely blame the other if something goes wrong. In this case, something probably will.

Ironically, one of the reasons that many individual investors don't manage their own money is that it's nice to have a money manager to blame if things go wrong. This is not said pejoratively. Managing money can be a lot of fun, but it can also be a great burden. It takes time and effort, the likes of which not everyone has. But as long as the average American household spends seven hours a day watching television, I'd say we have a pretty good source of time right there. I hope the methods of this chapter will enable you to use that time to advantage.

3 ❑ Investing in Fads

Each chapter in this book deals with the investment ramifications of a subject so highly visible that anyone with a pulse would know at least something about it. Weather, television—so far, so good.

The focus in this chapter is on *products,* a wide-open category if one ever was. But when you put the "visible" label on, the category shrinks dramatically. Many products that have made for great investments at one time or another—Merck's Vasotec, Ashton-Tate's dBase software, Insituform's pipe linings—were barely visible at all. It is our fate that products that do meet the visibility standard—Cabbage Patch dolls, wine coolers, Teenage Mutant Ninja Turtles—are almost by definition faddish. They arrive with a force that seems utterly unsustainable, and, inevitably, it is. This is not the sort of stuff successful investments are supposed to be made of.

In fact, many investors feel duty bound to look the other way when anything even *appears* faddish. It even sounds smart. But here's what they're missing:

Unexpected Longevity

When Reebok arrived with its initial public offering in 1985, many investors took a show-me attitude. Aerobic shoes just *had* to be a fad. The offering attracted a lot of attention, but the stock wasn't priced expensively relative to earnings, on the grounds that the company's growth wasn't destined to last.

Now we know better. The aerobics fad kept going and even spawned its own subcategories such as step aerobics. As for 1985, shoe production couldn't keep up with demand, margins were high, and analysts started tripping over one another raising their earnings estimates. Within a year of its initial offering, Reebok shares had quintupled.

First Team Sports is right out of the same mold. Its primary product since inception has been Ultra-Wheels, an in-line roller skate. "In-line" is of course the name of the category pioneered by privately held Rollerblade, Inc., and is usually referred to by that company's generic name. And Rollerblade, Inc., was always concerned that its product was merely a fad—as in the roller disco craze of the late seventies, as embodied by Olivia Newton-John, Ringo Starr, and Cher.

Rollerblade's fears were not realized. Not only were in-line skates not a quick-burning fad, the category proved large enough for Ultra-Wheels to prosper as well. Ultra-Wheels secured the endorsement of the Great One himself—Wayne Gretzky—and sales at First Team Sports moved from $1.7 million in 1989 to $26.2 million in 1992. The stock surged over fifteenfold in the 1990–91 period, and all you needed to participate was an appreciation that it might *not* be a fad. The company was still growing nicely several years later.

These stories aren't limited to exercise stocks. MTV surely looked like a fad when it debuted in November 1981. Who would believe in twenty-four-hour rock videos? Yet even though its shares didn't hit Nasdaq until the summer of 1984 (at $14 per share), MTV still proved a good buy, because Viacom bought the company for $33 per share in March of 1986.

For that matter, the expression "fast-food fad" was around some thirty years ago, when McDonald's went public. No need to go through the numbers this time: Suffice it to say that being fad-averse does not always lead to good investment decisions—it sounds good, but, like just about anything else, you can take it too far.

The underlying fallacy is the notion that a responsible investor must know in advance whether or not the damned thing is going to be a fad. It sounds all too reasonable, until you realize that there is an alternative: investing, then selling if the product starts to die an early death. If it doesn't, the stock can be held for years, to potentially great reward. And even if the product in question is a fad, one of the signs that the fad is getting out of hand, as we shall see, is that the stock price starts to rise out of control. Surely a responsible investor can live with that.

Blue Chips

To fad-averse investors, stocks like MTV and Reebok represented merely opportunity costs; you can't lose money in stocks you never invest in. But if you think you can avoid fads by sticking with blue-chip stocks, guess again.

In 1989, and for many years before, there was no bluer chip than Kellogg. Earnings had gone up for thirty-eight consecutive years, as had dividends. As the market-share leader in the cold cereal business, Kellogg had that vital asset called pricing flexibility (a bowl of cereal doesn't cost much, and Kellogg was consistently able to increase prices without consumer backlash). That feature enabled Kellogg shares to outperform even the prime of the great bull market, moving from a split-adjusted price of $5 in early 1982 to over $40 by mid-1989.

Then problems began surfacing. That year, Kellogg lost a full two points of market share because of the oat bran craze. Corn Flakes and Rice Krispies are wonderful cereals, but their very names let it be known that they contained no oats. The possible health benefits of oat bran—specifically, for the heart—were enough to create an enormous swing in the public's tastes. General Mills, maker of (oat-based) Cheerios, gained three share points in 1989, and its stock advanced almost 40 percent for the year. Kellogg wasn't as lucky. By year-end, its stock was down 15 percent from its mid-year high—all because of a stupid fad.

Professionals Do It, Too

Two of the best equity investors of the modern era have shown how a short-term orientation can pay off for mutual fund investors, as long as the *fundholders* don't lose their long-term perspective. As an example, when Ken Heebner's CGM Capital Development Fund underperformed the market by more than 20 percentage points in 1994, the financial press was suddenly all over him. Heebner's strategy of "investing in anticipation of surprising earnings growth" had backfired by leaving him with too many economically sensitive stocks, which didn't fare well when the Federal Reserve raised interest rates to slow the economy down. Had he lost his touch?

What people forgot was that any long-term Capital Development fundholder was still doing fine; the fund was the single best performing mutual fund for the ten years ending June 30, 1993 (and for many other ten-year periods, I should add). In particular, no one complained about Heebner owning such stocks as Bombay Company and International Game Technology during his early-nineties winning streak, even though those companies' explosive earnings-growth records smacked of faddishness.

Heebner isn't the only one to look to fads. In *The Alchemy of Finance,* the legendary Quantum Fund manager George Soros outlined his approach to the conglomerate boom of the sixties. The background was that corporations whose track record enabled them to be valued expensively by the market (LTV, Teledyne) began acquiring less richly valued companies so as to increase earnings per share. It made no difference what businesses the acquired companies were involved in; as long as the companies were cheap, their acquisition would prove antidilutive—that is, adding to earnings.

Investors rewarded the higher reported earnings of the acquiring companies by driving their stocks even higher, enabling them to make additional acquisitions that drove earnings higher still. Between 1964 and 1967, LTV rose from $10 to $160; Teledyne from $6 to $60. These moves were based on a classic pyramid scheme that would have to end someday. Many investors saw the whole thing coming and stayed out; no problem with that.

Soros reacted differently. He recognized the pyramid scheme early on but invested anyway (as if saying, hey, I know it's doomed, but other people might just fall for this). Then, knowing just how fragile these companies' earnings were, when the stocks started to unravel he went *short*, meaning that he borrowed shares from his broker and sold them, in hopes of profiting by buying the shares back at a lower price. It worked. Teledyne fell from $60 per share to $12, while LTV fell from $160 all the way to $8. Soros won on the way up and on the way down. He called this process a "boom/bust" sequence. We might call it a fad.

So Why Can't I?

Why can't the rest of us be more like Heebner and Soros? Well, if everyone could analyze and invest the way they do, they wouldn't be considered special. And perhaps not everyone should try. Following the two of them is no more a formula for investment success than "Be like Mike" is a path to basketball stardom.

And yet we should try to overcome some of the reasons we find it difficult to emulate this particular pair of investors. Beyond the issue of analytical ability, the general populace has a host of psychological barriers that make these styles so elusive.

The culprit is usually an attachment to long-term investing. Mind you, I have nothing against investing for the long term; the turnover rates of a Heebner or a Soros should not be the guideline for the rest of us. But the concept of long-term investing is constantly abused. Long-term investing naturally assumes that you are *willing* to wait many years for good things to happen. It does not mean that you *have* to wait. There's a big difference.

A number of perverse things can happen to the DLTI (dedicated long-term investor). To a DLTI, one of the worst things that can happen is for a recently bought stock to go up very rapidly!

Consider the case of a good friend who in 1986 bought shares of Carter-Wallace, a diversified consumer products company best known for making Trojan condoms. The reasoning behind the investment was that condom usage would increase as the public became more and more concerned about sexually transmitted diseases such as HIV. The reasoning proved impeccable. Condoms were not a fad, they were serious business. But Carter-Wallace stock surely had a component of mania as it moved from $35 per share to $75 by early 1987. Not only did this percentage gain far outpace the increase in actual condom sales, but it meant that Carter-Wallace was trading at over thirty times earnings, an unusually high level for a consumer health-care company.

The dilemma facing my friend the DLTI was that had he taken short-term profits, he would have felt like all the other short-term predators that were stalking the market back then. Instead, he found a research report that cited other products within Carter-Wallace's line, including antiperspirants and deodorants, that might make the company a viable long-term investment. He decided to keep holding the shares.

Unfortunately, the condom mania is what was driving the stock, and it didn't last. The stock fell back to the $50 level, then fell below $25 during October's market crash. (It came back, but it took five years to do so.) Had the initial gain taken years to achieve, selling the stock wouldn't have been as difficult psychologically. Taking short-term profits is anathema to many of us, but only because we confuse the willingness to wait with the requirement that we *must* wait.

The Fallacies of Risk and Timing

The very term "fad stocks" makes them sound more risky than others. But consider the chart below, which compares the price movements of two unrelated stocks at two different time periods.

The first stock is Playmates International, holder of the exclusive U.S. license for Teenage Mutant Ninja Turtle action figures. The second stock is International Business Machines.

The shapes are almost identical. The main difference is that it took IBM ten years to carve out an up-then-down cycle, whereas Playmates required only two years. Ken Hakuta, whose success with Wacky Wallwalkers gave him the name of "Dr. Fad," notes: "In Fad Standard Time, a day is a year." Everything happens much more quickly.

But does that make Playmates a riskier stock? Which is more dangerous, bungee jumping or an uncovered manhole? The most insidious risk in the stock market is the risk that comes unmarked, and fad stocks fare pretty well on that score—at least, they have the courtesy

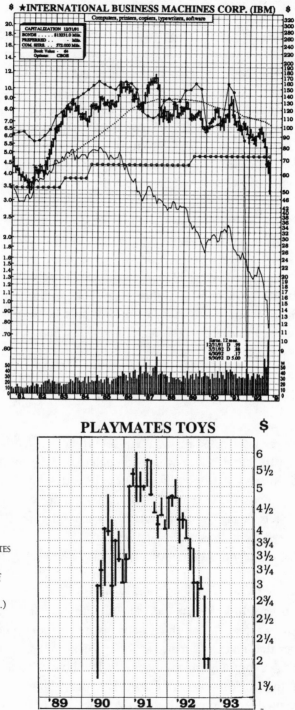

Fig. 31
IBM/PLAYMATES
INT'L CHART
(Courtesy of
Securities
Research Co.)

to advertise their risks. Besides, for every investor who held Playmates too long, there were fifty who made that mistake with IBM.

What about timing? It is said that you need perfect timing to possibly make money in fad stocks, simply because they move up and down so fast. Not so. If you had bought Playmates International in 1990 at $1 per share and sold it at $3 later that year, your timing would have been atrocious. You would have missed a 150 percent gain off the bottom and a 100 percent gain before the top. Yet for all that wretchedly bad timing, you tripled your money in a matter of months. And even though this gain came rather swiftly, how long does it take to call your broker?

It could be argued (in fact, I'm making the argument right here and now) that real timing is required if you want to make money in ALCOA, Caterpillar, or some other "cyclical" stock—so called because they tend to move up and down with the cycles of the overall economy. These stocks needn't be higher in the year 2000 than they were in 1990, yet they are perfectly investment-worthy. But precisely because the moves in these stocks are not as great as with a bona fide fad, you need to catch their price swings with unusual precision to make the effort at all worthwhile.

And who says that having extra time leads to better investment decisions? Isn't it perfectly possible to watch IBM slink downward for years, hoping that it would come back? Many DLTIs did just that.

The real problem is as follows: *Many investors hide behind the "long-term" protective umbrella simply because they have never developed an effective sell discipline.* And that's where looking at fads can truly help out, even if you never intend to invest in one.

WINE COOLERS: THE FAD MODEL

How do you go about converting the irrational into something rational? By observing patterns. Once enough crazes fit a prescribed pattern, they don't seem nearly as crazy. From the standpoint of investment action, a fad's life cycle consists of five distinct stages:

1. Humble beginnings   A time to prepare
2. Tip-offs   A time to buy

    3. Positive negatives   A time to worry
    4. The peak   A time to disregard
    5. True negatives   A time to get out
                               (if you're still in)

By number five, it is all over. Different fads will of course emphasize
different stages of the process, but wine coolers do a pretty good job of
showcasing all five. In fact, their history forms a model for *all* fads.

Humble Beginnings

Even though a fad is by definition something that bursts upon the
public scene, the truth is that most fads have waited years before
enjoying their days of outlandish popularity. Erno Rubik invented his
famous cube in 1974, seven years before all of America went crazy
over it; CB radios, a fad of the mid-seventies, had actually been around
since 1958. In effect, even the most short-lived fad represents a long-
term investment for someone: The rest of us must wait to be tipped
off.

   The modern-day wine cooler was introduced in the 1970s—where
else?—on a California beach. The innovators were a couple of
twentysomething guys named Michael Crete and Stuart Bewley, whose
original wine-and-fruit-juice concoction was literally blended in a
beachside bathtub. Spurred on by the favorable beach party reception,
the two launched the California Cooler, the first entry in the wine
cooler category. Crete and Bewley hand-delivered their coolers from a
1953 pickup truck. That was 1981, a year when the entire cooler
market amounted to only seven hundred 9-liter cases.

   The wine cooler pioneers did a lot of things right. They sold the
coolers through beer distributors, not wine distributors, so as to better
reach the mass market. The California Cooler's 12-ounce green bottle
packaging made it look like an imported beer (like beer, wine coolers
were kept cold). The packaging was also consistent with high retail
prices, which translated into high profit margins for distributors. Everyone involved in the process was winning.

   Within three years, Crete and Bewley took the wine cooler national. Cooler shipments moved from their standing start of 1981 to

12.4 million cases in 1984. Competitors had begun to enter the marketplace, but California Cooler remained by far the dominant brand, with a market share exceeding 50 percent. As a private entity, California Cooler was outside the grasp of the investing public, and so were the assorted regional wineries that provided most of the early competition. Enter Canandaigua Wine, makers of the Sun Country wine cooler.

Prior to 1984, Canandaigua was best known as a maker of high-alcohol wines such as Richard's Wild Irish Rose. The company's earnings (and share price) depended on unfamiliar factors such as grape supplies and fructose prices. Wall Street's indifference was understandable: The company's revenues for 1983 were only $79 million, which isn't all that much in the world of public companies.

Size is relative, though, and Canandaigua's immediate advantage with its Sun Country coolers was a built-in national distribution network that the California Cooler lacked. By committing to a national rollout early and waving off test-marketing, Canandaigua was the first to market coolers in many Eastern states. Revenues moved up to $90 million in the fiscal year ending August 1984. The following year, the company began to set records.

The Tip-off

All this success isn't much good unless you know about it. With fads, the dominant investor perception is that by the time you do hear about the fad, it's too late; in other words, only the early birds (i.e., Crete and Bewley) get rewarded, while the Johnnies-come-lately like you and me lose our collective shirts. That's a myth: Most fads are widely known well before the associated stocks have peaked.

That doesn't mean that everyone gets tipped off at the same time. In Canandaigua's case, I suppose those who actually drank the stuff had an advantage, because they could have read the small print on the Sun Country package to determine its source. But I want to stress that you don't have to participate in a fad to be made aware of it, as my unglamorous experience with Canandaigua Wine will illustrate.

I first heard of Canandaigua Wine while reading through some earnings reports in *The New York Times* one Saturday morning in the fall of 1985. (For those readers inclined to make personal judgments about someone who reads earnings reports on Saturday mornings, let me say that I've since gotten a life.) As earnings reports go, this one was pretty interesting. The company's sprawling name made it stand out more than, say, Cabot Corporation (two slots above), and the numbers were positively screaming for some attention.

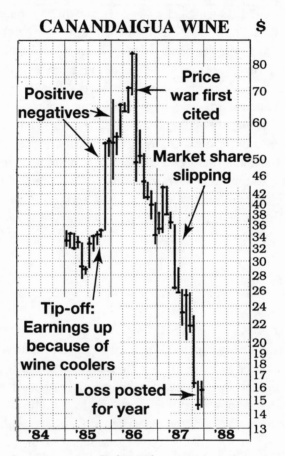

Fig. 32 CANANDAIGUA CHART #1 ('85–'87) (Courtesy of Securities Research Co.)

Sales for the fiscal year ended August 31, 1985, were $134 million, up almost 50 percent from fiscal 1984's level of $90 million. Earnings came in at $4.97 per share versus $3.24 in 1984—an increase of greater than 50 percent. The little "A" next to Canandaigua's name indicated that the stock traded on the American Exchange: Sure enough, a few pages away, there it was, at $35 per share. That's seven times earnings for a company whose earnings had jumped over 50 percent. Something was going on.

In retrospect, the correct move would have been to buy right then and there, sight unseen. Irresponsible? Of course, but it would've been better than watching the stock go up. Which it did; it was up four points when trading resumed the following Monday, three points on Tuesday, and another three and a half points on Wednesday. Moves like that are quite unusual, but a stock with such a limited float (back then Canandaigua had only 1.9 million shares to its name, an ultra-small number) can get pushed up a lot by any rise in demand. The combined three-day gain was a sprightly 30 percent.

Somewhere during this giddy spree, I found out that the Sun Country wine cooler was behind the sales gain. I had seen the Sun Country TV ads (the ones with Ringo Starr and Donna Mills in polar bear suits), but I had never made the connection to Canandaigua Wine. It felt too late to invest. But history showed that it wasn't even close.

Positive Negatives

As a fad stock climbs, investors must confront all sorts of signs—both qualitative and quantitative—that the phenomenon is getting out of hand. These are what I call "positive negatives" because they are impressive and worrisome at the same time. We will find that fad stocks cope surprisingly well during this phase.

For wine coolers, the most visible positive negative was the absolute inundation of cooler ads on TV even as far back as the fall of 1985. Gallo, the nation's leading winery, had launched a tremendous success with its Bartles & Jaymes campaign, featuring a couple of yokels named Frank and Ed (wrongly identified by the rumor mills as Ernest and Julio Gallo themselves). Then Seagram came along with its Golden Wine Coolers, with ads featuring a white-suited Bruce Willis sashaying through a series of swank bistros.

What was positive about this is that the wine cooler category was clearly deemed worthwhile by the major companies. In fact, these ads served to broaden the demographic, if you'll pardon the adspeak. Bartles & Jaymes appealed to older customers, while Bruce Willis made coolers more "cool." But the inundation of cooler ads was so out of control it served as a warning sign: How long could the craze last?

Despite these worries, the cooler category kept growing, and Canandaigua's stock kept rising, moving above $60 per share in early 1986. Then the stock suffered its first setback. On January 10, 1986, it dropped 11 points, from 63½ to 52½.

I mention this because fad stocks always encounter a few bumps on the way to the top. As precipitous as the decline was, though, nothing bad had happened to Canandaigua. The drop was simply caused by investors taking their profits after the stock's six-week, 80 percent move, and was made more dramatic by the small, illiquid market for Canandaigua's shares.

If you had actually held the stock at the time, could you have been this sanguine? Not necessarily. But even if this move had looked like the beginning of the end and scared you out of the stock, you'd still have been up almost 50 percent from November 1985, just two months prior. Selling too soon is hardly the worst crime in the world, especially when it comes to fad stocks.

In general, you shouldn't hold any stock if the negatives become too much to bear. But it's worth noting that an environment chock-full of positive negatives tends to be *good* for a fad stock. Remember the market maxim "A bull market climbs a wall of worry"? In that spirit, a fad stock could be said to climb a wall of sheer terror. If you choose to stand on the sidelines, fine. But the one thing you shouldn't do is sell a stock short during the positive negative period—no matter how doomed the fad may appear—because betting against a mania can be even riskier than betting with it. Besides, as we will see, a short seller's odds improve dramatically as we continue through the fad cycle.

The Peak

Adjusting for Canandaigua's 5-for-2 stock split in 1986, our November 1985 entry price of $35 per share becomes $14. In these post-split terms, the stock didn't peak until August 1986, when it hit $38 per share.

There is a Sir Edmund Hillary syndrome in all of this that makes us think that getting out at $38 is the whole idea. That's nonsense. The ill-advised search for the peak is one of the reasons that some well-meaning investors fare so poorly with stocks such as Canandaigua, because they tend to hold on too long. No one could have possibly told you when this stock (or any stock, for that matter) was going to stall out. Hillary had the advantage of knowing where his peak was; we don't. People will tell you that you *can* identify a peak—that it occurs at that moment of maximum investor optimism or when that last naysayer has thrown in the towel—but these things are true only by definition and not in a constructive, usable way.

Actually, there are some good reasons *not* to be around at the top! That's because fad stocks are especially likely to reach their top via a short squeeze—meaning that people who short the stock, hoping for a decline, at some point get so frightened by its continued rise that they close out (or "cover") their positions. But this is done by buying, which adds to the upward pressure on the share price. Ironically, the more overvalued a fad stock might look, the more likely it is to attract short sellers who one day may produce a short squeeze that sends it even higher.

The way to avoid the Hillary syndrome is to recognize the greed that underlies the notion of selling at the top. To repeat a prior point, fad stocks cover so much ground that you can make a lot of money from them even if your timing is terrible. Being close is enough, and far easier: As Louis Rukeyser wrote many years ago, "You never quite know when you're at the top, but you know when you're in the clouds." That should be enough.

True Negatives

I define a "true" negative as a tangible indication that the fad *has* taken a turn for the worse (as opposed to a positive negative, which is merely a sign that it *might*). The investment advice for times such as these is quite simple: If you're still holding on when true negatives start appearing, get out, once and for all. This chickenhearted strategy is recommended because the odds are overwhelming that the first true negatives will be followed by many, many more.

The first true negatives may be subtle and, unlike the fads themselves, they can be overlooked. With Canandaigua Wine, an early clue came from the July 1986 issue of *Adweek,* which reported that the major wine cooler producers had lowered prices by $1 per case. That's all it said. There was no bold type to guide you, nor was there any *Lost in Space* robot to yell "Warning!" With fad stocks, though, any concrete indication of a reversal should be heeded.

The alleged price war the *Adweek* article was referring to had a companion problem in the form of market share. Share figures for wine coolers have always been imprecise, but by late 1986 there was no question that Seagram and Gallo were winning the marketing battle. By that time, each had a market share in excess of 20 percent, while Canandaigua's share, which had peaked somewhere around the 15 percent level, was at 13 percent and slipping. The difference may not look like much, but the trend is everything, and this one was pointing the wrong way. By the end of the year, on the basis of these negative trends, Canandaigua stock had fallen from $38 to the low $20s—but it still wasn't too late to get out.

The decisive true negative came in the form of advertising expenditures. In 1986, Canandaigua spent over $25 million on advertising for Sun Country, an eye-popping number for such a small company. Remember, just two years earlier Canandaigua had made inroads on California Cooler by using its size advantage, but now it was victimizing itself trying to keep up with companies with much deeper pockets.

The key investment point was that Canandaigua had already committed itself to a big advertising budget for fiscal 1987 before the nasty combination of lower market share and lower product prices had made its appearance. The need to plan ahead is precisely why companies can become so vulnerable to a fad's sudden reversal. The net was that Canandaigua lost $10 million in 1987, or $1.32 per share. The stock, which even in early 1987 could have been sold north of $20 per share, was down into the mid-teens by late summer. The October crash then knocked it down to the $9 level, barely one-fourth its high of the prior year.

This stunning reversal is actually quite typical of fad stocks. Once the first true negative signs come in, there are inevitably far worse ones to follow, and those investors who stoically hang on simply don't understand the fad dynamic. Note that there was plenty of time to get out; it took Canandaigua shares fifteen months to move from peak to trough.

Wine coolers as a whole peaked in 1986 and settled down into a steady but unspectacular segment of the overall wine market. Although over a hundred brands entered the derby at some point in the mid-eighties, the trends of 1986 have been fully borne out. Today, the category is dominated by Seagram's and Bartles & Jaymes. You can still buy Sun Country coolers in some parts of the country, but its overall market share is minuscule.

The Takeover Test

Before applying the wine cooler model to other product fads, I should point out that manias and crazes don't always revolve around products that the average citizen can go out and buy. The corporate takeover/ leveraged buyout binge of the 1980s is a case in point. But does the model fit?

The humble beginnings stage certainly doesn't fit. There has never been anything humble about one company acquiring another—not in the eighties, not in the conglomerate binge of the sixties, nor even before that.

But in the more important area of tip-offs, we fare quite a bit better, because any takeover of consequence was a major media event. Even if you missed the oil takeovers of the early eighties, there was plenty of time to hop aboard. Among food companies, Carnation was bought by Nestlé in 1984; General Foods and Nabisco Brands were acquired in 1985 by Philip Morris and RJ Reynolds, respectively. There was simply no way to miss what was going on.

How to react to the takeover binge was another matter. For our purposes, it's safe to say that anyone who recognized the fad dynamic underlying the takeover era had a tremendous investment advantage.

Admittedly, putting "fad" and "takeover" in the same context seems to disregard the legitimate strategic considerations underlying many of the decade's most important mergers. Yet strategy was often just a cover for the monkey see, monkey do atmosphere that spurred many corporate boards into action. If you understood that viewpoint, you'd also realize that an acquisition within any particular industry—packaged foods, publishing, entertainment, you name it—would inevitably inspire more.

Knowing how the takeover frenzy played out in the boardroom also provided a logic to the fact that the initial takeover bid for a company was rarely the final bid. In the mid-eighties, if you did nothing but invest in takeover targets *after* an initial bid was made (i.e., after the original price advance, however big), you could have done awfully well.

Many analysts took a pen-and-pencil attitude toward predicting when the takeover boom might end. For example, for a given industry, it might have been "provable" that no acquisition that cost more than, say, ten times the acquired company's cash flow could possibly be justified. But did that mean the boom would stop once stocks in that industry started to be valued at ten times cash flow? No chance. In a true fad, the phenomenon would continue long after it made financial sense. And that's what happened.

Different CEOs justified their acquisitions in different ways. When Union Pacific Railroad acquired leading trucking company Overnite Transportation in 1986, Drew Lewis (formerly Secretary of Transportation and then chairman of UP's rail unit) said, "If you are going to get the best, which we think this is, you pay a higher price than you would for another trucker." (The purchase price was five times Overnite's book value, which, if you've boned up on your accounting, means that Union Pacific's earnings would be pinched for years to come by the so-called amortization of goodwill. In other words, they may have paid too much.) Philip Morris chairman Hamish Maxwell was more candid. Upon acquiring General Foods for twenty times earnings in 1985, Maxwell said: "That's not to say this is as easy as falling off a log. We paid a full price. It's no bargain."

That's where another important fad parallel came into play. As with your average, everyday fad, takeovers put long-term investors in an uncomfortable psychological position. For many, investing in takeover targets for their own sake was far too predatory a strategy to even contemplate. Besides, how long could the craziness possibly last?

Longer than you might have thought. Recall that our fad model suggests that signs of excess occur well before the fad actually dies out. These signs are the positive negatives, and there was no shortage of them in the takeover era. On any given day in 1985, the front page of *The Wall Street Journal* was odds-on to contain at least one takeover announcement. We got used to it.

Another positive negative came in January 1986, when *Money* magazine published a list of ten takeover candidates for the year ahead. Before the year was out, four of them—Color Tile, Dart & Kraft, Sheller-Globe, and Sterchi Brothers—had either been taken over or brought private. That's batting .400, which is every bit as extraordinary here as it is on the playing field. Was it simply good research or was the game getting out of hand? Perhaps the most memorable positive negative, though, was Michael Milken's LBO-inflated 1987 salary of $550 million. Surely *that* couldn't last. But when would it all end?

My personal hunch at the time was that leveraged buyouts would keep going until one of them went bankrupt (a "true negative," in our fad parlance). However, even that would have pulled the plug way early: The first LBO failure was Revco Drug Stores in July 1988, barely midway through what turned out to be the biggest acquisition year in history.

In retrospect, there *was* a peak to the craze—the $25 billion buyout of RJR Nabisco in December 1988. But the strain of over-buying didn't truly show until the next year, in the form of headline failures such as Robert Campeau's disastrous buyouts of Allied and Federated Department Stores. The coup de grâce came in October 1989 with the failed buyout of UAL (the parent company of United Airlines). At that point you knew for sure that the takeover landscape had permanently changed.

Once that change occurred, the odds were overwhelming that it would endure, and that's exactly what happened. The number of corporate acquisitions dropped from the 1988 peak of 462 to only 148 by

1991. By then, hundreds of arbitrageurs, junk bond managers, and other symbols of the eighties had cashed in their chips.

I have noted that many long-term investors didn't like the idea of playing the takeover game. Many elected to sidestep the issue by investing in franchise or brand-name companies such as Disney, Columbia Pictures, Cheseborough-Ponds, Washington Post, and so on. Buying a piece of a true franchise was a nice semantic twist because it enabled the purchase to be made under the cover of a long-term strategy. Meanwhile, the investor could secretly hope to hell that the company would get taken over. Many of them did.

The significance of this type of semantic rationale is as follows: The long-term investor will never participate in faddish-looking situations unless he or she is able to put a more positive spin on what is happening.

Getting back to product fads, the best positive spin is to treat them like a game, where the object is to identify the fad dynamic as it unfolds and pinpoint what stage of our fad model is taking place at any given time. Like any game, this requires practice, so here are five of the biggest fad stories of recent years laid out according to this new model.

Video Games: A Rare Comeback Story

Humble Beginnings

Back in 1972, a young man named Nolan Bushnell, toiling for an obscure California company called Syzygy, began dabbling with the concept of using computers to play games—as opposed to processing accounts receivable. Bushnell's first effort, a game called Computer Space, earned him nothing but anonymity. His second game, Pong, started an avalanche for Syzygy, which deserved and received a new name: Atari.

Like so many once-revolutionary products, Pong looks positively medieval by today's standards. The game was nothing more than a white square traveling back and forth against a black screen, propelled by a "blocker" on either side. No color graphics, no high resolution.

And no matter, because it was *new*. Next came Tank, a game more in keeping with the modern era in that it involved high-tech warfare. Tank debuted in 1975. The very next year, Atari was bought by Warner Communications, a transaction that gave the public a chance to participate in the video game revolution.

It seems difficult to believe that Atari, a company whose revenues were then only $40 million, could have affected the fortunes of an entertainment giant such as Warner. Again, though, our modern perspective is getting in the way. Today, Warner is part of Time Warner, a multibillion-dollar entertainment Goliath, but back then it was a somewhat more modest collection of businesses: Warner Brothers studios, Warner Amex cable, and the Elektra, Atlantic, and Asylum record labels. Not long after the 1976 acquisition, Atari would be outearning them all.

The Tip-off

Recall that to play an early game like Pong or Tank, you had to go to an arcade, bar, or some such public arena. In 1977, Atari made a more visible imprint on the game-playing public when it introduced the Video Computer System (VCS) 2600, a game machine that plugged into a television set. Game cartridges were sold separately. The graphics of these games were by no means up to arcade standards, but, from that point on, the player could stay at home.

If the VCS 2600 wasn't enough of an investment tip-off, more would be coming in the next few years, in the form of the games themselves. In 1979, Space Invaders arrived from Japan, and Atari won exclusive rights to the home game license. Warner was then trading at $15 per share, up 150 percent from its level at the time of the Atari buyout in 1976. But, in keeping with prior patterns, Warner stock wasn't through by a long shot.

Pac-Man, perhaps the most famous game of them all, became a fad unto itself in the early eighties and a gigantic winner for Warner. As this video game history was unfolding, Warner's earnings and stock price kept going up. From a split-adjusted level of $6 per share in mid-1976, the stock hit $60 in early 1982. That was a tenfold increase overall—and a fourfold increase even after the Space Invaders tip-off.

Positive Negatives

We have been applying the term "positive negative" to signs that a given trend has reached faddish proportions and must inevitably come down. In the case of video games, though, there was a lot of good, solid growth before an investor should have even considered exchanging his glee for skepticism. We will pick up the story in 1982, which turned out to be the crescendo year for the first phase of the video game industry.

There were some staggering numbers to be found. In 1978, Atari sold 800,000 VCS units; by 1982, that figure had reached 12 million. Industrywide, over 60 million game cartridges were sold in 1982. Atari owned more than 80 percent of the home video market—defined as the combination of hardware (VCS) and software (game cartridges). Atari's revenues for 1982 exceeded $2 billion, or fifty times their level of 1976, the year of the Warner buyout.

As these numbers suggest, Atari's importance to Warner was growing steadily throughout this time. In the first nine months of 1982, Atari accounted for almost one-half of Warner's $3 billion in revenues and two-thirds of its $500 million operating income.

This increasing dependency may have been a warning sign by itself. But there were other, qualitative signs of excess that were more available to the investing public. The emergence of the Top 40 song "Pac-Man Fever" by Jerry Buckner and Gary Garcia in the spring of 1982 was surely a positive negative, because the time it takes for a song to be recorded and produced can amount to a significant portion of a fad's lifetime. (The precedent was the song "Convoy" by C. W. McCall, which made it all the way to number one in January 1976 because of the CB radio craze. By the end of that year, the craze had fallen apart.)

Other nonfinancial positive negatives included *People* magazine's first celebrity Pac-Man contest in May 1982 and a Saturday morning Pac-Man cartoon show on ABC (neither quite caught on). But a big warning sign of 1982 came from none other than the stock market.

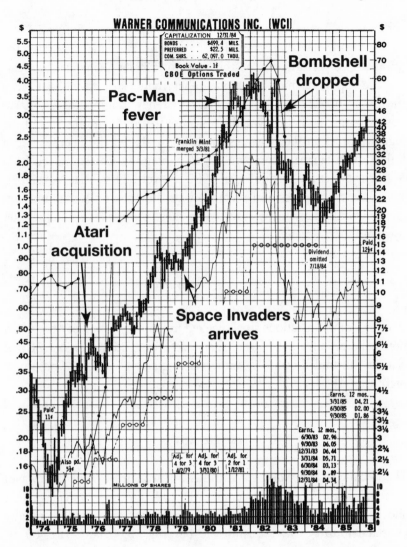

Fig. 33 WARNER COMMUNICATIONS CHART (Courtesy of Securities Research Co.)

Video game stocks such as Warner, Mattel (which manufactured a competing home video game system called Intellivision), and Bally Manufacturing (a leading arcade game maker) were strong even as the market struggled in 1981 and early 1982. In August 1982, the Dow Jones Industrial Average bottomed out at 777 and then took off, finishing the year at 1046. Economically sensitive stocks did especially well, and of those none did better than Chrysler, which moved from $3⅜ to $17¾ during 1982, a gain of 426 percent. But that was only the number-two performance on the New York Stock Exchange that year.

The top performer was none other than Hartford-based Coleco Industries. Coleco made Colecovision, a new competitor to Atari's home system, and also owned the license to Donkey Kong, one of the biggest names in video games (actually, it shared the license with a little-known Japanese company called Nintendo). Coleco moved from $3 per share at the beginning of 1982 to over $24 by that November. Yes, Coleco's graphics and memory were superior to Atari's, but you had to wonder how many video game success stories the stock market was going to tolerate.

The Peak

Warner Communications stock peaked in February 1982 at $63. It did not make an abrupt fall from that level—even in November of that year, it still traded at $59½. However, the stock would not hit a new high until 1987.

True Negatives

The decline of the video game industry (or at least of its first wave) came all at once. On December 8, 1982, Warner's management shocked the investment community by announcing that the company expected fourth-quarter earnings to be only $0.60 per share, off almost 50 percent from the $1.17 per share posted in 1981's fourth quarter. Warner stock dropped from $51⅞ to $35⅛ in one trading session, a decline of 33 percent.

Clearly, the earnings reversal had caught Wall Street by surprise. Analysts had been expecting earnings for the quarter to come in between $1.60 and $2.00, or three times the actual number. The earnings decline was the first in almost eight years, a period that included the entire history of Warner's ownership of Atari.

Were there ways of seeing the decline coming? Well, an article in *The Washington Post,* dated October 24, 1982, contained a few seeds of the decline. Notable among these was an estimate by Ralph Lally, publisher of *Play Meter* magazine, that the average arcade video game machine would eat up $109 a week in quarters in 1982, down from $140 per week in 1981. The saturation of game machines was one contributor, the lack of follow-up hits to Pac-Man and Donkey Kong was another. This was a true negative, and any shareholder who saw this article had over one month to sell. (In theory, the home market dominated by Atari was separate from the arcade market, but with fad stocks it doesn't pay to split hairs.)

One of the factors underlying the Atari/Warner collapse was that cartridge orders from distributors were made well in advance. In 1981, the problem had been a shortage of product, so, not surprisingly, distributors ordered more than they thought they would need for 1982, just to make sure they didn't get cut out.

Even that wouldn't have been a problem, but with competition moving in and offering a wide assortment of cheap games compatible with Atari hardware, the company's market share dropped, and cancellations from dealers poured in. *That's* why the profit decline was so severe. The high profit margins of the cartridge business were great while they lasted, but once competition sets in, high profit margins can be a liability because they represent profits that will disappear in the struggle for market share.

There are many other interesting aspects to the industry's decline, but that would be overkill. According to classic fad analysis that you've doubtless mastered by now, you'd expect the situation to get worse before it got better, and that's what happened. Warner Communications lost $3.22 per share in 1983, and $2.17 in 1984. The stock, which had fallen to $35 per share on that fateful December 1982 trading session, didn't bottom out until July 1984, when it hit $17.

The Nintendo Footnote

It should come as no surprise that many video game investors who got burned in 1982 were not hanging around to see Warner stock recover (culminating with the Time-Warner merger of 1989). But the bigger missed opportunity came from the comeback of video games themselves.

Recall that one nicety of the video game craze of the late seventies and early eighties was that it provided a big investment opportunity within a stock market that was otherwise struggling. However, turnabout is fair play. When the Atari/Coleco bubble broke, it did so at a time when the overall market was healthy again—thus magnifying the scorn that investors felt toward this group. Investors who took this scorn too far missed out on Nintendo, one of the great investment stories of the eighties. "Nintendo? Video games? Don't waste my time." (Remarks of an imaginary portfolio manager, circa 1985.)

Talk about humble beginnings. Nintendo was founded by a gentleman named Fusajiro Yamauchi in 1899 and started out as a manufacturer of playing cards. The company's first claim to video fame was the arcade game Donkey Kong, released in 1982. Posterity awaited the 1985 release of the Nintendo Entertainment System.

Nintendo did a lot of things right. The company kept the price of its system down (to between $70 and $140, depending on the accessories involved). It kept strict control over software licensing—thereby avoiding the plight of Atari, whose would-be customers became confused and disenchanted by the glut of low-quality games available for both Atari and rival machines. Plus, Nintendo's technology was simply better: faster, better graphics; better sound; and more memory. These advantages enabled Nintendo to capture an astonishing *80 percent* share of the video game market in both Japan and the United States.

Of course, the game market had declined precipitously—the domestic market dropped from $3 billion in sales in 1982 to just $100 million in 1985. But the advanced technology of the Nintendo system, coupled with the key fact that many Nintendo players weren't even alive during the first video game wave, created an opportunity for new growth. Nintendo shares didn't become available (in the form of American Depository Receipts) until early 1989, but that still wasn't too late. By the summer of 1990, they had quadrupled.

To add insult to injury for the fad-averse, the video game second wave wasn't even over. Shares of NASDAQ-traded Electronic Arts—yet another video game software company—appreciated fifteenfold between the end of 1990 and the middle of 1993, buoyed by strong sales of sports-related games such as John Madden Football, NHL Hockey, PGA Tour Golf, and basketball games such as Bulls vs. Blazers.

All you needed to participate in these gains was a little open-mindedness—at least, enough open-mindedness to realize how inaccurate a fad label can be.

HOME SHOPPING NETWORK: SHORTS TO THE RESCUE

Humble Beginnings

Even measured against its faddish brethren, the rise of Home Shopping Network was positively meteoric. The company began almost accidentally in the winter of 1977, when a cash-strapped advertiser on Florida AM radio station WWQT made its payments to the station in the form of electric can openers; station owner Lowell Paxson seized the opportunity and sold the can openers on the air. He then hooked up with a businessman named Roy Speer to take the enterprise beyond can openers and eventually to a different medium—the show moved to TV in 1982.

Originally, the Home Shopping Club television program was broadcast on cable to a small but loyal following in the Pinellas County area. The network went national in 1984 as part of a strategy to preempt the competition in all markets rather than concentrating on just one.

The Tip-off

Whatever progress was made in those next two years, Home Shopping Network remained essentially an unknown commodity when it went public in May 1986. However, *the offering itself* created an unusual amount of publicity and was the main tip-off to investors that a new sales medium was coming of age.

If you weren't in on the original offering, it looked as though you were out of luck; the stock was sold at $18 per share and closed at $42 the same day. (Lead underwriter Merrill Lynch was chided for underpricing the shares, in keeping with Home Shopping's image as the purveyor of cheap merchandise.) Of course, if the other fads we have looked at mean anything at all, Home Shopping Network had a long way to go, even after its first-day gain of 133 percent.

Positive Negatives

Before listing some of the factors that made Home Shopping look like an outright fad—and a particularly dangerous investment—let me divulge that the stock's high for 1986 was $133 per share, three times its first-day closing price. And in January 1987, the all-time high was reached: $282 per share. (Actually, the stock split 3-for-1 and 2-for-1 in 1986, so that dollar figure wasn't actually reached. Nonetheless, an $1,800 investment in Home Shopping Network in May 1986 was worth $28,200 by the following January—a gain of almost 1,500 percent.)

Mind you, I'm not suggesting that anyone actually bought at $18 and sold at $282. As with all the stocks in this chapter, the point is that you could have made out extremely well with only a small portion of the maximum available gain.

Throughout this stunning rise, many positive negatives came from the stock market itself, since all a company had to do to win investor approval in 1986 was announce an intention to get into the home shopping business. The mere intention to enter the business was enough; no existing operations were required, much less earnings. That's how stocks like Financial News Network, Entertainment Marketing, Horn & Hardart, and C.O.M.B. gained anywhere from 50 to 100 percent that year.

Another sign of investor mania was the talk that Home Shopping would put Kmart out of business—never mind that Kmart's revenues were over a hundred times HSN's.

The vast majority of portfolio managers were scared away, but Ken Heebner was not one of them. His Zenith Capital Growth Fund returned 95 percent that year, and Home Shopping Network was the single biggest contributor.

Years later, he admitted to me that he bought shares at the offering almost solely because it was a hot deal. Then his quantitative wheels began spinning, because the story was even better than he thought. Home Shopping used the cash from its public offering to acquire UHF stations across the country. Heebner, by extrapolating past sales performance to the wider base, came up with earnings estimates far in excess of most analysts' predictions. His sell strategy was concocted in advance: When the company had bought its quota of stations or when

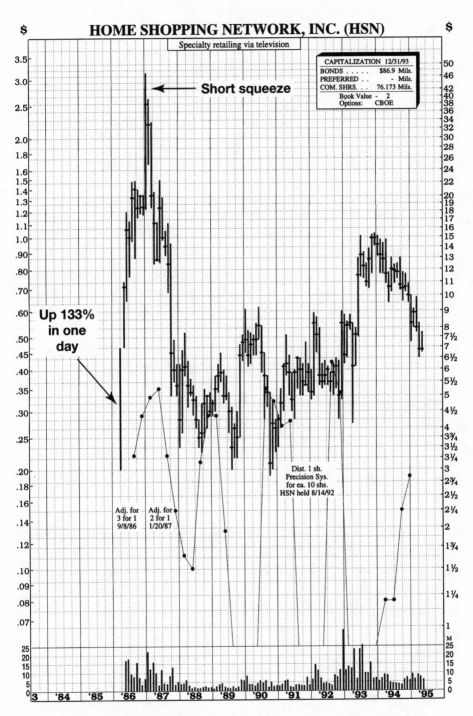

Fig. 34 HOME SHOPPING NETWORK CHART (Courtesy of Securities Research Co.)

sales volume began to level off at individual stations (as he pointed out, this was something you could see by turning on your television set), it was time to get out. What the stock price would be when these things happened was anybody's guess, but in this case the timing gods were on his side. All his sell indicators started flashing at once.

The Peak

As noted, the peak came in January 1987, at a split-adjusted price of $47 per share. At that price, the stock market was according Home Shopping Network a total market value of over $3 *billion*. In January alone, the stock had doubled.

As I suggested earlier, one of the reasons not to focus on getting out at the top is that short sellers often dominate the market at that time. When enough short sellers have tired of losing money, they cover their positions by *buying*, thus sending the stock even higher and making an already ridiculous valuation even more so. Even if you own a million shares (nice thought), you can get rid of your position by selling into this demand. That's what Heebner did, aided by the knowledge that short sellers accounted for a preposterously high 20 percent of Home Shopping's total float. When the January giddiness subsided, he was out of the stock for all time.

True Negatives

In 1987, the bubble burst for the home shopping business. Competitors learned that entry into the business wasn't as easy as the stock market seemed to think just one year before. Airtime was expensive and not available to everyone who wanted it. If Home Shopping Network, CVN, and QVC were already represented in a particular market, that might be it.

That phenomenon might have helped Home Shopping Network, but the company faced problems of its own. It encountered difficulties in filling sales orders and, in some cases, in obtaining the orders. In late 1987, the company ingraciously filed suit against GTE, claiming that some $500 million of telephone orders never got through because of GTE's negligence in installing and maintaining Home Shopping's phone lines. That number was almost as big as actual revenues for 1987. (Note: Shifting the blame didn't work. HSN not only lost the suit but was hit with a $100 million libel action by GTE.)

As a result of these snafus, earnings for 1987 came in at $0.33 per share, a 50 percent increase over the $0.22 earned in 1986, but well below analysts' estimates, which in early 1987 had run as high as $0.75 per share. The stock fell from $47 in January to low double figures by the fall, and hit just $5 in the aftermath of October's market crash. It would stay there for the next five years.

Sotheby's and the Art Boom: As Faddish as the Rest

Humble Beginnings

The art market doesn't have the same type of humble beginnings as the other fads we have looked at. There is a difference between something that debuts as a fad and something that has always been around —whether it be a work of art or tulip bulbs—suddenly finding itself in the middle of a mania.

For our purposes, though, the whole decade of the seventies can be considered a humble beginning for the art market. Art prices cannot be charted in the same way that stock prices can, but both markets languished during the seventies before picking up dramatically in the early eighties. And by the late eighties, one particular art company— the subject of this story—made its way to the American Stock Exchange.

The Tip-off

When did the art market begin sending signals that something big was brewing? *Time* magazine cited the 1980 sale of *Juliet and Her Nurse* by J.M.W. Turner as an early sign. The selling price of $6.4 million now looks puny, but that's the whole point. The craze was just beginning.

In the next few years, the buying spree pushed the works of a wide range of artists to record prices. Sotheby's itself became part of the action in 1983 when the company was bought by a group headed by Bloomingdale's chairman A. Alfred Taubman. Core operations were shifted from London to New York, and more than ever the art market became a playground for the rich and famous. In one especially rewarding intra-eighties transaction, Humana president Wendell Cherry bought *Yo Picasso* for $5.83 million in 1981 and sold it for $47.85 million in 1989.

For most of this time, the art market wasn't approachable by those with average household budgets. Shares of Christie's were available on the London Exchange, but most U.S. investors had to sit on the sidelines until 1988, when the Taubman group finally sold a piece of Sotheby's to the public.

The Sotheby's stock offering had been delayed for several months following the 1987 stock market crash, an event that many observers worried would carry over into the art market. That didn't happen. In November 1987, a mere month after the crash, Sotheby's handled the most expensive art transaction in history—the $53.9 million purchase of Van Gogh's *Irises* by Australian entrepreneur and renowned overspender Alan Bond from John Whitney Payson. As a follow-up, Sotheby's sold a collection of Andy Warhol knickknacks in early 1988 for $25 million, well above expectations. Warhol's cookie jars and salt and pepper shakers, with an estimated value of $100 to $150, went for $23,000. The art market was thereby pronounced healthier than ever, and in May 1988 Sotheby's went public at a split-adjusted price of $9 per share. What happened next defied belief.

Positive Negatives

To say that there were warning signs at the time of the public offering is a massive understatement. Some observers felt that the very existence of the public offering meant that Taubman thought the art market was peaking. *Irises* was of course another such positive negative—a sign that the art world had gone crazy, but also that craziness was alive and well.

It couldn't last forever, of course. Once Alan Bond and his like got their egos satisfied, where would the buyers come from? Even in the eighties, the world wasn't exactly swarming with billionaires. The Japanese were doing more and more of the buying, in keeping with the torrid pace then being set by the Nikkei Dow. How long could that last?

But the theory of positive negatives suggests that the Sotheby's shares would go up despite these storm clouds. The fact was that Sotheby's revenues and profitability were both increasing rapidly. Consider that earnings in 1987—at that time, a record year—had been $39 million, or 14 percent of revenues; in 1988, they jumped to $63 million, 18 percent of revenues. This amounted to $0.56 per share. The stock, still at the $9 level as 1989 began, was ready to put on a show of its own.

The last year of the eighties turned out to be Sotheby's best ever. More and more major collections were put up for sale to capitalize on high art prices, and Sotheby's was the beneficiary of this snowball effect. In 1989, the company would end up earning $113 million, or 25 percent of revenues. That amounted to $1.96 per share, and, as this earnings picture developed during the year, the stock could hardly stand still (stocks tend not to stay at five times earnings for long—certainly not in the eighties). By April Sotheby's shares had passed the $15 mark, and by August they had reached $25.

The Peak

In October 1989, Sotheby's traded at $37 per share, four times its level at the beginning of the year. That's also as high as it would ever get.

True Negatives

A list of true negatives for Sotheby's is probably as long as the list of overpriced paintings swept up in the initial craze, so I won't be able to list them all. But I'll try.

First of all, it was entirely fitting that the stock peaked in October 1989. That same month featured the failed buyout of UAL, the parent company of United Airlines. This was the event that punctured the

SOTHEBY'S HOLDINGS, INC. (BID)

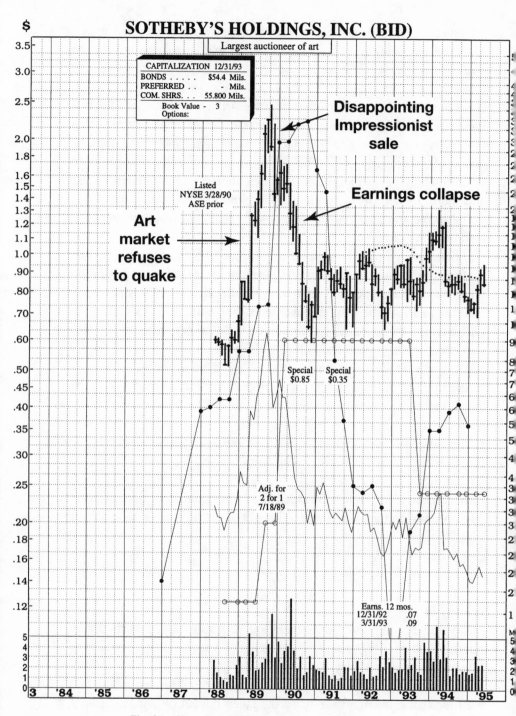

Fig. 35 SOTHEBY'S CHART (Courtesy of Securities Research Co.)

leveraged buyout balloon—and with it, collectors such as Alan Bond. The Dow Jones Industrial Average dropped over 100 points in a single day.

One month later, another negative sign appeared. Picasso's *Au Lapin Agile* was put up for sale by Linda de Roulet (John Whitney Payson's sister) amid expectations that it would become the highest-priced painting ever sold at auction. Instead, publisher Walter Annenberg bought the painting for a mere $40.7 million. Still an extraordinary price, but, in the context of a true craze, disappointing and worth noticing.

Sotheby's Impressionist sale of mid-November produced mixed results (again, "mixed" simply won't do when expectations are high, especially within the Impressionist category, which had been carrying the entire art market on its back). Although a dozen price records were set for individual artists, a Renoir didn't reach preauction estimates and was never sold. A Christie's auction of the same month was plagued by similar "buy-ins," again a function of high expectations. By this time, Sotheby's stock had fallen from its $37 peak to just over $30.

In late November, all of America was given a sell signal when *Time* magazine ran a cover story about the art market. The article disclosed what those in the business already knew—that Sotheby's was engaging in the dubious practices of guarantees and loans. A guarantee meant that a seller would be paid a fixed price for a collection (with the auction house implicitly making up the difference if the bidders didn't come through). A loan simply meant that Sotheby's was willing to front certain buyers up to 50 percent of the purchase price. Sotheby's was in essence artificially propping up both sides of the auction process. The vulnerability of the high prices created under such a system was a flashing red light.

Not only that, but the nineties were right around the corner and a new set of values was in sight. Said *Time,* "The art market has become the faithful cultural reflection of the wider economy in the eighties, inflated by leveraged buyouts, massive junk-bond issues and vast infusions of credit. . . . How much art can dance for how long on this particular pinhead? Nobody has the slightest idea."

I borrow liberally from *Time* not only because writer Robert Hughes captured the precariousness of the art market but also because his phrases were patently available to the investing public. They alone made Sotheby's stock an outright sale.

Why might a holder *not* sell? First and foremost would be the perception—typical for times when a specific stock is absolutely reeling—that the stock market was already discounting the bad news. After all, by the end of November, Sotheby's shares were hovering at around $20, down 45 percent from the peak of just one month before. It feels stupid to sell after such a serious decline. Not only that, many analysts' estimates for future earnings hadn't done the about-face you might have expected. For example, analysts at brokerage firm Alex Brown still projected Sotheby's earnings to increase from 1989's $1.96 per share to $2.35 in 1990 and $2.82 in 1991.

These earnings estimates held firm even after a disappointing London Impressionist sale in April 1990. With the estimates as a benchmark, the stock (at $20 per share) appeared to be trading at only seven times expected 1991 earnings—apparently a great value. But that's the most important lesson of Sotheby's and other fad stocks: After a craze has soured, a low price/earnings ratio means nothing—except perhaps that the analyst making the estimates is living in the past.

One early-1990 recommendation of Sotheby's cited the company's impressive four-year annual sales growth rate of 44 percent. Also cited was the company's sensational performance in 1989, during which auction sales rose 61 percent. Nice numbers, to be sure, but nothing about them could be extrapolated into the future.

Analysts are human beings. Part of the fabric of their earnings estimates has to do with the nature of their recent experience. For example, when the Japanese stock market began to decline in 1990, it was all too easy to conclude that the art market wouldn't be affected—hadn't the art market survived the 1987 crash in fine form? But the fall of the Japanese stock and real estate markets was different, because speculation was much more pronounced and valuations were so much more out of line. When those problems proved enduring, the art market had lost a significant group of buyers.

The bloom was off the rose. Sotheby's earnings declined in 1990 to $1.66 per share, sinking to just $0.25 per share in 1991 and $0.07 in 1992. Remember how, at $20 per share in late 1989, it was so easy to conclude that the damage had already been done? Well, Sotheby's stock dropped to $9 per share by late 1990, the same price at which it had come public just two and a half years earlier. Fads tend to come full circle.

Teenage Mutant Ninja Turtles: The Need to Look Overseas

Humble Beginnings

Until 1984, Peter Laird and Kevin Eastman were a couple of struggling artists: Laird was drawing eggplants for a gardening page of a Northampton, Massachusetts, newspaper, while Eastman, an amateur cartoonist, was earning his keep as a short-order cook. Then, in a couple of madcap moments, they devised four characters and dubbed them the Teenage Mutant Ninja Turtles. Laird and Eastman's comic books introduced the quartet to an unsuspecting world.

For those who don't know the story of the Turtles, here goes. Four previously normal turtles—named Leonardo, Donatello, Raphael, and Michaelangelo [sic]—get trapped in radioactive sewer slime and emerge as human-sized creatures with a humanlike intelligence. Raised by a giant rat named Splinter, who happens to be a ninja master, they develop a healthy dose of street smarts as well as a craving for pizza. The Turtles' special argot is dotted with such items as "Hey, dude" and "Cowabunga" (stolen from Chief Thunderthud of Howdy Doody fame). That's pretty much it.

The Turtles parlayed their catchy name and likeable personalities to become an enormous hit when they came to Saturday morning television in 1987. They were nothing less than the Rocky and Bullwinkle of the eighties. In fact, at risk of sounding heretical to my own generation, they became quite a bit more.

The Tip-off

It may go without saying that investors with children had an early advantage in catching on to the Turtles phenomenon. However, at the time the Teenage Mutant Ninja Turtle television show first appeared, there wasn't any stock market play—at least, not a domestic one.

The first widespread tip-off came in March 1990 with the release of the first feature film starring the TMNT (the full name gets cumbersome after a while). There were two stocks that offered an investment play on the film: New Line Cinema (the film's maker) and LIVE Entertainment (the distributor of the videos).

The movie's numbers told the success story. On its first weekend in the theaters, gross revenues came in at $25.4 million—the biggest opening in history for an independent film. The Turtles' movie went on to gross $138 million, easily surpassing *Dirty Dancing* as the biggest-selling independent film ever. All this for a film that cost only $15 million to make. I should add that these sales figures were achieved even though most of the tickets were sold to kids, at kids' discount prices.

Unfortunately, to make money in the stocks of either of the two film companies, you pretty much had to buy prior to the film's release, defeating the point of using the movie as an investment tip-off. As 1990 began, New Line Cinema traded for $4 per share, LIVE Entertainment for $15. By March 30, the movie's release date, New Line was at $8 and LIVE at $20. The stocks hadn't peaked, but it was getting late in the game.

The stock that had longer legs was Playmates International, the Hong Kong company we met earlier that held the exclusive rights to the TMNT action figures. This was the stock that truly defined the Turtles and truly defined a fad. During the first three months of 1990, it soared from $0.40 to over $1 per share, but it wasn't done by a long shot. Before the year was through, the stock had pierced the $4 mark, meaning that you could have quadrupled your money even *after* hearing about the film's stunning debut.

Positive Negatives

I don't think it's news to anybody that the Teenage Mutant Ninja Turtles were everywhere: lunch boxes, toothbrushes, Halloween outfits, breakfast cereals, skateboards. There was even a Teenage Mutant Ninja Turtles air freshener, their sewer heritage notwithstanding.

The saturation could be quantified. By 1991, Teenage Mutant Ninja Turtles accounted for 60 percent of the action figure toy market. It was estimated that over *90 percent* of American boys between the ages of three and eight owned at least one Turtle. Playmates' revenues exceeded $500 million. The company's profits exceeded $100 million, the first toy maker ever to exceed that amount in a single year. In July 1990, *The New York Times* gave Playmates credit for helping to rescue the entire Hong Kong stock market.

There were also some qualitative signs of the mania. Schoolchildren started getting into trouble by imitating the ninja aspect of the Turtles' culture. In Encinitas, California, the five-year-old daughter of a sewer maintenance worker asked her father, "Hey, Daddy, can I go to work with you and play in the slime?" Apparently, it looked like fun in the movie. In England, the foursome was called the "Teenage Mutant Hero Turtles" in deference to the British Home Office's ban on the sale of ninja weapons.

Playmates shares dropped from $4½ to $3 in the second half of 1990, but the decline related more to overall market weakness than to the fad dropping off (the Dow was dropping from 3000 to 2400 during this time). Playmates still had some life left.

The Peak

Playmates peaked at $6 per share in the first quarter of 1991, having increased 500 percent in just twelve months.

True Negatives

The downward stage of life was a bit different for Playmates International than some of the other fad stocks we have seen, because the company did an unusually good job of managing the Turtles fad. Playmates chairman Thomas Chan went out of his way to keep costs down. Head count was low, corporate headquarters were spartan, and, most important of all, product inventories were consistently kept low, even if that meant undersupplying the marketplace.

In fact, Chan claimed in 1991 that even if Turtles sales dropped to $100 million a year (from the $500 million level of 1990), Playmates would still make money. Shareholders in 1990 might also have taken comfort from the fact that the stock sold at a seemingly ridiculously low multiple of three times earnings (by comparison, the overall market hasn't sold at under ten times earnings since 1982, before the bull market began). The situation seemed under control.

When you have a true fad on your hands, however, even the best preventive measures can't stem the negative tide. The simple problem was that Turtles sales *did* decrease, from $500 million down to $200 million. Yes, the company was still profitable, as Chan had predicted, but it is hard for a stock not to drop in the face of such a dramatic sales decline; when earnings start to go down, even a low price/earnings multiple may not provide much cushion. Although *Teenage Mutant Ninja Turtles II* gave Playmates stock one final push, propelling it to $4.25 per share in 1992, what followed was a negative spiral that took the stock down to the $2.50 mark by mid-1993.

However, let's close the story with a note of appreciation. Even after this decline, Playmates was still trading at *ten times* its level of late 1989, just before the original Turtles movie hit the big screen. With moves like that, who needs timing?

BASEBALL CARDS: NO INSULATION FOR THE LEADER

Humble Beginnings

The concept of a baseball card goes all the way back to the 1880s, when tobacco companies added them to their products as a marketing device. The modern bubble gum and card era was ushered in by the Brooklyn-based Topps Company, which began its sports card business in 1948. When Topps bought out its chief competitor Bowman in 1955, the entire baseball card business had come to Brooklyn. And the Dodgers won the World Series. All was well.

For years, kids traded cards, flipped them, or clipped them to the spokes of their bicycles. (How humble can you get?) Obviously this was no way to treat items of great value, which is to say that cards were collected for collecting's sake. Then, in the 1980s, one hundred years after their debut, baseball cards took a giant leap forward.

The Tip-off

The tip-off process actually consisted of two steps, because Topps's history as a public company is divided into two distinct chapters.

The first significant change in the baseball card market came in 1980, when New Jersey–based Fleer Corporation won a longstanding court battle challenging Topps's monopoly of the card market. Fleer entered the market in 1981, joined also by Donruss (originally, a subsidiary of General Mills, later bought by Leaf, Inc., out of Illinois).

Ordinarily, the loss of a court decision and the emergence of competition is the last thing a shareholder would want. Yet Topps remained the industry leader and its shares awoke to the bull market's dawn in 1982, moving from $5 to $20 within that year. The stock doubled again in the first half of 1983, still trading at $20 *after* a 2-for-1 split that spring. In February 1984, Topps was taken private by Forstmann Little & Company in a leveraged buyout. The price tag was $98 million, or $26 per share. That concluded chapter one.

After three years as a private company, Topps was again sold to the public in 1987. The split-adjusted offering price of $4 per share, with 47 million shares outstanding, gave the company a market value of $188 million—90 percent higher than its buyout level. On the surface, it looked like a reverse LBO sucker play, meaning that the owners had bled all of the value out of the company and were now offering the anemic remains to the public. Not so. Much had happened in those three years to make Topps an even more interesting investment than it had been in chapter 1.

No single factor triggered the surge in baseball card trading, collecting, and investing; it was more of a combination of factors. One was the emergence of new superstars in important media markets, notably Don Mattingly of the Yankees, Dwight Gooden of the Mets, Wade Boggs and Roger Clemens in Boston, and Rickey Henderson wherever. Another factor was cable television, which exposed the public to more baseball games than ever before.

Other tip-offs were more directly tied to investments. Old Mickey Mantle cards that sold at auction for tens of thousands of dollars rejuvenated many old collectors. Beckett Publishing introduced a monthly in 1984 that gave price updates for the most volatile cards, giving the card market an appearance of liquidity it had never had.

The entire industry was growing rapidly, and Topps's revenues for 1987 came in at $149 million, twice their level of three years earlier.

The most significant investment tip-off came from a competitor: Privately held Upper Deck, which entered the baseball card market in 1989, started offering glossy cards at twice the standard price (i.e., $1 per card pack instead of the usual $0.50 cents). These premium cards, produced at least initially in limited runs, had the effect of raising the price standard for all new cards. The days of the 50-cent card pack were disappearing, and the profit margins of the card makers were on an impressive uptrend.

Sound like something to invest in? Well, Topps shares doubled in 1989 as the stock market began to appreciate the company's improved profitability. Topps's revenues kept rising—from $149 million in 1987 to $199 million in 1989 to $290 million in 1991, the year Topps introduced its Stadium Club premium cards. The share price moved from the $4 offering price in 1987 to the mid-teens by 1991, representing an annual return in the neighborhood of 40 percent per year.

Positive Negatives

So far, the competition has appeared as a welcome force. But there certainly can be too much of a good thing, and the possibility of a crowded marketplace was cropping up even as Topps shares were heading higher. A partial roster of new entrants would include the following:

1987	Classic
1988	Score
1989	Upper Deck, Skybox International, Pro Set
1990	Action Packed

And so on. Altogether, over twenty companies entered the business between 1980 and 1990. In 1980, Topps's last year as the sole provider, its total sales were in the $35 million range. By the end of the decade, the industry's annual sales had soared to $1 billion, representing a compound growth rate of 40 percent. But $1 billion is a lot of trading cards.

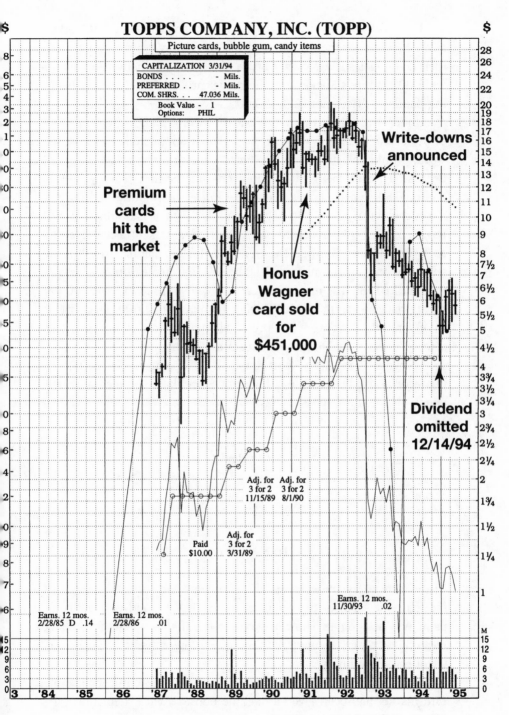

TOPPS COMPANY, INC. (TOPP)

Picture cards, bubble gum, candy items

CAPITALIZATION 3/31/94
BONDS . . . . .   - Mils.
PREFERRED . .   - Mils.
COM. SHRS. . .   47.036 Mils.
    Book Value -   1
    Options: PHIL

Premium cards hit the market

Honus Wagner card sold for $451,000

Write-downs announced

Dividend omitted 12/14/94

Adj. for 3 for 2 11/15/89

Adj. for 3 for 2 8/1/90

Paid $10.00

Adj. for 3 for 2 3/31/89

Earns. 12 mos. 11/30/93   .02

Earns. 12 mos. 2/28/85 D .14

Earns. 12 mos. 2/28/86   .01

'84   '85   '86   '87   '88   '89   '90   '91   '92   '93   '94   '95

Fig. 36 TOPPS CHART (Courtesy of Securities Research Co.)

The most headline-making sign of the mania came in 1991, when a 1910 Honus Wagner rookie card was bought by Wayne Gretzky and then Los Angeles Kings owner Bruce McNall at a Sotheby's auction for $451,000. Topps's Mickey Mantle rookie cards from 1951 were changing hands at prices north of $50,000.

Underneath the mania was a blatant incongruity. If the very rarity of yesteryear's cards was what made them so valuable, why in the world would the new mass-produced cards also be rising in price? Because demand was greater than ever—for the time being.

In 1984, when *Beckett's Baseball Card Monthly* published its first issue, the magazine was 36 pages long. By 1991, it had grown to 128 pages. Anyone who followed cards (and, ideally, kept a few back issues) could have followed the trend. As for circulation, in 1986 the subscription base numbered 30,000; 1991's circulation was a cool million. In 1986, the magazine's card show listings numbered 200 per month nationwide; in May 1991, they hit a peak of 2,600. That's right: In one month, there were 2,600 get-togethers of dealers and collectors across the country. Doesn't that seem a trifle high?

To make a long story short, baseball card companies were reporting record earnings because of high prices and high volumes, a combination that couldn't possibly last.

The Peak

Topps shares peaked at $20 in January 1992.

True Negatives

There were a few unwelcome developments for Topps in 1992, although none seemed to portend disaster. First, by mid-year the company was starting to show negative comparisons—Wall Street talk meaning that a given quarter's earnings are lower than the same quarter of the preceding year.

This dip seemed understandable. In 1991, the entire collectible card market had been given a onetime boost by cards depicting various aspects of Operation Desert Storm, so a decline the following year was to be expected. The sports card business, still the mainstay of Topps's operations, remained healthy, at least according to the company's account.

Other events cast considerable doubt. Even the previous year there were signs of a downturn. The circulation at *Beckett's Baseball Card Monthly* was beginning to drop by mid-1991, as were the number of dealer shows. Of special note was the slowness in November and December; this period is ordinarily quite active in the baseball card business because the baseball season is over and the game's stars can make personal appearances at the trading shows to boost card sales. Any slowness during that time frame had to be taken seriously.

In 1992, things got worse for a number of companies. Score Board, which had gone from a standing start in 1988 to a $60 million marketer of cards and other sports-related memorabilia by 1992, saw its business drop off and its stock price drop from $40 to $12 in four months. Skybox International and Pro Set were in financial distress, the former cutting its staff by 75 percent and the latter filing for Chapter 11.

The fundamental problem was that collectors were becoming confused by the vast array of cards and sets available to them. Not knowing what to buy, many didn't buy at all. The football card business was in particular disarray, as competing licensees flooded the market with new products.

A different sort of true negative came in September 1992, when Fleer was bought out by comic book publisher Marvel Entertainment for $265 million, or $28 per share. (Marvel made the acquisition so that Fleer could produce its comic cards, a hot new item.) It seemed curious that Fleer, a company with the best card mix in the business, little to no debt, and seemingly outstanding growth prospects, would agree to be bought out at a price that amounted to only ten times earnings, hardly a premium valuation. Did they know something?

By that time, Topps's management, never known for its candor, had already publicly conceded that business looked soft for the second half of the year. All this negative news wasn't great for Topps stock, which backed off its $20 high and spent most of the year trading in the mid-teens. But that's hardly disastrous. It was tempting for shareholders to conclude that their company was insulated from the woes of the industry—and that was the trap. When an industry is sufficiently troubled, *everybody* gets hurt, and it's not much consolation to get hurt less than the other guy. Any seasoned fad-stock follower would have known that the worst was yet to come.

On January 27, 1993, Topps announced that card shipments for the quarter ending February 27 would be "significantly lower" (versus the year before) and that write-downs of unsold cards would force the company to report a loss for that period, its first quarterly loss in ten years. The stock dropped $4 immediately, to just over $8 per share. All told, the stock had dropped 60 percent in just one year.

I should mention that rebound investors soon began to emerge. Throughout 1993, there was talk that the major participants were cutting back production and that the market would return to its prior health. And the industry did have its bright spots—such as Shaquille O'Neal, who carried the basketball card market on his shoulders.

I remember getting a call that year from one Topps shareholder, puzzled that I was retaining Topps on my sell list. Didn't I know that the stock had *already* gone down? Or that analysts were estimating earnings of over $1 per share, making the stock dirt cheap? My response was that I was sticking to the basic fad model, which suggested that the $1 earnings estimates would have to come down.

The simple truth was that bright spots such as Shaquille were masking deterioration elsewhere—notably, a steady outflow of collectors leaving the business for good. Given the role that collectors played in creating the mania in the first place, their retreat suggested that baseball card stocks should be avoided for some time to come. Topps earned just $0.56 per share in 1994, and the stock fell from $8 to under $5 by the end of the year. The model had come through again.

After the Fall: A Different Set of Strategies

In looking at the stories of the last section, one pattern was abundantly clear: Once the downward slide of a fad stock begins in earnest, it keeps going. Practically any sale of a fad stock is a successful one, even if it looked way too late at the time it was made. In particular, investors should be reluctant to get back in to fad stocks, however washed out they might look. Video games were the exception, but only because of a combination of a new generation of computing power and a new generation of potential game players. Nonetheless, there are ways in which a fad's decline can create buying opportunities in the stock market.

The Victims' Revenge

As a fad approaches its manic crescendo, it is easy to overlook the basic fact that its sales may be at the expense of some other product. These victims are worth identifying for reasons of symmetry: When the fad dissipates—as it must—a sales increase is probably in store for whatever it was that the fad displaced.

The oat bran craze of 1989 provided just such a scenario. Recall that Kellogg's thirty-eight-year streak of rising earnings was broken that year because of the oat bran craze, which benefited competitor General Mills. In response, Kellogg shares declined from their then all-time high of $40 to under $30 by early 1990.

If you happened to have identified oat bran for the fad it was, you were in luck. The way to profit from this perception was simply to buy Kellogg shares as they fell; if you already owned the stock, you could always buy more. One can't ever suppose buying at the absolute bottom, but with any luck on timing, you could have picked up shares in the low 30s. When the oat bran fad ended, Kellogg's earnings quickly resumed their uptrend, cracking the $500 million barrier in 1990. By early 1991, the stock had made up all of its lost ground, having gained over 25 percent in just one year.

Knowledge of the Kellogg example can pay off because these patterns tend to repeat themselves. Late in 1990, I was a guest on Ken and Daria Dolan's *Smart Money* program on CNBC. The market was in the midst of a serious downswing at that time, coping with a recession at home as well as the escalating tensions in the Persian Gulf. The Dolans were apparently in search of some comic relief, so I was called upon to provide a review of some famous fad stocks. Everything was going fine until I was asked about some *current* fads that just might be investment worthy.

Stuck for an answer, I suggested a backdoor play. At the time, both Nintendo and Teenage Mutant Ninja Turtles toys appeared to be losing sales momentum. It seemed reasonable to think that a conventional toy maker such as Hasbro would benefit as those fades continued—as the makers of G.I. Joe, Hasbro competed with TMNTs in the action figure category, while the company's conventional board games competed directly with Nintendo.

As the pair of charts suggests, the "sell Nintendo, buy Hasbro" strategy worked like a charm—much better than I could have ever anticipated. Hasbro was trading at $7 at the time (adjusted for subsequent splits). Within a year, in a stronger stock market, it had risen to over $20. Meanwhile, Nintendo shares dropped 50 percent even *before* the major decline in the Japanese market in 1992. (As for Teenage Mutant Ninja Turtle toys, they got a boost from the second TMNT movie in early 1991 but declined sharply thereafter.)

Timing like that is serendipitous, but for me it was a great entrée to the Hasbro investment story, which got even better as time wore on. In 1991, the company acquired Tonka Corporation, bringing both Tonka trucks and Parker Brothers under the Hasbro umbrella. Having acquired Milton Bradley some years earlier, Hasbro now dominated the board game market. The diversification created by these acquisitions gave it an earnings predictability far above the average toy company (even themselves—a few years before). This argued for a more generous valuation than the market typically accords a toy stock. And that's what happened: Hasbro shares continued to rise, hitting $35 by mid-1993, 500 percent above the levels of late 1990. The net result is that a fad can lead to good long-term investments.

Fad Stock Comebacks

An important underpinning of the "victims' revenge" strategy is that the fizzled fad isn't apt to turn around quickly. It is a general rule that *fads cannot come back,* at least not with anything close to the initial excitement. Erno Rubik devised many puzzles after his cube, some of which were advertised as being every bit as intricate as the original. But the public didn't buy in to the sequels, because intricacy wasn't the point. Novelty was the point, and true novelty cannot be cloned.

Fad *stocks,* however, *can* come back, but that usually requires that the company in question find a different way to drive its earnings back up. I should stress that these comebacks are typically many years in

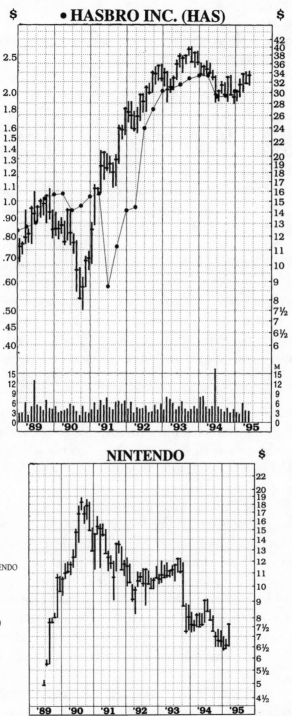

Fig. 37
HASBRO/NINTENDO
CHARTS
(Courtesy of
Securities
Research Co.)

the making, meaning that, as an investor, you don't have to be a hero and rush back in to the stock. As before, wine coolers form a working model for a fad-stock rebound.

Shares of Canandaigua Wine sat idly for years following the 1986 wine cooler boom. Following the stock market crash of 1987, Canandaigua traded down to $6 per share. In late 1990, when the whole market was weak, the prevailing price was still $6. Not once in the intervening years did it ever get north of $10; that's what you'd call true stagnancy.

It's also what you'd expect, when you consider how tumultuous a fad can be for both a company and its investors. Canandaigua's earnings, which peaked at $1.47 per share in 1986, gave way to losses of $1.35 per share in 1987 and $0.71 in 1988. Deficits of this type are part of the fad experience. It costs money to close down production capacity, to sell product at a discount, to service the debt incurred in the original expansion, and fads from coolers to Cabbage Patch Kids often have to deal with this "hangover" effect. Said Cowen & Company analyst Harold Vogel, an unsurprised observer of such bankruptcies as Coleco and Worlds of Wonder (makers of Teddy Ruxpin), "Investors have to realize that these companies can lose a significant part of what they made."

In Canandaigua's case, the demise of the wine cooler business didn't lead to a bankruptcy filing because the company had a solid spirits business to fall back on. The key observation was that the company's single biggest expense associated with wine coolers was the $20 million–plus advertising budget of 1986, an expense that could be and was eliminated at the stroke of a pen.

In addition, Canandaigua systematically pulled Sun Country out of markets where sales were weak, keeping the brand only in regions where sales could be sustained without extensive advertising. And once the cooler red ink stopped flowing, the company could concentrate on its basic business. The acquisition of the Cisco dessert wine from Guild Wineries & Distributors in 1987 enabled Canandaigua to redeploy some wine cooler bottling capacity. Also, just as it had done with Sun Country, Canandaigua used its national distribution network to broaden Cisco's base.

These positive steps notwithstanding, even after a company has regained its footing—a process that can take years—it can take even

CANANDAIGUA WINE CO., INC. (WINEA)

Produces wines, imports beer

CAPITALIZATION 8/31/94
BONDS . . . . . $289.1 Mils.
PREFERRED . . - Mils.
COM. SHRS. . . 12.618 Mils.
Book Value - 13
Options:

Vintner's acquisition announced

1986 peak: corresponds to 90 on old chart, after adjusting for splits

Vintner's Int'l. acq. 10/15/93

Barton, Inc. acq. 6/29/93

Initial wine cooler earnings announcement

Guild Wineries & Distilleries acq. 10/1/91

Three full years to sit back and assess

Fig. 38 CANANDAIGUA CHART #2 ('85–'95) (Courtesy of Securities Research Co.)

longer for investors to start accumulating the stock once again. The fad label is a very destructive one and can live in investors' memories long after the company has turned over a new leaf. Apathy is common. One of the few analysts following the company was Paul Szczygiel (pronounced *she-gul*) of Bear Stearns. Said Szczygiel of the typical Canandaigua investors' meeting of the late eighties, "It was just me, Mario Gabelli, and some other guy I didn't know."

Mario Gabelli is, of course, a renowned value investor, and not a bad guy to run into at one of these meetings. And whoever the third guy was, he's probably pleased with his patience. Canandaigua showed how successful an acquisition strategy can be in a fragmented industry. In October 1991, it bought the remainder of Guild, picking up such well-known brand names as Cook champagnes and Dunnewood wines. In 1993, Canandaigua acquired Vintner's (Paul Masson, Taylor's), thereby pushing past Heublein to become the nation's second-biggest wine company, after Gallo. The stock market, which usually penalizes companies in the short term when they make acquisitions, was willing to make an exception. Canandaigua shares rose from $18⅜ to $21½ in the two days following the announcement of its intent to acquire Vintner's.

Today, Canandaigua's share of the wine market is more than double what it was before the advent of the wine cooler. In fiscal 1992, Canandaigua's earnings finally exceeded their 1986 peak, and so did the stock price. A $10,000 investment in late 1990—by which time the resumption in earnings growth was quite apparent—would have been worth over $80,000 by mid-1995. The key here was being able to separate the company, which reemerged as a good investment, and the fad product (wine coolers), which never came back.

Other fads have duplicated this pattern of crash, long recovery period, and eventual upswing. For example, Home Shopping Network sat idly for years following its own surge (1986–87). HSN traded as low as $3 per share in 1989 (down from $47 in early 1987), and basically traded between $5 and $10 through the end of 1992.

One telling aspect of the late eighties and early nineties is how much investor views toward Home Shopping were changed by its faddish history: The reckless optimism surrounding HSN's early offering had turned to sour pessimism. In July 1988, the Strong Income Fund—then a high-yield fund run by Milwaukee-based investment managers Strong, Corneliuson—was taken to task by *Barron's* for "questionable holdings such as Home Shopping Network." Potshots were easy to take.

But investors gradually came to appreciate that home shopping (the concept is in lowercase, the company in upper-) could well play a significant role in the future of retailing, even if it wasn't going to put Kmart out of business. The home shopping concept had clear-cut advantages over catalog retailing: Customers could see the product more clearly, and inventory problems were almost nonexistent. In 1992, when Diane von Furstenberg sold $1.2 million worth of merchandise in two hours on QVC, it was time for would-be Home Shopping reinvestors to awaken from their five-year layoff.

The fact that von Furstenberg was accompanied to QVC headquarters by media mogul and longtime friend Barry Diller turned out to be an even more powerful buy signal. When Diller assumed leadership of the QVC Network in late 1992, portfolio managers came out of the closet en masse to show their support for the home shopping concept. As the two companies flirted with a merger in 1993, HSN shares moved to $15, three times their 1992 low. During this same ten-month period, shares of QVC quintupled. The moral is clear: Fads don't come back, but fad stocks can.

PUTTING IT ALL TOGETHER

The multitude of examples in this chapter may have opened your eyes to the money that can be made riding a faddish wave. Or perhaps it's convinced you that there is money to be lost. If you feel you belong to the latter group, consider fast-forwarding to the last section—on "normal" investing.

Before you do, though, realize that it's no joke: Knowing your psychological tolerance to stocks that make enormous moves is something that should be nailed down well before you phone in your first buy order. With fad stocks, knowing what you're getting into is an absolute precursor to success. Treating them like long-term investments by buying and holding (a euphemism for buying and forgetting) is the surefire route to failure.

When do you get in? The tip-offs to a fad's upward phase will be different for different people. If you feel chronically out of it and have good reason to believe that you *are* always the last person to know, don't buy. Period. If you get the bulk of your current events knowledge from the nightly news, likewise, forget it. By the time Callaway Golf made it to *ABC World News Tonight* (August 1993), it had more than quintupled off its 1992 offering price and the downturn was not far away. Prime-time stories are notoriously out of phase, yet that's precisely when the Merrill Lynch switchboard starts lighting up. Don't do it. Call your aunt instead.

If nothing else, recognize the fallacy of the dedicated long-term investor, who feels a need to *prove* that the product in question has long-term staying power before committing a single dime. It's crazy. Cabbage Patch Kids sold to the tune of $600 million one year and then died down; Barbie is now over thirty years old and stronger than ever. You're trying to tell me you can predict this stuff? No one can. Investing is not about eliminating surprises; it is about dealing with them when they occur.

Is it a fad or is it a trend? John Naisbitt, of *Megatrends* fame, says that "Trends are bottom-up, fads top-down. . . . New trends and ideas begin in cities and local communities—for example, Tampa, Hartford, San Diego, Seattle, and Denver, not New York City or Washington, D.C." As it happens, the Wacky Wallwalker was born in the nation's capital; score one for the trend man. The California Cooler is probably worth another point.

But before you as an investor feel compelled to bring out your gazetteer, remind yourself of that one point that so many investors forget: If the product does turn out to be a fad, you can *sell*. Although this book was not intended to editorialize, if you don't feel comfortable selling, you shouldn't invest in common stocks. Ever. Besides, unless you are horribly unlucky with your timing, one of the signs that a product is a fad is that the stock goes up too far, too fast. As I said before, shouldn't investors be able to live with that?

One way to get out of the fad-versus-trend way of thinking is to recognize that you can be flexible about the *amount* you invest. Even if you are fad averse, it's silly to turn down a potential big winner on the grounds that it is too risky when you can dilute that risk by buying less than you ordinarily would. If your normal position is $10,000, commit $1,000 to $2,000 instead. This type of flexibility admittedly is easier accomplished with a large portfolio (alas, another reason why the rich can get richer), but even if your normal position is quite a bit less than these amounts, there's no reason you can't approach things the same way.

As to when you should get out, we've seen two choices: Either you sell when the positive negatives become too much for you to bear, even if the stock is going up, or you sell when you get your *first* sign that the party is over—whether it be a bad auction, a drop-off in baseball card shows, or the number of quarters people stuff into arcade games.

Whichever approach you use, the sell point should be independent of your buy point. If you were unlucky enough to buy at the absolute top and face a 30 percent loss when that dreaded first piece of bad news comes in, take the loss. A couple of years down the road, that sale should look good enough to wash out your 30 percent sorrows.

Applications to "Normal" Investing

On the assumption that less is more, even those people who will never, ever invest in a fad can still come away from this chapter with one nugget to guide their future investing: When a company experiences true negative change, sell.

What is true negative change? An example far away from the fad world would be the hospital management business in 1983, the year that "diagnostic reimbursement guidelines" (or DRGs) were instituted as a means of controlling Medicare expenditures. Another would be MCI, not too much later, when its "access charges" to local phone lines were raised. This posed a significant threat to the price advantage versus AT&T that was MCI's very reason for being, and MCI stock dropped 25 percent in one day.

Inevitably, you didn't anticipate the news. Worse, by the time you *do* hear about it, the stock has fallen sharply, perhaps by 10 percent or more. You're faced with the decision of whether to hold or sell. How could you possibly sell the next day—or the day after, or the day after that—without feeling like a dope? Isn't it easier to say that the damage has been done, the news has been discounted, and that a long-term investor knows enough to hang on?

In a word, no. The smart investor must forget how satisfying selling *before* the news broke would have been. More to the point is that even those steep price declines didn't make it too late to sell. The DRGs weren't something that the hospital management industry was just going to shrug off; it was going to take time to realign cost structures to meet the challenges of the new environment. Some of the hospital management chains were selling at the same price ten years after the DRGs were first instituted.

Same story for MCI. Even after the initial stock price drop, it wasn't too late to sell. Earnings disappeared altogether and the stock traded down from $28 to $3 before a reversal was in store. It didn't reach a new record high until 1989. Similar to some of the fad comebacks we looked at, you had four years to study the situation and get back in before another big gain.

It could be argued that I'm picking these situations merely because they reward those who sell after the bad news is out. Obviously, stocks can rebound from bad stretches. For example, bank stocks plummeted in 1990 and then staged a sensational recovery—who's to say that during 1990 they didn't look like the hospital companies and MCI in 1983? To many people, they looked worse!

The point is this: In making judgments about which downturns are transitory and which are not, there will be errors; that's to be expected and is clearly forgivable. What isn't forgivable is to feel that a downturn may be permanent but to hold on anyway.

Fad stocks provide the ultimate case where you *know* things won't ever be the same, because of the onetime character of the fad dynamic. But the applicability is far greater than that. You know that the changes in question will take years. Being a long-term investor doesn't mean that you have to hang on. Instead, merely follow the story to see if the company in question can thrive in the new environment. Once you get positive signs, invest again. You won't get in at the bottom, but so what? You could save five years or more of valuable waiting time.

If you still can't bear the thought of selling, try selling *part* of your position (ideally, a big part). Technically, a partial sale can't ever be right: Either the stock goes down (you should have sold it all) or it goes up (you shouldn't have sold *at* all). But the benefit of a partial sale is that you can continue to follow the story as a shareholder: Realistically, it is very hard for any of us to get back into a stock that we used to own, especially if it represents a difficult memory. If you hold on to a little piece throughout, you just might get over that hurdle.

Promise me this, though. If you really think that it was a fad all along, make that little piece as small as possible.

4 □ Presidents and the Stock Market

As you are probably aware, the influence of presidents and elections on the stock market is a subject that hasn't exactly suffered from inattention. Every four years, we the people are bombarded by an avalanche of investment spins on the presidential election.

Just as World War I did not live up to its billing of "the war to end all wars," this chapter does not aspire to be the presidential investing treatise to end all presidential investing treatises. However, there are a few important holes for us to fill. I will start by attempting to undo some of the outright myths that get kept alive by the never-ending literature on presidents and markets.

Myth 1: Republicans Are Better for Stocks than Democrats Are

The truth is that the two parties are running in a virtual dead heat.

One of the difficulties in establishing a winner is the measurement process itself. Do you measure the stock market's performance for a given president starting on election day, or do you wait until the actual inauguration?

The choice of measurements makes a difference. For example, Jimmy Carter took the oath of office on January 20, 1977, when the Dow Jones Industrial Average stood at 968.67. On his final day in office—January 19, 1981—the market stood at 970.99. His gain of 2.32 points in four years isn't much, but at least it's a gain: If you measure by calendar years instead (1977 through 1980), stocks actually *declined* 4 percent during the Carter administration—a rare achievement, as we will see. (Measuring by calendar years, which essentially splits the difference between Election Day and Inauguration Day, is the simplest approach.)

Even the choice of the Dow Jones Industrial Average as the measuring device is open to debate. The S&P 500 is a much broader-based index, and for that reason is the benchmark used by most institutional money managers. The two indexes often move in sync, but in Carter's case the choice again made a big difference. In 1980, the S&P 500 gained 30 percent, buoyed by inflation beneficiaries such as oil, oil service, and gold mining stocks. Meanwhile, the Dow, for which these stocks constitute a much smaller portion, gained only 15 percent. Altogether, the S&P 500 rose from 103.85 to 134.37 during the Carter years, a gain of 29 percent.

The following table provides the stock market's performance for each twentieth-century president, using calendar years and the Dow as a basis. The results make you wonder how the myth of Republican superiority ever got started. Since 1901, the average gain for a Republican term is 32.2 percent, while the average gain for a Democratic term is 34.9.

One way to make the Republicans look better is to wait until after World War II to start the meter running. Since 1945, the Republican average is 36.9 percent, well above the 25.4 percent figure posted by the Democrats. However, the statistical significance of this advantage is limited, simply because the data pool of presidents is so small.

What if Dwight Eisenhower had been a Democrat instead of a Republican? (He was wooed by both parties after leading the Allied victory.) During Eisenhower's eight years in office, stocks more than tripled. And what if Ronald Reagan had remained a Democrat instead of switching parties? Reagan's eight years turned out to be even better

PRESIDENTIAL TERMS AND THE DOW JONES INDUSTRIAL AVERAGE

Percentage Change in the DJIA

PRESIDENT	First Year		Second Year		Third Year		Fourth Year		All Four Years
Republicans	Year	(%)	Year	(%)	Year	(%)	Year	(%)	(%)
William McKinley/T. Roosevelt	1901	−8.7	1902	−0.4	1903	−23.6	1904	41.9	−1.6
Theodore Roosevelt	1905	38.2	1906	−1.9	1907	−37.7	1908	46.6	23.8
William Howard Taft	1909	15.0	1910	−17.9	1911	0.4	1912	7.6	2.0
Warren G. Harding/C. Coolidge	1921	12.7	1922	21.7	1923	−3.3	1924	26.2	67.5
Calvin Coolidge	1925	30.0	1926	0.3	1927	28.8	1928	48.2	148.9
Herbert C. Hoover	1929	−17.2	1930	−33.8	1931	−52.7	1932	−23.1	−80.0
Dwight D. Eisenhower—1st term	1953	−3.6	1954	44.0	1955	20.8	1956	2.3	71.1
Dwight D. Eisenhower—2nd term	1957	−12.8	1958	34.0	1959	16.4	1960	−9.3	23.3
Richard M. Nixon	1969	−15.2	1970	4.8	1971	6.1	1972	14.6	8.1
Nixon/Gerald R. Ford	1973	−18.7	1974	−27.6	1975	38.3	1976	17.9	−1.5
Ronald W. Reagan—1st term	1981	−9.2	1982	19.6	1983	20.3	1984	−3.7	25.7
Ronald W. Reagan—2nd term	1985	27.7	1986	22.6	1987	2.3	1988	11.9	79.0
George H.W. Bush	1989	27.0	1990	−4.3	1991	20.3	1992	4.2	52.4
Average		5.2		4.7		2.8		14.3	32.2
Average since 1945		−0.4		13.3		17.8		5.4	36.9

Fig. 39 PRESIDENTIAL STOCK TABLE (Information from "Forecasting Stock-Market Performance Via the Presidential Cycle" by Robert Stovall, *Financial Analyst Journal*, May/June 1992)

Democrats

Woodrow Wilson—1st term	1913	−10.3	1914	−5.1	1915	81.7	1916	8.1
Woodrow Wilson—2nd term	1917	−21.7	1918	10.5	1919	30.5	1920	24.3
Franklin D. Roosevelt—1st term	1933	66.7	1934	4.1	1935	38.5	1936	200.2
Franklin D. Roosevelt—2nd term	1937	−32.8	1938	28.1	1939	−2.9	1940	−27.1
Franklin D. Roosevelt—3rd term	1941	−15.4	1942	7.6	1943	13.8	1944	16.2
FDR/Harry S Truman	1945	26.6	1946	−8.1	1947	2.2	1948	16.4
Harry S Truman	1949	12.9	1950	17.6	1951	14.4	1952	64.6
John F. Kennedy/Lyndon Johnson	1961	18.7	1962	−10.8	1963	17.0	1964	41.9
Lyndon B. Johnson	1965	10.9	1966	−18.9	1967	15.2	1968	8.0
Jimmy Carter	1977	−17.3	1978	−3.1	1979	4.2	1980	−4.0
Bill Clinton	1993	13.7	1994	2.1				
Average		4.7		2.2		21.5		34.9
Average since 1945		10.9		−3.5		10.8		25.4

than Eisenhower's. Of course, it could be argued that that's the whole point: They weren't Democrats! But it simply isn't well recognized that the Republicans' stock market advantage rests *entirely* on these two men.

Elsewhere, the Republican slate comes up short. The two biggest one-year gains in the history of the Dow Jones Industrial Average came under Democrats: The Dow rose 81.7 percent in 1915 under Woodrow Wilson and 66.7 percent in 1933 under Franklin Roosevelt. And the only two presidents to leave office with the Dow lower than when they started were both Republicans: Under Herbert Hoover, the average dropped from 319.12 to 53.84 (down 83 percent), and, under Richard Nixon, it dropped from 935.54 to 784.89 (down 16 percent). Jimmy Carter's calendar-year loss of 4 percent seems mild by comparison.

The knock on the Democrats is that they represent a more populist party, intent on denying the interests of major corporations. And it's not all hype: When a reporter once suggested to JFK that big business had him exactly where they wanted him on one of the issues of the day, the president paused, reflected, and replied with a big smile, "I can hardly believe that *I'm* where big business wants me to be."

JFK himself provided one of the most dramatic reasons why investors might be wary of populist presidents. In April 1962, when the steel companies announced what they thought was a modest price increase, Kennedy replied, "The simultaneous and identical actions of United States Steel and other leading steel corporations increasing steel prices by some $6 a ton constitute a wholly unjustifiable and irresponsible defiance of the public interest." Faced with an unrelenting chief executive, the companies accepted defeat —and so did the Dow Jones Industrial Average, which fell from the 750 level to under 550 within three months. Jimmy Carter's windfall profits tax on the oil industry was another case of the Democrats trying to spoil the party. The main difference in Carter's case was that the earnings (and stock prices) of the major oil companies didn't come down until after he left office.

Episodes such as these have left a strong anti-Democrat bias in the eyes of many money managers. Like any other bias, though, this one often gets applied when it shouldn't, creating an opportunity for investors to bet the other way. One classic opportunity came in 1992, when the transfer of power from Republican to Democrat was taking shape. But to participate you had to shift your attention from stocks to bonds.

THE CLINTON BOND RALLY.   By the time Bill Clinton was elected in 1992—in fact, by the time it *looked* like Bill Clinton was going to be elected—there was a preordained sense of fear that swept through the ranks of money managers nationwide. You could almost feel the thought process: Clinton. Tax and spend. Wider deficits. Higher interest rates. Many money managers reacted by getting out of long-term bonds. Between mid-September and Election Day 1992, the price of the 30-year Treasury bond declined 5 percent—a small decline in the world of common stocks but a bloodbath by Treasury bond standards.

However, anything that Pavlovian just has to be suspect. The truth was, the run-amok pessimism about Clinton was enough to make bonds a wonderful buy on the day he was elected.

First, a bit about bonds. You'd think that a bond is the simplest thing in the world, but even the most basic types of bonds—which pay their owner a fixed amount of money every year for a fixed number of years—have a way of being complicated. As none other than Clinton strategist James Carville joked, "If there was reincarnation . . . I want to come back as the bond market. You can intimidate everyone."

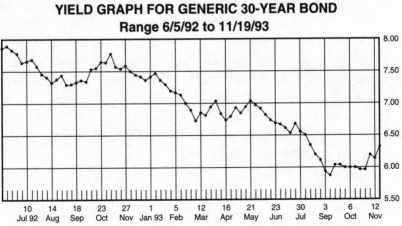

YIELD GRAPH FOR GENERIC 30-YEAR BOND
Range 6/5/92 to 11/19/93

Fig. 40   CLINTON BOND YIELD CHART (Courtesy of Bloomberg)

In that spirit, the accompanying bond chart may require some explanation, because the line is going down after Election Day, not up —as my phrase "wonderful buy" might have suggested. The reason for the inversion is that the chart tracks bond *yields,* not bond *prices.* Bond yields are really the same thing as interest rates—and, as the textbooks will tell you: *When interest rates go down, bond prices go up.*

Why is this so? Well, the italicized adage is in some sense backward. Bonds are the things that get traded, not interest rates, so the first thing to understand is that as the price of a bond moves up, its own interest rate (i.e., its current yield) goes down.

The process isn't nearly as complicated as it sounds: If you have an 8 percent bond trading at 100, that means that you receive $8 per year for every $100 you have invested. If the bond's price goes up—to, say, 105—you are now receiving $8 per year for every *$105* you have invested. Your new yield works out to be 7.6 percent, a lower number. The situation is no different than a dividend-paying stock whose price goes up; when you next check the newspaper, its yield will be lower.

The wrinkle in the bond world is that new bonds are issued all the time, at different rates. Whereas in one year new bonds might be issued to yield 6 percent, the next year new bonds might yield 8 percent. Typically, this increase occurs when investors become worried about inflation; in periods of high inflation, investors require high yields on fixed-income instruments, such as Treasury bonds, because the perception is that the inflation will eat away at future income streams. (The fact that the Treasury issues new bonds and retires old ones is why bonds are conventionally measured in terms of yields, not prices.)

This brings us to the punch line. If new Treasury bonds are at 6 percent, how does the market treat the old Treasury bonds that were issued at 8 percent? Well, two bonds of the same issuer and the same credit quality must have the same yield—the market is at least *that* efficient. Therefore, the price of the old bond has to go up. In this case, the price of the old bond should rise to 133.33, because its yield will then be precisely 6 percent ($8/133 = 6$ percent). Perhaps the adage should be, "As interest rates go down, the prices of *existing* bonds go up." That way, there's really no mystery.

Assuming that you're still with me, let's get back to the Clinton bond rally. If you bought bonds on the heels of Bill Clinton's election in November 1992, you made the right move. Because, as anyone who bought a house or refinanced a mortgage in 1993 could tell you, interest rates came down sharply throughout that year. One by one, investors became persuaded that the new Democratic president was in fact capable of fiscal restraint. By July, the yield of 30-year Treasury bonds had dropped from 7.7 percent to 6.5 percent—but the rally wasn't over.

When the long-awaited budget agreement was passed by Al Gore's tiebreaking vote on August 6, the bond rally got a second leg. Yields on the 30-year Treasury bond dropped to 5.8 percent by October, the lowest yield level in the history of the long bond. Altogether, the decline in yields from 7.7 percent to 5.8 percent corresponded to a price gain of about 35 percent—one of the biggest one-year moves in bond market history. If you add in the interest on the bond itself, you would have made over 40 percent in a single year!

Best of all, you really didn't need to understand much about interest rates to make this call. You simply needed to be enough of a contrarian to make a move that was opposite to the conventional wisdom. Even if you missed that rally, you can benefit in the future from knowing that old investment adages can steer you the wrong way.

Myth 2: Election Years Are Particularly Good for the Stock Market

The reason this myth gets promulgated is that the articles connecting the presidency to the stock market tend to be written in election years!

I should know. I wrote one such article for *Worth* magazine in the spring of 1992. One of the basic conclusions of the article was that, within the four-year presidential cycle, *the year before* an election year is historically the best time for common stocks. Whereupon my editor exclaimed, "Why didn't we do this piece last year?!"

The answer, as we both knew, was that no one would *read* the article in a nonelection year. But that's the persistent rub of financial publishing: It is easiest to sell an article about a specific investment style when that style is most in vogue, which almost by definition is the time that you shouldn't be considering it! Over the years, industries such as biotech or even gold mining have gotten the bulk of their press *after* they've turned white-hot. Prior to that, the articles might have been unsalable.

Despite this complaint, I should stress that election years aren't *bad* for the stock market. Since 1888, election years have produced up markets 70 percent of the time, compared with a 59 percent success rate for nonelection years. However, the years prior to presidential elections have done much better. The most telling statistic is this: Between World War II and 1995, the Dow Jones Industrial Average posted sixteen down years, and not one was the year prior to a presidential election!

During this time, the average gain for the third year in the presidential cycle was over 14 percent. The other three years in the cycle are clustered far behind, in the 4 to 6 percent range (election years come in second).

There are always risks in molding explanations to conform with published statistics, and the "third year" principle is no exception. However, it's worth noting that the year before an election is when the government is most likely to take action to help the economy. In 1991, for example, the Federal Reserve under Alan Greenspan initiated a succession of discount rate cuts to stimulate the economy, and these cuts gave the stock market a series of helpful pushes. And whereas 1994 was a year of rate *hikes* and a treacherous stock market, these hikes disappeared in the "year-before" year of 1995, and the market soared.

In general, an incumbent has an enormous incentive to get the economy in good shape as the election approaches. But waiting too long to take action—that is, until the election year—can be disastrous: Either the recovery comes too late for the election or the efforts at economic restoration appear too politically motivated. Gerald Ford's "Whip Inflation Now" (WIN) buttons were a little of both. They helped pushed the stock market sharply higher upon their introduction in January 1976, but they could not secure Ford's reelection. An earlier introduction might have worked out better.

In fact, aside from 1987—the crash year—there have been only two occasions since World War II where the market's performance the year before the election has been lower than that of the election year itself: 1971 and 1979. But even these years weren't without presidential intervention: In 1971, Richard Nixon instituted wage and price controls, and, in 1979, Jimmy Carter appointed Paul Volcker to head the Federal Reserve, clearly a strong anti-inflation statement. For the record, the market was up 6.1 percent in 1971 versus 14.6 percent in 1972, and 4.2 percent in 1979 versus 14.9 percent in 1980.

To combine myths 1 and 2, I should mention that within the four-year election cycle, it is the year *following* an election that most substantiates the market's anti-Democrat bias. Starting at the beginning of the twentieth century, the twelve months following a Republican victory have witnessed an average gain in the Dow of 9.6 percent, compared to an average gain of 1.7 percent in the twelve-month periods following a Democratic victory. This advantage comes despite the fact that the Democrats have Franklin Roosevelt in their column—without FDR, the twelve-month average for the Democrats becomes *negative* 4.2 percent. However, note that Theodore Roosevelt is in the Republican column, and the market, such as it was back then, rose 45.3 percent in the year following his 1904 reelection.

These patterns are interesting and they're fun, and I could go on and on. But I won't. Having a couple of things to think about is better than having a dozen to get confused by, one of the real dangers in "presidential investing."

Myth 3: The Stock Market Is a Valuable Election Indicator

The specific myth is that if the stock market goes up at the beginning of an election year, it presages a victory for the incumbent party, while a down market means a win for the challenging party.

Theoretically, this connection would be of more interest to pollsters than to investors, but there is an element of circular logic that investors sometimes get caught up in. Early in an election year, if the Republican candidate appears to be at risk of losing to a Democrat, some investors (those who haven't read this book) want to flee well before the transition takes place. And what is one clue that the election might not go well? Why, a down market early in the year, of course. In essence, some investors worry that the market is going down early in the election year because it might be going down later.

Surprisingly, some of this jibberish makes sense. The stock market, whatever its supposed party preferences, has an understandable hatred of uncertainty and change, so you might expect a down period when a presidential transition is in store. And the market isn't the worst predictor in the world, either: Using the first quarter of the election year as our time period, the market has made correct election predictions as far back as 1956, when its 4.8 percent rise in the first quarter corresponded with incumbent Dwight Eisenhower's victory that November.

For many years after that, the election predictor worked like a charm. In 1960, the market was down 9.2 percent in the first quarter, and the incumbent party lost. In 1964, the market rose 6.6 percent in the first quarter, and incumbent Lyndon Johnson was reelected. And so on. In fact, for the five elections between 1956 and 1972, this indicator had an unblemished record of 5-to-0, which is probably why it became an indicator in the first place.

Unfortunately, its record for the next five elections—from 1976 through 1992—was a mere 2-to-3, registering accurate signals only in 1980 and 1988. In particular, despite a flood of reports suggesting the contrary, the strong market of early 1992 did not keep George Bush in office.

Actually, 1992 sounded the death knell for a variety of election predictors, predictors that I will inundate you with for the remainder of this section. For starters, schoolchildren polled by *The Weekly Reader* had picked the right candidate in every election after World War II—but they picked George Bush in 1992. (Why *The Weekly Reader* had been successful is unclear. Maybe parents displayed an honesty to their kids that they withheld from the pollsters.)

Speaking of honest indicators, Crook County, Oregon, had voted for the winner in every election since 1884—but they, too, voted for George Bush in 1992. The defeat doubtless made residents there feel they had lost a special stature, but that was an illusion: Given the vast number of counties in the United States, and given the limited number of elections in our young nation's history, it would not be surprising to find that *some* county had been right every time.

On a more technical level, Yale professor Ray Fair spent years forming an election model that used economic data to predict presidential elections. The critical variables in Fair's formula were the inflation rate in the two years prior to the election and the growth rate of the economy in the first and second quarters of the election year. An advantage for the power of incumbency was also woven into the formula, which, other than the close Democratic victories of 1960 and 1976, would have accurately called every election between 1916 and 1988, with a standard error of just 3 percentage points. But in 1992 the environment of low inflation fooled the model—badly. Ross Perot's third-party candidacy was another monkey wrench. Throughout 1992, Fair's formula had Bush winning 56 percent of the popular vote, which turned out to be off by almost 20 percentage points. Oh, well.

These economically based "predictors" are arguably the most dangerous, in that their highbrow character gets people to take them more seriously than they should (although, in defense of the creators of such models, they are probably more aware than anyone of their fallibility). The same could be said of many technical stock market indicators: The more data you compile and the more lines you draw, the more people you can fool.

Contrast that with the Super Bowl indicator, which no one takes seriously despite its remarkable success. The principle is that an NFC victory in January suggests an up market, while an AFC victory suggests a down market. Eventually, people realized that in a league where the NFC usually wins (nineteen out of the first twenty-nine) and a market that usually goes up (twenty-one out of twenty-nine for the same period) some correlation between the two is not surprising. In fact, if it weren't for the market going up on each of the four Pittsburgh Steeler (AFC) victories, this indicator would have been right a stunning twenty-four times in twenty-eight years.

If AFC victories and presidential transitions are both bad for the stock market, you might even think about putting them together. If so, you'd have a terrific record: Whenever an incumbent president has either resigned, decided not to run, or been defeated in the general election, the AFC has won the Super Bowl the following January. When Lyndon Johnson opted out of the race in 1968, the Jets went on to their famous victory in 1969. The AFC Steelers won in 1975, the January following Richard Nixon's resignation. Gerald Ford's loss in 1976 presaged an Oakland Raider (AFC) victory in 1977, and Jimmy Carter's loss in 1980 gave the Raiders another nod in 1981.

All of which should have given the perennially frustrated Buffalo

Bills cause for optimism for the 1993 Super Bowl, following George Bush's defeat. But the Bills lost anyway. As I said earlier, the 1992 election turned a lot of indicators upside down.

In sum, many of the indicators covered in this section—even the hokey ones—have had pretty good records. And indicators with good records aren't to be sneezed at; after all, you don't have to be right all the time to make money in the stock market. Ironically, the real flaw with these market myths is the notion that they have to be right all the time. If I've imparted anything, I hope it's that the next time you see a horde of investors betting on an age-old myth, you'll give some thought to betting the other way.

More Presidential Indicators

Somehow I feel as though I should apologize for the previous section. Investment writing that only talks of myths can be maddening to the reader/investor, because for the most part these myths only tell you what *not* to do. Such naysaying is often not nearly as smart as it sounds, because the long-term upward bias of the market tends not to reward those who sit on the sidelines. With that in mind, it's time to shift gears and talk about some presidential observations that just might lead to a positive investment action down the road.

Presidential Popularity

Read the following paragraph and try to figure out what "it" is.

"It is perhaps the most closely watched number our country has ever known. It has functioned for generations as a barometer of American self-worth, reflecting how we feel about our country and about our economic strength. It can be moved by emotion and perception as much as by cold hard facts. When it falters, or when it soars, the entire nation is sure to know."

The point is that there are two possibilities for "it." The Dow Jones Industrial Average is one; the Gallup index of presidential popularity is another. The fact that these two different numbers can be linked by a

common description suggests that one might be used to help understand the other. Establishing that link is our very next task.

The idea of using Gallup polls as a stock market tool is not a new
one: Popular culture analysts Paul MacRae Montgomery (of Baltimore brokerage firm Legg Mason) and Robert Prechter (of *Elliott Wave
Theorist* fame) both include poll watching within their vast bags of
tricks.

The underlying idea behind a Gallup/Dow tie is this: Although
corporate earnings and interest rates are probably the two most important influences on the stock market, they certainly don't account for
everything. Stock prices also fluctuate according to the national mood
—and presidential popularity is the single best numerical gauge of
that mood. Before applying Gallup poll readings to investment decisions, however, I should point out three basic limitations of Gallup
theory.

One obvious limitation to the correlation of presidential popularity
and the stock market has to do with direction. The market, as we
know, tends to go up over time. Presidents, unfortunately, move in the
opposite direction—they tend to get *less* popular over time.

The chronic inability of our presidents to sustain their initial approval ratings has been explained every which way by the academic
literature. It has been suggested that initial presidential ratings are
artificially high because they are based on a combination of hope,
patriotism, and bipartisanship that is in itself unsustainable. Then
there is the "coalition of minorities" effect, which holds that the more
decisions presidents make, the more people they alienate. It is noteworthy that Eisenhower is one of the few presidents to have sustained
his popularity throughout his tenure; not coincidentally, he has also
been roundly criticized for his failure to take as a president the same
decisive steps he took as a general.

The second problem is that the Dow Jones Industrial Average and
the sitting president's approval ratings are perfectly capable of moving
in different directions in the near term. During national crises, for
example, the stock market tends to get frightened, while the sitting
president tends to get more popular. This "rally round the flag" effect
boosted Reagan's approval ratings as he recovered from the Hinckley
assassination attempt, Carter's ratings at the beginning of the hostage
crisis, and JFK's ratings in the wake of the Bay of Pigs fiasco ("The

worse I do, the more popular I get," was Kennedy's famous lament). Needless to say, none of these events helped the stock market one bit.

The third and final caveat for our hoped-for Gallup indicator is that sometimes the effect can be backward, meaning that the stock market can influence how the population feels about the president, not the other way around. Reagan, for example, didn't receive good economic approval ratings until two years into his administration. This surely reflected the bull market that had already begun—as opposed to being a helpful indicator that a bull market might begin. Similarly, although Herbert Hoover predated the Gallup era, he found his image inexorably linked with the 1929 stock market crash and the Great Depression. He is *not* remembered as being the last president to have balanced the budget, although he is just that.

These three caveats notwithstanding, presidential popularity has had some remarkable successes as a stock market indicator. For example, it is no coincidence that JFK, whose average favorability rating of 71 percent is history's loftiest, also enjoyed a record Dow during many stages of his thousand days. At the other extreme, Richard Nixon left office with a record low 24 percent favorability rating, shortly after which the Dow *permanently* bottomed out at 570.

The Gallup/Dow connections don't stop there. Nixon, Ford, and Carter turned out to be the only presidents whose average approval rating was below 50 percent—and during their collective twelve years in office, the Dow rose just 35 points. (That's right, 35 *points,* not 35 percent.) In the twelve subsequent years, under the more popular Reagan and Bush administrations, the Dow's gain exceeded 2,000 points.

In putting presidential popularity to use, it is essential to recognize that it is a *contrary* indicator. In other words, all other things being equal, a high Gallup poll reading is a bearish stock market indicator because it suggests that the next direction for presidential popularity—and the market—is inevitably down. Likewise, a low Gallup number can be bullish for the market. The second half of the Bush administration provided a couple of terrific opportunities to put this principle into action.

During his first year and a half in office, Bush actually confounded the conventional logic and *increased* his popularity. The wimp factor that had dogged his vice presidential years seemed to evaporate. More and more Americans felt that, yes, George Bush had trained years to be where he was and he looked comfortable being there.

But in late 1990, just before the halfway point of Bush's four years in office, both his popularity and the stock market were dragged down by the domestic recession and the grave uncertainties posed by the situation in the Persian Gulf. The president's approval rating fell from 69 percent in mid-June to 53 percent by October; meanwhile, the Dow Jones Industrial Average fell from the 2950 level to under 2400. The two numbers were moving in sync, just as the theory would suggest.

The decisive moment for the Gallup poll as a stock market indicator came in March 1991—right after Operation Desert Storm—when Bush's favorability rating soared to 89 percent, the highest in the history of the polls. The stock market had been rising, too, from 2490 as war broke out in mid-January to 2973 on March 6. Of course, that may look like a low number now, but it was a euphoric level then, and the unprecedented presidential popularity rating offered some perspective. Said one White House official, "When he was at 70 percent it was great . . . but 90 percent was just plain silly."

Enter Paul Macrae Montgomery. Said Montgomery, "When Bush's favorability rating reached 89 percent, I suggested that the market wouldn't go any higher [in the near term]." To Montgomery, the high rating was significant because it quantified the exuberance in the national mood. And, as he knew, overexuberance on Wall Street translated into stock prices that had gotten ahead of themselves. That didn't mean that stocks couldn't go higher—it just meant that they had to find another reason! As things played out, the stock market was in fact stagnant for much of 1991, struggling to stay above the 2900 level.

The rebound didn't occur until December 1991, when Bush's approval rating dipped below 50 percent for the first time—and the Federal Reserve dramatically cut the discount rate (one of the short-term interest rates controlled by the Fed). "I suggested that [the low rating] might start a rally," said Montgomery. Sure enough, by early January, the market had jumped from 2900 to 3200.

Wait a minute, you might say. The market wasn't reacting to the low approval rating; it was reacting to the discount cut!

Maybe so, but that does nothing to diminish the usefulness of the Gallup poll as an indicator. Is it unreasonable to suppose that the two events might have been connected? Even though the Federal Reserve is outside the executive branch of the government, there can be no question that it shares an interest in getting the economy moving. Bush's low favorability rating was tangible proof of the public's unhappiness, and it demanded a response.

As it turned out, Bush's 50 percent approval rating, although a low at the time, was not the low of his administration—he dipped below 30 percent in August 1992. Nor was the December 1991 action by the Fed the last time that the discount rate was lowered—several rate cuts followed in 1992. Collectively, the lower interest rates were the single most important stimulus to the stock market, which proceeded to move into record territory that year.

As a perverse footnote, George Bush's popularity didn't recover until his defeat that November. The final Gallup poll of his administration (for the period January 8 through January 11, 1993) gave him an approval rating of 56 percent.

The *Time* Man of the Year Indicator

In cases where favorability ratings aren't extreme enough to answer the question "How high is high?," pop culture analysts have the option of turning to *Time* magazine. The abiding rule is that a *Time* cover appearance for a politician—much like a *Sports Illustrated* cover for an athlete—is a jinx. A cover appearance can suggest that the president has peaked in the near term, and there can be a ripple effect in the financial markets.

The Man of the Year designation is especially double-edged. Nixon won Man of the Year honors for 1972; as we know, though, it was all downhill from there, and the next twelve months shaved 41 points from his favorability rating and 30 percent from the stock market. Similarly, after Reagan was named 1980 Man of the Year, 1981 was a down year for the stock market—the only down year of the decade. Even Reagan's repeat Man of the Year designation of 1984 was linked to a brief pause in the great bull market.

To justify using magazine covers as contrary indicators, you don't have to look any further than the law of averages. For example, if the Detroit Tigers begin the baseball season with a 35-to-5 record (as they did in 1984), they *should* make the cover of *Sports Illustrated* (and they did). Yes, they slacked off somewhat after that (their final record was 104–58), but the cover shouldn't be seen as a jinx, merely as an ode to a pace that was unsustainable. More generally, the popular press is responsible for simply telling things the way they have been, not the way they might be. But sometimes the very appearance of these cover stories is a reminder that something extreme is going on.

Where the stock market is concerned, the most famous magazine cover of all time was the August 13, 1979, issue of *Business Week,* which heralded "The Death of Equities." According to the theory of the day, hard assets such as gold and diamonds were supposed to put the stock market out of business. A few years later, it was clear that the correct investment response to the cover would have been the exact opposite: selling gold and buying stocks instead. That's why someone like Paul MacCrae Montgomery uses presidential covers as contrary indicators.

There is still room for coincidence in the world of magazine covers. For example, it was probably serendipitous that the market staged its "minicrash" in October 1989, just two months after a *Time* cover story heralded President George Bush as "smarter than Reagan, less driven than Carter and savvy like Nixon." The trigger event for the 100+ point single-day decline was the failed buyout at UAL, not anything emanating from the White House.

However, three presidential covers later (1990 Man of the Year), the results were more telling. Unlike most presidential Man of the Year designations, the tone of this one was *negative.* Pictured on the cover were two George Bushes, one controlled, one vacillating; it was *Time's* way of asking who was running the show.

If a positive presidential cover such as Richard Nixon's 1972 Man of the Year is bearish for the market, then a negative cover would have to be bullish, and in this case the results were dramatic. *Time's* perceived schizophrenia, dreamed up in the depths of the prewar Persian Gulf crisis, was quickly supplanted by the Desert Storm victory, an event that quickly vaulted the president and the stock market to record levels. Popularity had come full circle.

A few postscripts on the Man of the Year. Since Charles Lindbergh received the initial designation in 1927, only two presidents have failed to receive the honor at least once: Herbert Hoover and Gerald

Ford. FDR, not surprisingly, is the leader in total designations, with three. Tied with two are Harry Truman, Ronald Reagan, and Richard Nixon. Nixon, who shared the award with Henry Kissinger in 1972 after being the sole designee in 1971, is the only person to have received at least a piece of the award in successive years.

Between 1927 and 1993, a U.S. president was Man of the Year no fewer than sixteen times. In retrospect, the timing of the award is sometimes curious. JFK, for example, won it in 1961—the year of the Bay of Pigs—and not for his election of 1960 or for his handling of the Cuban Missile Crisis in 1962. Dwight Eisenhower, the only president to have won the award in another role (1944), didn't receive his presidential designation until 1959, in what looks like a now-or-never decision by the editors.

However, there is one pattern worth keeping in mind. The most common time for a president to achieve the Man of the Year designation is the election year: FDR (1932), Truman (1948), Lyndon Johnson (1964), Nixon (1972), Carter (1976), Reagan (1980), and Clinton (1992) were all honored in this manner.

The reason I point this out is that these election year appearances are quite harmonious with what we know about stocks and the election cycle. In the previous section, we saw that the first two years of a president's term are historically the years when the stock market struggles the most: On average, the market goes up 5 percent in such years, compared to an average gain of over 10 percent for the third and fourth years. Putting that together with the *Time* election year covers, it looks as though the nation's excitement about a new administration creates a type of emotional peak that the stock market has a hard time living up to. The forces that push stocks higher from these emotional peaks have to be strong enough to overcome the return to reality once the new president's honeymoon is over.

PRESIDENTIAL IMAGE

Many of the indicators we have looked at tacitly assumed that the U.S. president can control the economy. Not everyone would agree: In the exasperated words of Herbert Hoover, "Once upon a time, my political opponents honored me as possessing the fabulous intellectual and economic power by which I created a worldwide depression all by myself."

It may be too late to exonerate Hoover, but it is not too late for investors to take another tack. Apart from economic power, presidents wield an entirely different type of power merely by continuing to be themselves under the newfound world spotlight.

For example, Dwight Eisenhower had *always* played golf, but his doing so as President Eisenhower is what stirred interest in the game nationwide. John Kennedy happened to be an excellent golfer, but chose to downplay that fact and ended up glamorizing sailing instead. Ronald Reagan single-handedly revived the jelly bean business. Bill Clinton and his morning jogs created a second running boom, quadrupling the new membership applications for the New York Roadrunners Club.

Even if we're looking for investment indicators, we should realize that presidential sidelights such as pork rinds and killer rabbits get a lot more press than Laffer curves or the term structure of interest rates. As newsman Sam Donaldson commented in 1981, "A clip of a convalescent Reagan waving from his window at some circus elephants is going to push an analytical piece about tax cuts off the air every time."

With that in mind, it's good to know that an understanding of the president's image can be a very valuable investment tool. A good place to start is with an uncanny contrast from a few administrations ago. When you look at the disparate personal styles of Jimmy Carter and Ronald Reagan, their disparate experiences with the capital markets fall eerily into place.

In 1976, all that we knew of Jimmy Carter was that he sought to transform the presidential image. And he may well have succeeded. After his inauguration, he walked from the Capitol to the White House. He was informal: He routinely wore blue jeans for the paparazzi. Frugal, too: Within a year, he had sold *Sequoia,* the presidential yacht, thereby trimming the national deficit by $286,000. Finally, he was honest to a fault, as in his observation about the "great American malaise."

If this backdrop seems at odds with cork popping on Wall Street, it should. Not that Carter was entirely to blame for the dual perils of high interest rates and high inflation that plagued his administration. But under his administration, stocks underwent a malaise of their own. As we saw earlier in this chapter, on Carter's Inauguration Day in 1977, the Dow Jones Industrial Average stood at 968.67. When he left office, the Dow was at 970.99. Four long years and two lousy points.

The contrast in styles provided by Ronald Reagan was on display from the very first moment. Reagan's inaugural clothes cost six times as much as Carter's. His trip back to the White House was in a limo, not on foot. And once there, the Reagans gave their residence an immediate and lavish facelift, the first since the days of Jacqueline Kennedy. Inevitably, some negative publicity ensued, and Nancy bashing became the order of the day.

Yet there were also some positive chords. As Lance Morrow wrote during Reagan's first year in office, "The presidency is a form of national theater; even in difficult times, Americans may still like to see a little sumptuousness there. . . . Lacking royalty, Americans need at least a little regality in their four-year constitutional rulers." As it happened, America decided that four years of Reagan wasn't enough. During his eight-year tenure, stocks nearly tripled.

No, Reagan didn't *create* the bull market. But a Goldman, Sachs study found that only one-third of the eighties' bull market could be accounted for by fundamentals such as rising earnings or falling interest rates. The rest came from the shrinkage of the equity market; that is, stock repurchases and corporate takeovers. What we forget is that Reagan's laissez-faire attitude toward takeovers was an important part of the equation. We also forget that this attitude was entirely predictable.

Think about it this way: Would the takeover mania have remained unchecked under Jimmy Carter? Would Carter have allowed passage of the 1986 tax bill, the one that encouraged corporations to assume more debt? Would he of the windfall profits tax and the proposed $50 per person tax rebate have stood idly by while Michael Milken parlayed leveraged buyouts into single-year earnings of $550 million? Unthinkable. Under Carter, the most leveraged portion of the eighties' bull market would almost certainly have been truncated, either by example or by the brute force of legislation. The deal makers themselves seemed to sense their privileged terrain. The biggest leveraged buyout of them all, the $25 billion takeover of RJR Nabisco, was consummated in December 1988, just one month before Reagan left office.

But if presidential image is so damned important, why in the world was the market so strong during the administration of Gerald Ford? (I happened to have voted for him, but I had to overlook his bumbling image to do so.)

First, the numbers. When Gerald Rudolph Ford assumed the presidency on August 9, 1974, the Dow Jones Industrial Average stood at 784.89. By the time Jimmy Carter was elected on November 2, 1976, the market had risen to 966.09, a gain of 23 percent. Not a bad result, and not what you'd expect from someone who tripped down airplane stairs and konked golf spectators on the head with errant tee shots.

However, there is a simple explanation. No one who lived through Watergate or studied the period in history class has to be reminded of the depths to which American self-esteem sank in the mid-seventies. In particular, the bear market of 1973–74 was one of the bleakest periods in Wall Street history, with the Dow plummeting from its 1972 high of 1000 to just 570 by late 1974.

When Nixon tried to reverse the downtrend—"If I weren't president, I'd be buying stocks"—he ran into a sharp-tongued response from one anonymous Wall Streeter: "If you weren't president, we'd be buying stocks, too." The rally that followed Nixon's resignation suggests that the Street was true to its word.

What Gerald Ford did—never mind his clumsiness at the airport or Pebble Beach—was reinstill the notion that the presidency was still a place for an honest man. Given the times, it was no mean feat. What an investor had to do in 1974 was look beyond the fear and say, "If Ford can restore credibility, stocks will go up." Sure enough, the market never looked back from there. Although 1982 is heralded as the beginning of the modern-day bull market, the turnaround year of 1975 has its own place in stock market history.

Putting Personalities into Practice: The Case of George Bush

So far, we have looked at the effect of image on the overall market. More common is that a president's character ends up influencing certain subsectors of the market. Finding indicators for individual companies or industries is what every other section in this book concentrates on, and this section now continues in that fine tradition.

Let's go back to January 20, 1989, the day that George Bush was sworn in as the forty-first president of the United States. How might an investor have put Bush's image to good use, right then and there?

The picture was not without confusion. On the one hand, there was George Herbert Walker Bush, whose patrician nameplate seemed very much in keeping with the Reagan regality: Big business. Big oil. On the other hand, there were the multiple address changes and the fly-fishing and pork rind affinities—all of which seemed to take the Connecticut Yankee out of King Arthur's court.

Actually, Bush was a man of dichotomies. He had been a public figure for twenty-five years, yet he remained surprisingly ill-defined. He aspired to the loneliest job in the world yet seemed strangely intolerant of his own company. What did all this mean?

If the call for a "kinder, gentler nation" truly meant a cleansing of eighties' values, then the stock market by all rights should have reacted negatively to Bush. But it didn't. In fact, anyone who was out of the market in Bush's first year in office had plenty of reason to be disappointed, because the Dow Jones Industrial Average rose 27 percent.

The most important Bush dichotomy for investors was best summed up by *Fortune* magazine during the Bush-Dole primary struggle of 1988: "The Vice President [Bush] loves to talk about international relations, while the minority leader [Dole] seems genuinely interested in the nuts and bolts of domestic economics." By implication, Bush was not.

The investment conclusion was stunningly simple and could have been posited the very day that Bush took the inaugural oath: During his administration, companies with extensive international exposure would be more rewarding investments than companies whose fate was linked to the U.S. economy.

And so it was. Although stocks in general rose during Bush's tenure, they didn't move up equally. One particular span shows who the real leaders were: On July 16, 1990, the Dow Jones Industrial Average stood at 2999.75; on April 17, 1991, it closed at 3004.46. Not much of a change. However, within the thirty companies that make up the index, there were some mammoth changes. Of the Dow thirty, the three biggest winners were Philip Morris (up 40 percent), Merck (up 28 percent), and Coca-Cola (up 23 percent). All of these companies had extremely strong international operations.

And the biggest losers? Seven stocks registered declines of more than 15 percent during the period in question, and they sound like a roll call of smokestack America: Allied-Signal, Bethlehem Steel, General Motors, Boeing, Westinghouse, Goodyear, and United Technologies. With the recession in full force, stocks linked to the domestic economy were bad bets. Said Elizabeth Bramwell, then manager of the Gabelli Growth Fund, "By choosing companies with a global focus, you've kind of hedged yourself against stupid management in Washington." A mite harsh, perhaps, but the idea is there.

As with other cases we have seen, it would be an exaggeration to say that Bush caused the recession; as his term began, he was already inheriting the nation's longest postwar economic recovery, and something had to give. But his image of domestic indifference clearly worsened the decline in consumer confidence, one of the factors that made his term-ending recession so stubbornly long.

As we know, the state of the domestic economy became the focal point of the 1992 campaign. Recession or no recession, the stock market was actually a good place to be for most of the campaign, as the Fed repeatedly cut short-term interest rates in an effort to get the economy moving again. Although these rate cuts were bullish for stocks, they weren't enough to keep Bush in power, and on January 20, 1993, William Jefferson Clinton took the inaugural oath.

PUTTING IT ALL TOGETHER: BILL CLINTON AND THE STOCK MARKET

Because this book was written during the Clinton administration, I thought that the sitting president should have a section all his own. As we'd expect from prior examples, a comprehensive investment response to the forty-second president of the United States involved a combination of policies, party affiliation, and image. We have already seen that bonds were a great buy in the early days of the Clinton presidency, precisely because so many people believed they wouldn't be. It remains to show how a knowledge of what Clinton stood for could have helped you out in the stock market.

Drug Stocks: The Most Important Sell Signal of the 1992 Campaign

I should warn you that I am going to tell this story in some depth, so if you don't care for or about drug stocks, you can fast-forward to the section called "The Lighter Side." However, the drug-stock sell-off of 1992–93 is a great example of how a president's focus on a particular industry can completely change the industry and the underlying investment psychology.

Suppose you had been invested in drug stocks in January 1993, the month that Bill Clinton took office. If you hadn't taken the new president's health-care preachings into account, the investment picture might have looked pretty favorable.

One thing you knew for sure was that drug stocks were down significantly from their highs and were now extremely cheap relative to their historic growth rates. For example, Merck, inarguably the research pioneer within the group, had seen its earnings rise from $0.54 per share in 1986 to $2.12 per share in 1992—a compound annual growth rate of 25 percent. The company was routinely listed among the most admired corporations in America. However, its stock had fallen from $55 in January 1992 to just $40 per share a year later. This was the sort of stock that you'd want to buy on weakness—ditto, the entire pharmaceutical group. Right?

Not exactly. The Clinton campaign had already given drug-stock investors some powerful warning signs. Here are the two most prominent red flags:

For the prescient or near prescient, the first warning sign that pharmaceutical stocks were in trouble came in December 1991, when Clinton signed on James Carville and Paul Begala as advisers to his campaign (as we know, Carville's role was destined to expand). The rising cost of health care was precisely the issue that Carville and Begala had exploited so deftly in engineering Harris Wofford's upset victory over Dick Thornburgh in Pennsylvania's off-year senatorial race of 1991. All by itself, the Carville appointment sent the signal that the cost of health care was politically charged enough to become a major issue on the national level. From that moment on, the notoriously high profit margins of the major drug companies would be under siege.

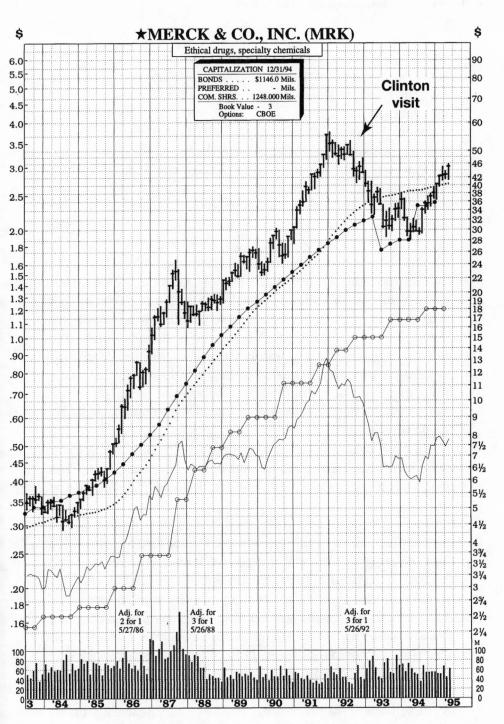

Fig. 41 MERCK CHART (Courtesy of Securities Research Co.)

If you sold at the time of the Carville appointment (December 2), you might consider toning down your prescience next time. Being ahead of the crowd isn't all it's cracked up to be—remember, after your farsighted stock sales, the unsuspecting crowd controls the market. Drug stocks rose a stunning 16 percent in December 1991 alone, continuing their multiyear bull market. At year-end, the S&P Pharmaceuticals Index was at 1736, an all-time high.

However, as the rhetoric of the campaign continued, drug stocks slowly and insidiously reversed their long-standing uptrend. By September 1992, the S&P Pharmaceuticals Index had fallen to 1380, down 20 percent from its high. But that was only the beginning. That month, a new sell signal came in the form of a visit by candidate Clinton to Rahway, New Jersey, the headquarters of Merck.

Clinton's visit was pure Trojan horse. Unsuspecting Merck officials, perhaps thinking that Clinton intended to extol the company's "best and brightest" workforce, got a tongue-lashing instead. Words like "fraud," "abuse," and "free rides" dotted the candidate's speech. Clinton was suggesting nothing less than that the major drug companies had abused their pricing power. The irony was that the price abuses, if that's what they were, had simultaneously created voter resentment and investor admiration. Because of Bill Clinton, that emotional gap would be closing.

To put the Rahway speech to work as a sell indicator, you had to understand that the strength of drug company earnings came from more than just innovative new products. In the mid- to late eighties, drug companies had the luxury of being able to profitably launch new drugs even without being the innovator. This was possible because me-too products for specific diseases or conditions often abided by the logic of the eighties (if it's more expensive, it must be better) and were priced even higher than their predecessors, whereupon the innovators would push the price of their existing product up to achieve parity. For example, the look-alike ulcer drugs Tagamet (SmithKline) and Zantac (Glaxo) underwent a series of look-alike price hikes—not declines, as the conventional view of competition might have suggested. That's what pricing power is all about, and the drug companies had it.

Actually, the potential for price abuse had long been woven into the health-care insurance system. Under so-called indemnity health-care plans, which once accounted for virtually the entire insured population, the patients were in control. They could choose their own doctors, and there was no monitoring of prescriptions, except for the record of dollars spent. Of the total bill, patients would typically pay 20 percent and insurance would cover the remaining 80. If drug companies raised their prices, the patient's 20 percent share became a bigger number, while insurers responded by raising rates. Either way, patients were left holding the bag—it was, in essence, the price of their freedom.

Even before Bill Clinton, the industry was trying to correct for these imbalances. The growth of so-called funded health plans in the eighties represented a massive effort to cap total pharmaceutical costs, as opposed to passing them on to someone else. One telling statistic is that in 1979, only 4 percent of insured patients faced restrictions on prescriptions (perhaps the best-known restriction is a requirement for generic substitution whenever available). By 1986, these restrictions applied to 22 percent of insured patients; by 1991, 35 percent. (Estimates for the year 2000 indicate the figure will rise to 80 percent.)

There were other pre-Clinton forces that loomed as long-term threats to the drug industry's profitability. The tracking of prescription dollars became a growth business in the eighties, and nothing exemplified this trend better than Medco Containment Systems, the pioneer of the mail-order pharmaceuticals business. Medco's revenues in 1984 were a scant $26 million; by 1992, they had reached $2 billion. As the company grew from a mere processor of prescriptions to a large-scale drug buyer and the owner of a valuable database of medical information, Medco developed the clout to force discounts from the major drug companies.

Time for two important questions. If all these forces had been in place before 1992, why in the world were drug company earnings still going up? And how dare I call Bill Clinton the catalyst of change?

The answer to the first question goes back to pricing power. Even if Medco had the clout to negotiate a 10 percent discount of a drug's list price, the manufacturer didn't have to suffer. They could simply raise it to make a 10 percent discount equal the original, "normal" price. And as long as earnings were going up, the stock market didn't seem to care why.

As for the second question, the Clinton campaign did more than any brokerage house to signal the public that the times were changing. The drug companies sensed the change and became more lenient in their pricing policies. Case in point: In February 1992, when Pfizer came out with its antidepressant Zoloft—similar in many respects to Eli Lilly's Prozac—it was forced to price at a discount to Prozac; when SmithKline Beecham then came out with Paxil (same category), it priced that drug at a discount to Zoloft. This was the exact opposite of the strong pricing environment that had prevailed just a few years earlier, and it had "sell" written all over it.

In cases such as these, where an industry is undergoing fundamental change, the result is often a slow, steady decline in share prices as more and more institutional investors reluctantly recognize the change and sell the shares that had provided so much prosperity in the past. The drug stocks fit this pattern perfectly. Even in January 1993, the stocks hadn't hit bottom. By August of that year, the S&P Pharmaceuticals Index had declined an additional 20 percent.

As for Merck, the stock traded at $40 per share in early 1993 but within the year would drop below $30. Along the way, the company acquired Medco Containment Services for $6 billion, an unprecedented merger of research and distribution capabilities. The merger confirmed what was in the air when Clinton visited over a year before: The pharmaceutical landscape was changing, possibly for good. (We'll return to the story later on.)

The Lighter Side

As the 1992 campaign wore on, the financial press eventually tired of tough issues and began searching for different angles on the election—any angle. As a financial writer, I lived and died by the "Clinton stock" frenzy without even trying.

In late 1992, I wrote an article that sifted through some of the stock market losers of that year in hopes of finding some winners for 1993. As we will find out, that can be a dangerous strategy, but for now (this *is* the lighter side) we will talk about the good part.

The article's first stock selection was Kellwood, a supplier of low-to medium-priced private-label apparel to Sears and other major retailers. One of the company's attractive features was that it was broadening its customer base and thus lessening its dependence on Sears. This was a long-term trend, one that led to my initial recommendation in 1990 at $8 per share. By the end of 1992, even after a 30 percent decline from its earlier year high, it sat at $25 per share, well above my original buy point.

I reiterated the recommendation in part because of the stock's decline and the fact that earnings were still rising. However, another positive and timely factor, which I was frankly too embarrassed to admit, was that the stock had a presidential kicker to it: Imagewise, the downscale Kellwood was to Hillary Rodham Clinton what the upscale Adolfo had been to Nancy Reagan.

Little did I know that 1993 was to become the year of the private label. The attack on brand-name consumer stocks in early 1993, although more visible in the food and tobacco businesses, was indicative of the tremendous opportunities available to a wide variety of private-label companies, Kellwood included. The company's sales increased 19 percent for the first three quarters of 1993. Earnings were up 15 percent for the same period, not bad for a stock that began the year trading at just twelve times trailing earnings. The results made many investors rethink their sell decisions of 1992, and Kellwood shares rose 60 percent before 1993 was through. (By the way, I "settled" for Kellwood because Hillary's real clothier, St. John Knits, hadn't gone public yet! That offering came in March 1993, at $17 per share, and the stock pierced $30 within two years.)

"Light" recommendations such as Kellwood—half serious, half silly—were quite popular around that time. In September 1992, a PaineWebber release featured two columns, one for Bush and one for Clinton, each with fifteen specific investment recommendations. For example, Tiffany was in the Bush column, while the more bourgeois Catherines Stores was the corresponding Clinton entry. U.S. Surgical was a Bush stock, Paramount a Clinton (fabulous call on both sides). Bush was Merrill Lynch, Clinton was Newmont Gold. (Sort of a cheap shot there: The idea was that a Clinton presidency would lead to higher inflation and, therefore, higher gold prices.)

In October, Smith Barney strategist Marshall Acuff went a couple of steps further with a piece called "A Day in the Clinton White House." "It's early morning when the Clinton family arises," he wrote. "Demonstrating their dedication to environmental purity, the family always brushes with Arm & Hammer baking soda (Church & Dwight). Daughter Chelsea is shampooing for her first day at school with Breck (Dial Corp.) while Bill is showering with Ivory '99^{44}/$_{100}$ pure' soap (Procter & Gamble). Over breakfast, of Grape Nuts (Philip Morris) and bran muffins (not baked by Hillary), President Clinton discusses how to get the economy moving."

You get the idea. Altogether, twenty-three stocks were mentioned before Acuff's piece was through—including McDonald's, the president's favorite food stop, and CBS, the network of his good friend Linda Bloodworth-Thomason. And the man hadn't even been elected yet! (And I'm not sure how many people at Smith Barney voted for Clinton. Dare I mention that SBHU—the initials of Smith Barney, Harris Upham—is an anagram of "BUSH"?)

Anyway, these types of articles offer great protection to the writer. If the stocks don't work out, the writer can always claim that it was written in fun; and if they *do* work out, well, I told you so. Silly or not, though, it was not unreasonable to think that presidential preferences would affect specific industries or even entire sectors of the market.

In fact, about the only major fallacy that sprang from the lighter side was the notion that Arkansas-based Wal-Mart was a Clinton stock —ditto, Dillard Department Stores, headquartered in Little Rock. For these companies, the pundits had it backward: The success of Wal-Mart and Dillard helped Clinton's image, not vice versa!

Dillard and Wal-Mart had attained leadership positions in their respective fields (department stores and discount stores) in large part because of their pacesetting implementation of superior computer systems—never mind that they came from the supposedly hick state of Arkansas. So when a desperate George Bush tried to label Arkansas "the lowest of the low," it simply didn't ring true. Think about it: Wasn't it harder to ridicule Omaha after you found out that Warren Buffett lived there?

Hillary Clinton, a onetime Wal-Mart board member, resigned that position when her husband launched his presidential campaign. But who's to say that Wal-Mart's success didn't help him get to Pennsylvania Avenue? One thing I can tell you for sure: Within a year of Clinton's election, Wal-Mart shares fell 25 percent. Wal-Mart was not a Clinton stock.

Stocks for the New Administration

When Bill Clinton actually entered office on January 20, 1993, one wonderful corollary was that you didn't have to hear the hackneyed phrase "Clinton stock" anymore. However, Clinton's influence over the financial markets was just beginning, and it didn't stop at drug stocks.

Perhaps the earliest image-related market call of the new administration was "sell Philip Morris." On Friday, April 2, Philip Morris cut prices on its flagship Marlboro brand, sacrificing near-term profits in hopes of clinging on to market share for the long term. The stock cratered following that announcement, but the Clinton sell signal came well before that.

The first clue came just weeks into the new administration, when Hillary Clinton banned smoking in the White House. It doesn't take long for presidential preferences to work themselves into the general population. Shortly thereafter, President Clinton's favorite haunt, McDonald's, announced that it would test a smoking ban in forty of its outlets. Events such as these marked a sea change in the public's tolerance for smoking.

The stock market eventually caught on to the Clinton stance. By late February 1993, Philip Morris shares had dropped into the low 60s (from the mid-80s the prior September) on fears that higher cigarette taxes would be invoked to pay for health-care reform. The stock then dropped to $45 in the wake of the April price reduction. Even though it was a company event (the price cuts) that triggered the biggest decline, anyone who believed in the power of the presidential image would have been out of the stock with months to spare.

There were many other stocks that were closely tied to the new administration. The Student Loan Marketing Association, or Sallie Mae, was another Clinton "sell," because investors rightly feared a Clinton-led reorganization of the student loan system that could bypass the agency altogether. Sallie Mae had weathered such concerns before in its ten-plus-year history as a public company, but this time

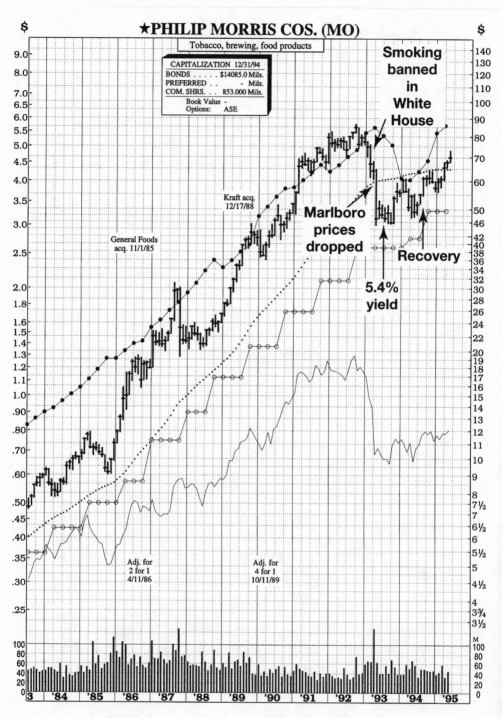

Fig. 42 PHILIP MORRIS CHART (Courtesy of Securities Research Co.)

the president meant business, and it wasn't long before a "direct lending" bill became reality. Although the near-term effect of the bill was to broaden the student loan market—a positive for Sallie Mae—it also created the possibility that Sallie Mae would someday not exist.

On the plus side, stocks such as Scholastic (education) and Ingersoll-Rand (infrastructure) were seen as potential beneficiaries of new government spending programs. The distance between these hopes and an actual boost to earnings was admittedly great, but clearly these businesses were on the right side of the coin.

The following tables summarize various picks and pans for the new administration. Two prices are given—one for November 4, 1992, when Bill Clinton was elected; the other, precisely one year later. The results are remarkable.

CLINTON "BUYS"

Company	11/2/92	11/2/93	Return (percent)
Paramount	$42⅝	$79⅛	+85.6
U.S. Healthcare	$43½	$50½	+16.1
Kellwood	$23⅝	$40	+69.3
Ingersoll-Rand	$30¾	$36½	+18.7
Scholastic	$32½	$48½	+49.2
Newmont Gold	$37¼	$41	+10.1
Average			+41.5

CLINTON "SELLS"

Company	11/2/92	11/2/93	Return (percent)
Sallie Mae	$68¾	$44¼	−35.6
Merck	$44⅜	$31¾	−28.5
Philip Morris	$77	$53¾	−30.2
Average			−31.4

These figures have to be taken with a couple of grains of salt. For one thing, there were more "buys" and "sells" featured in the financial press than the ones listed here, and not all of them would have produced the desired results.

Time Warner, for example, could have been considered a sell because of concerns that Clinton would clamp down on cable rates. Although those fears did make their way into the market for essentially one day—taking Time Warner down from $33 to $30 overnight—the media stock frenzy of late 1993 pushed Time Warner above $45, an 82 percent increase from where it stood the day of Clinton's election.

There was also an element of luck concealed within the table. Paramount was deemed a Clinton stock because of the company's textbook subsidiary, which was not the reason the stock went up. It went up because companies such as QVC and Viacom decided they wanted to own Paramount, and their bidding (Viacom was the winner) was surely not about textbooks.

Nonetheless, the important thing to remember is that these stocks were all widely discussed before the election, but the supposedly efficient stock market still hadn't accounted for the new president's power. In other words, these are more than just lists of winners and losers; they are lists of *widely predicted* winners and losers, purely on the basis of the changing of the guard at Pennsylvania Avenue. So even though the "Clinton stock" concept seemed tired and worn out by election day, its merits were not. In fact, for most of these stocks, buys

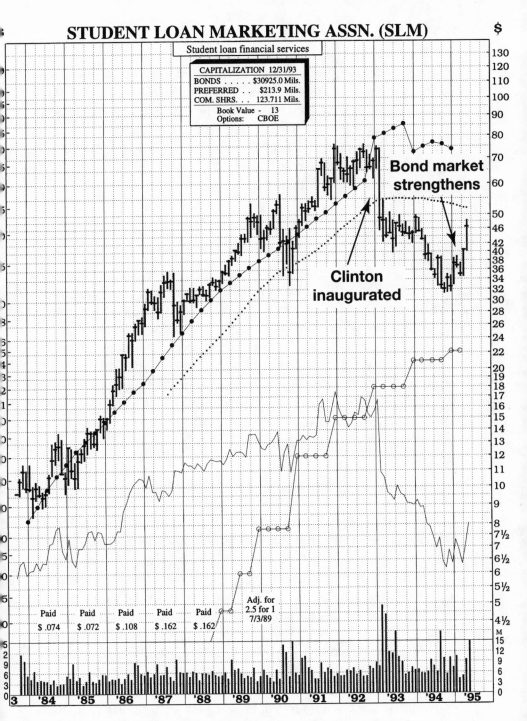

STUDENT LOAN MARKETING ASSN. (SLM)

$

Student loan financial services

CAPITALIZATION 12/31/93	
BONDS	$30925.0 Mils.
PREFERRED . .	$213.9 Mils.
COM. SHRS. . .	123.711 Mils.
Book Value -	13
Options:	CBOE

**Bond market
strengthens**

**Clinton
inaugurated**

Paid	Paid	Paid	Paid	Paid	Adj. for 2.5 for 1 7/3/89
$ .074	$ .072	$ .108	$ .162	$ .162	

Fig. 43 SALLIE MAE CHART (Courtesy of Securities Research Co.)

and sells alike, you could have waited until Inauguration Day and still made out fine. So much for the efficient market theory.

Unfortunately, given this spectacular record, the next election will probably produce even more presidential stock selections that we'll have to weed through. As these writings proliferate, it may no longer be possible to wait until Inauguration Day to take advantage. However, the 72.9 percent differential between buys and sells is a huge number, and it could be many years—if ever—before there is no investment advantage in knowing the quirks of a new president.

The Losers: When to Get Back In

Do the "Clinton sells" remain sells forever? Of course not. When was the last time that "forever" applied to Wall Street?

As to when you should get back in to any of these stocks, we saw in the case of drug stocks that people paid a price if they got back in too quickly. When an industry encounters turbulence, it is often best to sit on the sidelines—possibly holding on to a few token shares just to keep your interest—and taking some time to assess whether the good old days will ever return. But here are a few specific times when getting back in could be a good idea:

WHEN RHETORIC EXCEEDS POLICY. An investor has to monitor presidential rhetoric with one ear and presidential policy with the other. Such was the case with stocks of health maintenance organizations (HMOs) in 1993. HMOs such as U.S. Healthcare were supposed to be Clinton stocks because of the candidate's well-known preference for managed care over more expensive alternatives. But President Clinton gave the group a rude shock in his first State of the Union message when he suggested that the government might institute premium controls.

HMO stocks were hit across the board: U.S. Healthcare dropped from $60 to $37; United Healthcare, from $64 to $40; Pacificare plummeted all the way from $57 to $25.

As usual, there was no way of knowing exactly when HMO stocks would bottom out, and when you're in the middle of such a cataclysm, the notion that there might be a bottom at all seems hard to believe. But there were signs that the fall could not continue indefinitely.

The key observation, for which I'll thank my friend Ed Gordon at Morgan Stanley, was that such draconian measures as premium controls would have devastating implications for *employment* in the health-care sector. That is, the panic in HMO stocks was justified only if you believed that Clinton would adopt the label of "unemployment president" instead of "health-care president." Of course, Clinton was not about to make such a trade-off, and by early 1994 U.S. Healthcare had rebounded from $37 to $55; United Healthcare, from $40 to $68; and Pacificare, from its low of $25 to over $40.

Yes, the presidency is powerful. But remember that the president also has more than one issue to deal with.

WHEN THE STOCK'S PRICE SUGGESTS A FLOOR. That's a dangerous statement, on face value. As we saw with the pharmaceutical stocks, floors have a way of giving way underneath you. But in mid-1993, far away from the health-care group, there was a major buying opportunity in Philip Morris.

As a financial writer, recommending Philip Morris in print is difficult but not impossible. My standard way of dealing with ethically based objections is to say that my job is not to determine someone else's ethics but to advise which stocks look like good value and which don't.

In the summer of 1993, following a few months of wretched performance, Philip Morris had become excellent value: The stock had fallen to just $48 per share, at which price its dividend yield was 5.4 percent, the highest yield among the 30 Dow Jones Industrials. Whereas the dividend had been a secondary consideration when the stock was at $77, now it was pivotal. Better still, the dividend could essentially be paid out of income from the company's food operations, even if its tobacco operations went to zero. My feeling was that if the dividend was as safe as it appeared, the stock wasn't going to go much lower; I was willing to bet that good news would push the stock up before bad news pushed it down.

The "good" news came in November 1993, when the company and its competitors announced price increases for their discount brands. The stock, which had moved into the low 50s since its April low, shot up to $59 per share, a 23 percent increase from the time of my recommendation. Note that the stock's low price made a rebound possible even though the tobacco industry remained in the new administration's doghouse. In fact, it continued to rise—in fits and starts —over the next two years.

As Philip Morris was rebounding, Sallie Mae suggested itself as the next candidate among the Clinton "losers." The stock had fallen from the mid-70s in early 1993 and didn't seem to know when to stop. As it dropped, it seemed cheaper and cheaper relative to near-term earnings, but that wasn't enough; with the direct lending plan throwing a cloud over the company's future, near-term earnings no longer mattered. However, by the time Sallie Mae hit just $35 per share in mid-1994, its total market value was *less* than the value of the company's vast student loan portfolio. At that point, there wasn't as much reason to worry about the company's future because it was already trading at its liquidation value!

This alone didn't make the stock a sure thing—after all, if interest rates continued to go up, the liquidation value would go down. However, suffice it to say that when a stock is trading at liquidation value, it's often worth buying, on the chance that an upside catalyst will appear.

The catalyst came in the fall of 1994, when Sallie Mae and the government began active discussions to "privatize" the company, which would free it from some of the onerous fees that had just been legislated. You had to have good timing to profit, though. When the privatization possibility was officially aired, the stock popped up to $39—not a whopping success, but another indication that even the most out-of-favor stocks can eventually reach attractive purchase levels. Then, as the bond market strengthened in early 1995, Sallie Mae initiated a large-scale stock buyback that pushed its shares into the low 50s. This was nowhere near the all-time high, but it was a 50 percent gain off the 1994 low.

WHEN HELL FREEZES OVER. You shouldn't always be in a rush to find the bottom of a group or stock that has fallen out of favor. Consider the health-care stocks of 1993. While I avoided most of the industry, my one health-care selection of late 1992—U.S. Surgical— was as ill-starred as any of them.

Make that more so. Whereas my selection of Kellwood (from the lighter side) was triumph, U.S. Surgical was tragedy. Both stocks had been big market losers in 1992, and I harbored hopes of a rebound for each of them in 1993. Kellwood complied nicely. However, this type of rebound strategy is always dangerous because, by definition, you're culling from a loser list and some stocks are on the list for good reason. In the immortal words of the singer Meat Loaf, "There ain't no Coupe de Ville hiding in the bottom of a Crackerjack box."

How true. U.S. Surgical, which had fallen from $134 to $65 in 1992, before I chimed in, did even worse in 1993. It wasn't supposed to be that way. Fundamental to the bullish case was the company's leadership position in disposable supplies for laparoscopies, a less-invasive form of surgery that was growing at about 20 percent per year. Reusable medical equipment was being given increasing scrutiny in the era of AIDS, and surgeons clearly preferred U.S. Surgical's products to those of the company's main competitor, the Ethicon division of Johnson & Johnson. So what if the company's gross margins were a bit on the high side? In the long run, laparoscopies were cost-effective.

Well, in the short run, they weren't cost-effective in the least. Once Clinton came into the picture, hospitals were under more pressure than ever to cut costs. U.S. Surgical's biggest allies in the buying process, the surgeons themselves, now had to take a backseat to hospital administrators. And from the hospital's perspective, cost savings could be achieved either with reusables or with Johnson & Johnson disposables, which were priced 10 to 15 percent lower than U.S. Surgical's. Either way, U.S. Surgical would lose.

Whether laparoscopic procedures continued their growth rate or not, USS was no longer a beneficiary of that growth. The company's fat cost structure made it an absolutely terrible stock for the times, and a stock that any "Clinton first" investor would have avoided. As it was, between Kellwood and U.S. Surgical, I broke even on my selections, so the net result wasn't disastrous. But it could have been a whole lot better.

To close where we started—with drug stocks—the good news is that they eventually recovered from their extended funk. As with so many rebound situations, though, drug stocks weren't destined to go up for the same reasons they had in the eighties. And as with Sallie

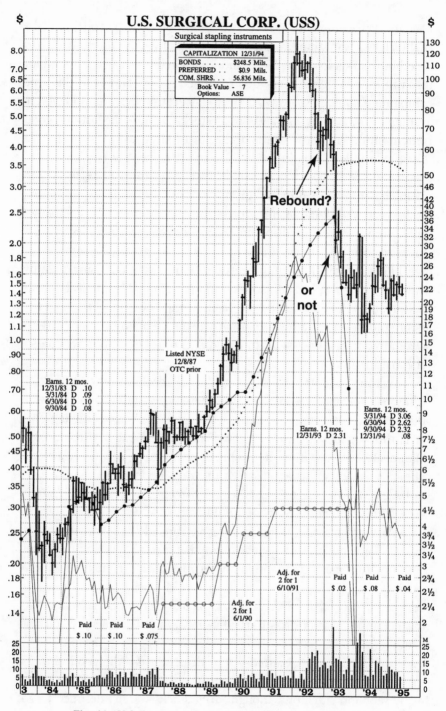

Fig. 44 U.S. SURGICAL CHART (Courtesy of Securities Research Co.)

Mae and Philip Morris, there was no reason to buy until a brand-new way of looking at the industry had arrived.

The most visible catalyst came in early 1994, when Roche Holdings of Switzerland made a bid for the oft-beleaguered Syntex, a drug company that suffered from a paucity of new products and above-average exposure to generic competition. Although Syntex had been rumored to be a buyout candidate for some time, the price offered by Roche was well in excess of analysts' estimates, and the market responded by pushing up the stocks of other takeover candidates— notably, Upjohn and Marion Merrell Dow. When American Home Products moved to acquire American Cyanamid in the summer of 1994, there was also a ripple effect throughout the industry, with shares of Warner-Lambert and others moving up in sympathy.

The other important stimulus to drug stocks in 1994 was that investors became increasingly convinced that Clinton's vaunted health-care plan, the scourge of the industry in 1992 and 1993, was simply not going to pass. As a result, stocks such as Johnson & Johnson and Merck posted nice rebounds, even though these companies were hardly takeover candidates, and even though their growth prospects were modest by eighties' standards. By the end of 1994, these stocks had posted nice moves during a very difficult year in the market, and both continued their rebounds in 1995.

However, to come full circle, if you had bought just about any drug stock in early 1992, you'd still have been showing a loss as 1994 came to a close. Although Clinton's bark was in some sense worse than his bite, his influence could not be ignored.

5 ❑ When Wall Street Meets Madison Avenue

If you think that advertising has other purposes besides giving us investment ideas, you're right. But there are dozens of ways in which advertising can help us make smart investment decisions.

Of course, there are thousands of ads out there, so part of our job is to know which ones not to spend time on. Sometimes this is obvious: For instance, the Avis "We're number two—we try harder" campaign was one of history's greatest, but Avis was a private company and therefore out of reach for the investing public. A related deterrent is "Speedy Alka-Seltzer" syndrome—a situation where the advertised product accounts for only a small percentage of the company's total revenues and therefore does not drive its stock. This syndrome is especially common among major packaged food and pharmaceutical companies, not to mention household products leader Procter & Gamble, perennially one of the biggest advertisers in the country. You can't point to a particular spot on P&G's historical stock price chart and say, "Ah, yes. That must be where George Whipple started squeezing the Charmin."

But even if advertising cannot explain near-term stock market action, it can say a great deal about long-term *corporate strategy*. Remember, advertising is nothing less than a company's chance to tell us what makes them special. It is in everybody's interest that those precious on-the-air moments are not spent in vain.

THE POWER OF POSITIONING

In our efforts to let ads do our stockpicking for us, there is no better place to start than with what is known as positioning theory. For all the commercial clutter that crowds the airwaves, there are ultimately just two kinds of ads—those that convey a position for the products they represent and those that do not. This lone distinction is probably the most important one an investor can make.

Instinctively, we have a pretty good idea of what a position is. For instance, we *know* that "I've got the eaties for my Wheaties" is a less-effective slogan than "Breakfast of Champions." The former is merely prattling, while the latter says the product stands for something—and that's a position. "Breakfast of Champions" alone has given Wheaties a healthy connotation, distinguishing it not only from the Cocoa Krispies and Count Choculas of the world but also from some equally nutritious flake cereals.

More generally, a position can be thought of as a mental lock on a particular market niche. For example, if you were asked to name a dandruff shampoo, the fact that Head & Shoulders comes quickly to mind suggests that H&S "owns" the dandruff shampoo position. The product doesn't lack for competition: Denorex and Selsun Blue, to name two others, have carved out territories all their own, mostly because they contain stronger antidandruff agents. But Head & Shoulders owns the concept of dandruff prevention in consumers' minds and could own it indefinitely.

Remember, these positions don't just happen, they are *created*, and advertising is inevitably a key part of their creation. Which appliance maker is "dependable"? Maytag, of course. But without the perpetually out-of-work Maytag repairman, we might not think of the company that way. Or take Crest, which remains the cavity fighter's toothpaste of choice. Why? Because Kathy Langley from Minneapolis, Minnesota, told us that her group got 21 percent fewer cavities with Crest. That was in 1962. Positions can last a long time.

The fathers of positioning theory are Jack Trout and Al Ries, chairman and president, respectively, of a marketing consultancy that bears their names. Through their pioneering efforts, positioning has become a well-developed field on Madison Avenue, but it has somehow remained an infant science on Wall Street. I'd like to change that.

Three classic advertising campaigns—Federal Express, Chrysler, and Philip Morris—turn out to be clever positioning strategies in disguise. These campaigns display many of the qualities investors should look for when turning to advertising as a source of moneymaking ideas.

Introducing a New Product: Federal Express

"America, you've got a new airline," came the original message for Federal Express, launched in a test campaign in New York and Los Angeles in 1974. The campaign quickly showed how the right advertising can make a great concept even better. During the test marketing period, FedEx's Los Angeles business increased 59 percent and New York business 87 percent—compared to growth of "only" 32 percent in the rest of the country.

Stock market investors couldn't participate in these early successes because Federal Express wasn't a public company yet; its initial public offering didn't come until April 1978, at a price of $3 per share (adjusted for later splits). But the FedEx example illustrates the entire strategy of this chapter, in that the company's advertising *by itself* was enough of a clue to take investment action.

Yes, I realize that corporate performance, not advertising expertise, is what ultimately makes stocks go up, so my intent is not to downgrade FedEx's remarkable business execution or the revolutionary "hub" strategy that made the company so different. But you and I were never given a private tour of the Memphis headquarters, nor did we ever meet Fred Smith, the company's dynamic chairman. FedEx's advertising, like that of any company, was its face to the world. Taking that thought a step further, part of the brilliance of the overnight delivery concept was that it lent itself to memorable advertising, because even the best-managed consumer business can't thrive without first grabbing the consumer's attention.

Suppose you had bought shares of Federal Express at the initial offering in 1978. As you kept up with the company via quarterly reports and 10-K forms and the like, here's the advertising that you would have been exposed to over the next five years:

One set of ads introduced the pathbreaking slogan "When it absolutely, positively has to be there overnight." Graphic comparisons were made between the reliability rates of Federal and its prime competitor, Emery Air Freight, which has since been left in the dust. The fact that Federal could come in and preempt the overnight delivery concept from an existing player in the field underscores the tremendous power of the campaign. The Post Office and UPS were likewise made to play catch-up.

The reliability angle was exploited further by the ad showing a hapless corporate soul hunkering under his desk as his boss ranted about who might be responsible for the vital package not being delivered on time. Actually, FedEx wasn't *guaranteeing* delivery, only a commitment to deliver. No matter: The ads tapped into the public's vast reservoir of negative feelings about the Post Office.

The people at Ally & Gargano—FedEx's ad agency—knew what they were doing. They hyped FedEx by noting that they used the service themselves to communicate between their Manhattan office and a client in Great Neck, Long Island—never mind the stopover in Federal Express's Memphis hub. The idea is now utterly commonplace, but it was revolutionary at the time.

By 1982, the advertising emphasis had shifted to pure speed. Guinness world record holder John Moschitta was recruited from the television show *That's Incredible* to play Federal Express's fast talker, now perhaps the most famous campaign of them all: "I-know-it's-perfect-Peter-that's-why-I-picked-Pittsburgh-Pittsburgh's-perfect-Peter-may-I-call-you-Pete?" Different ad, same message.

Together, these various ad campaigns ensured that FedEx had earned America's trust when it came to package deliveries; in our newfound terms, the company *owned* the overnight position. This gave FedEx the ability to charge more for its services, which is what great advertising is all about.

And that's precisely what *investors* want. A fast-growing business with a strong pricing environment? It's no mystery why those quarterly reports looked so good. Appreciating the positioning power of the ads would have made the decision to buy shares that much easier —a wise move, because by the end of 1983 that onetime $3 stock was trading at $48. For those keeping score at home, that's a sixteenfold increase from the initial offering price, for a compound annual rate of return of 63 percent.

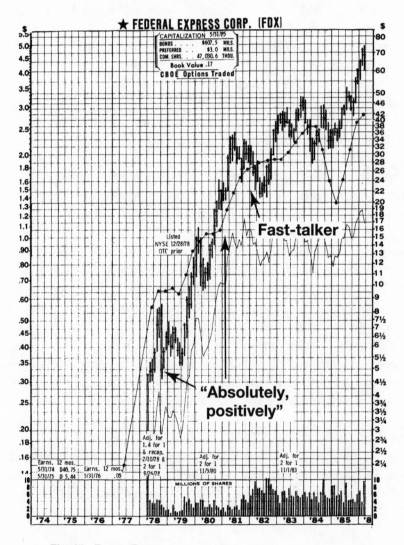

Fig. 45 FEDERAL EXPRESS CHART (Courtesy of Securities Research Co.)

Of course, the good times did not last forever; ironically, just as the bull market was beginning in 1982–83, Federal's best stock market performance was already behind it. Revenues continued to grow strongly, but profit growth was harder to come by in the years ahead. Competition developed for package deliveries, eventually squeezing domestic margins. Hundreds of millions of dollars were lost to international operations and Zap Mail. Fax machines circumvented overnight letters.

We'll see later how ads could have helped you get *out* of the stock. But even if you had held on from April 1978 all the way to early 1995, your compound annual return would still have exceeded 20 percent. It was a success you could have latched on to simply by watching the ads. Luckily for us, it is not alone.

Changing an Image: Chrysler

"If you can find a better car, buy it!" Thus spoke Iacocca in 1981 with a confidence that belied the inferiority complex that was haunting domestic automakers. Chrysler in particular, having staved off bankruptcy only by unprecedented governmental largesse, was as inferior as they could come. Iacocca's very appearance on the airwaves might have been seen as an act of desperation: To quote from an old ad agency maxim, "Only in the gravest cases should you show the clients' faces."

By now, of course, Chrysler's comeback from the dead is a classic American success story. For our present purposes, the Chrysler example shows that changes in perception created by advertising can translate into big turnarounds on Wall Street.

It helps my pro-ad-watching stance that some people saw the significance of these ads right then and there. Said Leo Kelmenson, chairman of Chrysler's ad agency Kenyon & Eckhardt (now Bozell, Jacobs, Kenyon & Eckhardt), "I begged, borrowed, and stole every penny I could to invest in Chrysler stock." And he wasn't living in a fantasy world. Said Ron DeLuca of the K&E creative group, "The Iacocca ads weren't supposed to be commercials; they were supposed to be a reflection of reality."

The beauty of the campaign was that whether or not the so-called reality existed at the time, it became a self-fulfilling prophecy once the public got behind the idea that "Chrysler" didn't mean "lemon." We all know how much America loves a winner. Well, for several glorious years, Chrysler had the winner position all to itself.

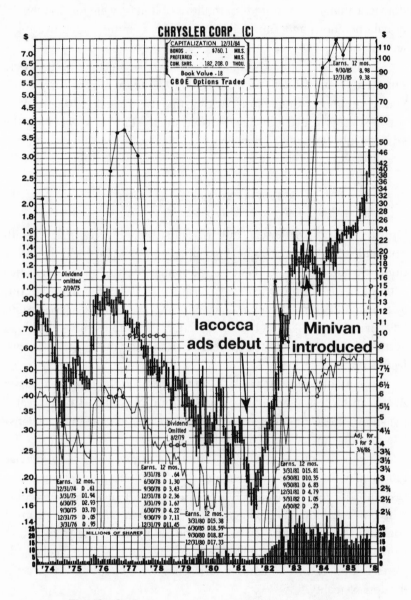

Fig. 46   CHRYSLER CHART (Courtesy of Securities Research Co.)

Until the ads ran, the reverse was true—a point that is central to the turnaround story. Chrysler had lost over $2 billion in just three years. Rebate programs practically begged customers to buy the company's cars. The company's idea of advertising was having Joe Garagiola yell "Get a check"—not much of a positioning statement. Said Iacocca in his biography of the same name, "In retrospect . . . it's clear that my appearing in the television ads was an essential part of Chrysler's recovery."

Leo Kelmenson and others were well rewarded for investing on the basis of this breakthrough campaign. The company's sales doubled within two years, and earnings topped $1 billion for five years running. Federal guarantees were paid back in full and well ahead of schedule. Between the trough of 1981 and the peak of 1987, Chrysler shares advanced fiftyfold.

I am not here to claim that ad watching would have led to *all* that gain. The minivan, not mere image, converted Chrysler's initial turnaround into a sustained recovery. But without the Iacocca ads, the minivan success never would have happened, because the battle of perceptions had to be won first. Besides, as the chart shows, the minivan didn't appear until 1984, and there was a lot of money to be made before then.

I should add that when the minivan took off, Chrysler changed its advertising to include the positioning tag line "The Minivan Company," lest there be any doubt of the company's pioneering role. This subtle move not only told investors where the profits were, it also aided Chrysler in protecting its dominant share of that important market.

A Bit of Everything: The Marlboro Man

As impressive as the prior entries were, for the most influential "investor's" ad of all time you have to go back to 1955, when the Marlboro cowboy first entered the national landscape. The Philip Morris story shows how a well-crafted position can work wonders in your portfolio.

First, a warning label of sorts: America's fondness for the cowboy notwithstanding, not everybody is fond of what this particular cowboy stands for. When investors screen stocks according to ethical guidelines, tobacco companies are often the first to be scratched out—and for good reason.

But step back for a moment and consider that this historic campaign began in 1955, nine years before the surgeon general's landmark health warning. It was a time when TV stars and baseball heroes could hawk cigarettes without penalty: Lucy, Desi, even Stan Musial. Lucky Strike sponsored *Your Hit Parade* and Brooklyn Dodger baseball. Times were different.

It was also a time when Philip Morris was the smallest domestic tobacco company; competitors Chesterfield, Lucky Strike, and Camel accounted for some 90 percent of the total cigarette market. The future of course was in filters—all the more so after a 1954 *Reader's Digest* article warned for the first time of the hazards of smoking. But RJ Reynolds, not Philip Morris, was first in filters with its successful Winston brand.

If this sounds bad for a potential Philip Morris investor, it gets worse. The company had spent most of its time and money advertising its house brand using corporate spokesman Johnny Roventini (a.k.a. the Philip Morris Man), a four-foot two-inch bellhop. As for Marlboro, the brand's trademark was a funny-looking red tip, marketed to women as a means of hiding lipstick marks. The angle wasn't working: Marlboro had acquired less than 3 percent of the overall market.

The breakthrough finally came when Leo Burnett, Philip Morris's new ad agency, realized the potential of the *masculine position* for a filtered cigarette. Enter the Marlboro Man.

The original Marlboro Man was actually a collection of American males from various walks of life, each sporting a tattoo with a naval insignia. The idea was to show that filters weren't for sissies—a strange thought today, but an extremely effective angle back then. Marlboro sales went up fifteenfold in the first two years alone.

When the company settled on the cowboy image a few years later, posterity awaited. "They tapped into the quintessential American myth with the cowboy," said Jay Nelson, beverage and tobacco analyst at Brown Brothers Harriman. "Independence, self-reliance. In a society where those commodities are in short supply, the Marlboro Man said it all."

Philip Morris stock soon showed signs of greatness, advancing 300 percent between 1957 and 1961, but the gains didn't stop there. The power of the cowboy gave Marlboro its pivotal boost when cigarette ads were banned from television and radio in 1971. The western image translated perfectly into print media, whereas Reynolds's jingle-dependent Winston ads did not. As a result, Marlboro soon became the nation's best-selling brand, a position it has never relinquished.

The brand's success continued for decades without any fundamental shift in advertising. By 1990, Marlboro's market share, including its various line extensions, was at 25 percent domestically and even higher overseas. Throughout this time, because of this high market share and the pernicious nature of the product, Marlboro's pricing power was as great as any brand in the world.

Philip Morris as a company now sports a very different look, what with the multibillion-dollar acquisitions of General Foods (1985) and Kraft (1989). But tobacco remains the profit center, and, as such, Philip Morris is not an investment that everyone feels comfortable with. In fact, many onlookers were delighted when the company finally had to lower Marlboro prices in April 1993 in response to competition from discount brands, an action that sent the stock tumbling over 30 percent.

While this proves that nothing lasts forever, including the strategy of riding companies with well-crafted market positions, the fact remains that if you had invested $1,000 in Philip Morris in 1955, your investment would have grown to more than $300,000 in the next forty years.

Positions Versus Commodities

To better understand what positions are all about, it helps to look briefly at what they are *not*. At the opposite end of the spectrum from companies with well-defined positions are commodity/cyclical companies. These include but aren't restricted to smokestack America and other basic industries.

Earnings of these industries are often dependent on the price of a particular commodity, such as steel, aluminum, paper, or even something like polyvinyl chloride. The "cyclical" label is affixed because earnings tend to move up and down with the overall economy, with

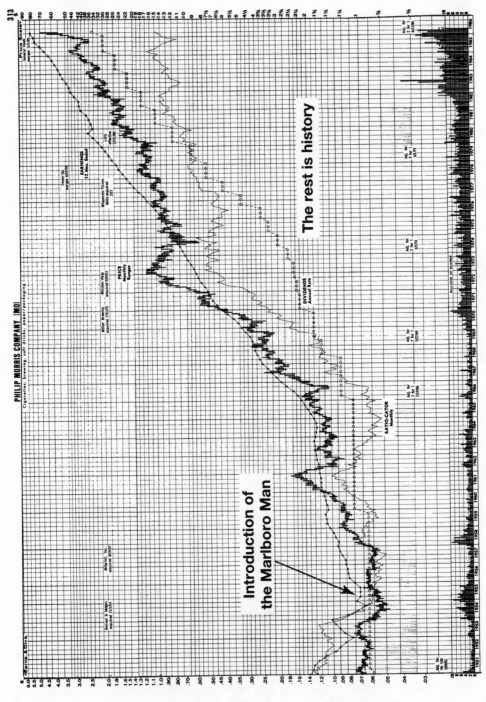

Fig. 47 PHILIP MORRIS CHART (Courtesy of Securities Research Co.)

no guarantee of net improvement over, say, a ten-year period. Catching the upswings is what investing in cyclical stocks is all about, and it's a complicated task. For now, the simple point I want to make is that commodity/cyclical businesses can be identified purely by the nature of their advertising.

Which of the following slogans do you like best?

"Fly the friendly skies."

"Something special in the air."

"You'll love the way we fly."

These slogans may be recognizable as those of United, American, and Delta Airlines, respectively. And the words are not without value. "Friendly skies" suggests a safe flight, obviously a favorable association. "You'll love the way we fly" suggests a comfortable flight, another plus. And whatever that "something special in the air" actually is, it hardly sounds bad.

Yet slogans such as these are not *positions,* because they do almost nothing to differentiate the companies involved. When companies have unique attributes, they'll *tell* you. Therefore, as a general rule, the more slogans you see in an industry's advertising, the more likely it is that the industry is a commodity.

It is important to note that commodity businesses such as the airlines are especially susceptible to price wars because price is one of the few competitive tools available. When these wars show up in television advertising, they represent good deals for the consumer but are anathema to an investor because, by definition, they suppress profits throughout an industry.

Small wonder that airline stocks tend to be uninspiring long-term investments. Their most recent glory days came in 1989, when it looked as though UAL was going to be taken private in a leveraged buyout. But that didn't happen, and, in the five years that followed, Delta dropped from $85 to $40, UAL from $280 to $140, and AMR (parent of American Airlines) from $100 to $50. Note that the different stocks tend to move together, as you'd expect from an industry with little differentiation. Most of them didn't rebound until late 1994.

Just to show that we're not picking on the airlines here, consider another commodity situation: the insurance industry. Anyone who has invested in insurance stocks over the last ten years can tell you how price-competitive the business is, and again, the commodity nature of the business is given away by the preponderance of slogans:

"The good-hands people." (Allstate)

"A piece of the rock." (Prudential)

"Aetna, I'm glad I met ya."

Yes, there will be times when insurance stocks can boost your portfolio. The 1984–86 period was one, 1992–93 another. But stocks such as Aetna and Travelers made little or no *net* progress between 1983 and 1995. (Travelers has an umbrella, not a slogan. Same difference.)

Ad watching can't solve all your problems when it comes to cyclical investing. However, one of the most common mistakes investors make with cyclicals is treating them like growth stocks and therefore holding on too long. Now that you can identify cyclical industries while sitting in front of your television set, you no longer have to make that mistake. In other words, we've made progress.

Autos: Where Positions and Commodities Meet

If you are still intent on including cyclicals in your portfolio (and if you're intent on getting clues from this chapter), my advice is to look for *positions* within commodity industries. In airlines, for example, that approach could have led you to Southwest, the low-cost, no-frills airline—and one of the few major carriers to reward investors in the bear market for airline stocks in the early nineties. (Southwest shares did drop more than 50 percent in 1994, but not before gaining *700 percent* in the 1990–93 period.)

However, the automobile industry is a more fertile hunting ground. To conclude this motivational section, let me quickly run through a few of the great individual stories in the annals of auto stocks, all of which came from companies whose advertising reflected well-defined positions.

For starters, it is well known that the American auto manufacturers' insistence on homogeneity in the late fifties left the door open for foreign manufacturers to enter the U.S. market. American auto executives were accused of being stodgy and complacent. However, their specific failing was that they didn't understand the power of positioning. Unfortunately for them, many of their competitors did.

Volkswagen's "Think small" campaign of 1962 was one of the greatest positioning ads ever, instantly distinguishing the VW Beetle from the clunkier models coming out of Detroit. On the strength of this campaign, Volkswagen's ugly little compact broke sales records held by the Model T. Another foreign coup of the sixties was Volvo's successful capturing of the safety position, which was left open following Ford's failed "Lifeguard design" advertising campaign of 1956. Volvo's ads, featuring crash dummies and tough Swedish roads, stole the position away from American carmakers who were convinced—incorrectly—that safety didn't sell.

Moving on to the seventies, Honda's achievement with the fuel economy position is now legendary. For example, in the second half of the seventies, you would have had a hard time making a dime on the Big Three, whereas you could have doubled your money with Honda.

And the first auto-stock success story of the eighties wasn't Chrysler; it was Subaru, whose sales moved from $744 million in 1980 to $1.9 billion in 1986. During this time, Subaru stock soared from $1¼ all the way to $39. The company's position? Low-cost four-wheel drive. You may remember the ads with the U.S. men's ski team stopping to rescue the Swedish women's team on a 45-degree mountain slope. Sexist now, profitable then.

When Korea's Hyundai entered the U.S. market in 1986, the company immediately claimed the low-cost position. All the ads did was give you the sticker price, but that was enough. Hyundai sold 168,882 of its Excel subcompacts in America in 1986, more than any importer had ever sold in its first year in the U.S. market. Americans couldn't buy shares of Hyundai Motor itself, but they could buy the Korea Fund, a closed-end fund traded on the New York Stock Exchange.

Between the beginning of 1986 and the fall of 1987, the Korea Fund was up 300 percent. Its biggest holding during that time was Hyundai Motor.

Finally, the United States achieved some redemption. We have already mentioned Chrysler's triumph with the minivan position beginning in the mid-eighties. The company was also helped by Jeep, owned by Chrysler since 1987. Jeep ads such as " 'Which way to Bakersville?' . . . 'Straight through those mountains, ma'am' " were keyed into the outdoor orientation of the nineties (which also spawned the success of Timberland and other manufacturers of rugged outdoor footwear). These ads helped the Grand Cherokee become a smash hit, which in turn helped push Chrysler's stock price up from just $10 in 1991 to $60 by early 1994.

As impressive as all these campaigns were, perhaps the best way to underscore the investment importance of well-defined positions in the auto industry is to consider what happened to companies *without* them. To that end, what was Studebaker's position? How about Rambler or Hudson? Clearly, it's hard to sustain life without a well-defined niche in the marketplace.

The truth is, many car ads can be ignored by the budding ad investor for the simple reason that they don't say anything. The Chevy Cavalier once used a tap dancer to advertise its superior braking system, but does Cavalier own the braking position? Hardly. Volkswagen's "Fahrvergnügen" was likewise a meaningless campaign; although the word means something like "pleasure ride" in German, such attributes tend not to overcome the language barrier. (The worst gaffe was the Chevy Nova, which didn't fare well in Spanish-speaking countries because "no va" essentially means "won't go.")

But the worst investor's auto ad of all time tried to own *too many* positions.

The campaign started with a two-page magazine spread showing an automobile carrier stocked with five cars, all covered in cloth. "These carriers with covered cars are headed in your direction," it said.

When the covers were finally taken off in a follow-up ad, the copy went as follows: "It says you chose elegant styling, luxurious comfort. . . . It also means you made a wonderful buy. . . . For of all medium-priced cars, this one really new car is actually priced the lowest."

Can one car really be all those things? Not a chance. By trying for everything, they got nothing instead.

"It" was the Ford Edsel.

PUTTING POSITIONING TO WORK

The reason that positions are worth creating in the first place is simple: Once you have a lock on the consumer mind-set, it can't be taken away from you. So says a main doctrine of positioning theory. We'll call it the principle of preemption.

Before you reject this principle as the most naive thing you've ever heard, let me explain what it really means. In advertising terms, the principle of preemption means simply that no product other than Ivory will ever be $99^{44}/_{100}$ percent pure. And nothing other than Rice Krispies will ever go "Snap, Crackle, Pop." These positions are *taken*.

Needless to say, this doesn't solve our investing problems: Pullman will always be the first name in railroad cars, likewise Western Union in telegrams, yet their wares are more appropriate to the Smithsonian than to your portfolio. However, the principle of preemption often gives investors one less thing to worry about.

For example, suppose you owned shares of Federal Express back in the late seventies. You might have conjured up plenty of legitimate worries: Could the company finance its expansion plans? Would the federal government stand in its way? Could this fly-by-night operation really work? And what about FedEx's competitors such as Emery Air Freight or even the U.S. Postal Service? What was preventing them from snatching back market share from the upstart overnight service?

Although part of FedEx's insulation came from the operational complexity of the overnight business and the company's ability to provide superior service, FedEx's ownership of the consumer mind-set was an even bigger barrier for competing firms. America wouldn't trust just anybody with its packages, a preference born out of brilliant advertising. Understanding that would have been your advantage as an investor.

Similarly, Philip Morris's Marlboro Man put RJ Reynolds (now RJR Nabisco) thoroughly on the defensive. As Bryan Burrough and John Helyar wrote in the best-seller *Barbarians at the Gate: The Fall of RJR*

Nabisco, "Reynolds tried a macho counteroffensive, with a campaign portraying loggers and sailors. It tried a 'working men of America' campaign, trying to celebrate the blue-collar brand it had become. Nothing worked."

Of course, given that Philip Morris owned the masculine position, nothing could have worked. You don't have to feel sorry for RJR shareholders, because the company did just fine in its own right. But if you had been a Philip Morris investor back then, there would simply have been no need to worry that RJR was going to dislodge the Marlboro Man. In general, being able to relax when other investors are needlessly worried is a good way to make money on Wall Street. It means you don't have to sell when everyone else is selling. You can even buy more.

The most important corollary of the principle of preemption will win no points for imagination but could earn many points in your portfolio: *When investing in consumer companies, it pays to stick with the leaders.* All else being equal, a long-term investor should choose McDonald's over Wendy's, Anheuser-Busch over Adolph Coors, Procter & Gamble over Colgate-Palmolive, even Wal-Mart over Kmart. All you ask of the leaders is that they stick to their guns and don't change a winning game.

Fundamental to this approach is that America loves winners. We may talk about the importance of competition, but in our heart of hearts we want somebody to rise to the top. It's certainly true in sports: The NFL has a parity system to protect the weak, but the public has always loved the dynasties—from the Packers to the Steelers to the 49ers to the Cowboys. And it's true on the consumer level as well. Over time, the consumer mind-set's simplicity seeking has enabled leaders in a wide range of consumer markets to steadily increase their market share. What better underpinning for a long-term investment?

This does not make ad-based investing as easy as finding companies with strong market positions and simply holding on, because even the best stocks can eventually run out of steam. Plus, as an investor, you get more bang for your buck by discovering a company like Federal Express *before* they become the industry leader. But investing in established leaders can be profitable for longer than most investors realize, despite some common objections to the strategy.

OBJECTION 1: THE MARKET IS EFFICIENT.   The efficient market theory holds that all publicly available information about a company is incorporated in the price of its stock. With that in mind, surely the stock market knows a leader from a follower. So even if a leader does have some fundamental operating advantages, wouldn't those advantages be fully reflected in the price of its stock?

The answer is no.

It's not that the stock market doesn't *try* to distinguish good from bad; it does, each and every trading day. Companies with superior prospects are accorded higher valuations than languishing ones. For example, between 1980 and 1990, Wal-Mart shares on average traded at over twenty times earnings, while Kmart traded at below ten times earnings.

But did these different valuation levels equalize the long-term stock price performance of Wal-Mart and Kmart? Hardly. High P/Es can be a warning sign, but companies that come through with consistent earnings growth tend to retain or even increase their premiums to the market. Wal-Mart's earnings growth rate was 34 percent per year for the decade, compared to only 10 percent annual growth at Kmart. Between 1980 and 1990, Wal-Mart shares increased fiftyfold while Kmart shares merely doubled. In effect, Wal-Mart was chronically undervalued even at *apparently* high price/earnings ratios.

Investors often forget that leaders are perfectly capable of increasing their already dominant market share. For example, in the early eighties, Gillette sold 48 percent of the razor blades in this country, and you'd be forgiven for viewing the company as a stodgy leader in a mature market. Except that by the end of the decade, Gillette's market share had risen to 56 percent—and, at this writing, it exceeds 60 percent. As these share gains were being made, Gillette was a sensational stock to own, appreciating some fourteenfold between 1982 and 1995.

The ability to increase market share is often a hidden trend in the leader's favor. Remember, Wall Street analysts are obliged to make earnings estimates on a year-by-year or even quarter-by-quarter basis, and it is extremely difficult to incorporate longer-term market share trends into a specific near-term estimate. So what happens? The leading companies, because of this "hidden" trend in their favor, are often the ones that produce upside quarterly surprises. For years, Wal-Mart,

Gillette, and Microsoft routinely generated better-than-expected earnings reports. These three are unusual companies, to be sure, but the point is that being number one can be a powerful advantage long after you got there in the first place.

OBJECTION 2: BRAND NAMES ARE DEAD. Another common objection is that going with leaders forces you to rely on the success of their brand-name products, and everyone knows brand names are dead, right? Wrong.

The apparent demise of the brand name began with the recession year of 1990, when private-label consumer goods gained market share at the expense of higher-priced brand-name products. This led to cries of "Advertising is dead," as well as a break in the multiyear bull market for consumer stocks. Because so many of the highly visible stocks in this sector—Philip Morris, Campbell Soup, Tambrands—were hit hard in the 1993–94 period, it is tempting to conclude that investing in leaders is only a fair-weather strategy for consumer stocks.

But what really happened is that brand names were only *temporarily* derailed, mostly because of their own greed. After years of aggressive price hikes in the eighties, many leading brand-name products became conspicuously overpriced relative to no-name, private label merchandise; at a certain point, shoppers began to move in the other direction. But the share-price losses that resulted were simply "givebacks" of prior gains, not harbingers of future underperformance. Frankly, unless you had bought consumer stocks very late in the game, you'd still be sitting on a large profit even after 1993—remember, those greedy price hikes worked to your advantage for a long time!

Besides, the idea of investing in leaders doesn't imply that the stocks won't have their bad patches; it simply means that they are preferable to the competition. And that can be especially true in difficult times.

One of the best examples of the dangers of second-tier consumer stocks is Borden. In August 1991, I had the good fortune to read a report on Borden written by food industry analyst Joanna Scharf, then at First Manhattan Corporation. The bold headline ran as follows:

UNDERINVESTMENT IN ADVERTISING WEAKENS BRAND FRANCHISES. The report revealed that Borden spent less than 1 percent of its sales on advertising, far less than the industry average of 7 percent.

If advertising were a waste of money, then Borden was making a brilliant move—but it isn't and they weren't. A survey taken at around that time revealed that virtually no one under the age of thirty had heard of Elsie the Cow (Borden's longtime corporate mascot). Not so coincidentally, Borden's dairy products found it difficult to cope with private-label competition.

Borden also experienced severe pricing pressures in the salted snacks business, where its Wise potato chips were up against formidable competitors such as Frito-Lay and Anheuser-Busch's Eagle Snacks. And Prince, Borden's pasta division, could no longer rely on Wednesday being Prince spaghetti day; their little boy, Anthony, had grown up, and Borden never really found an ad campaign to replace him.

The point is that Borden wasn't spending the money to truly position its products, and eventually the franchise crumbled. The combination of difficulties I just outlined caused earnings to fall dramatically, from the peak of $2.46 per share in 1990 to $2.30 in 1991, $1.67 in 1992, and $0.27 in 1993. In August 1991, Borden sold for $36 per share. By late 1994, when Kohlberg, Kravis, Roberts (KKR) made a move to acquire the company, it had fallen to just $12.

The Borden story also pokes another hole in the efficient market theory. At the time of Scharf's report, Borden was the cheapest stock in the packaged-food group; at $36 per share, it was trading at just fifteen times expected 1991 earnings, compared to twenty-plus multiples for first-tier companies such as Campbell Soup, Kellogg, and General Mills. But even this sharp discount wasn't enough, because Borden's ensuing 66 percent decline made it by far the worst performer of the group during the next three years. The moral: *When a company's fundamentals truly fall apart, even a low price/earnings ratio won't save you.* This is a recording.

OBJECTION 3: WHAT ABOUT IBM? Despite IBM's comeback under Louis Gerstner, many investors still hold this company up as the ultimate failure of investing in a leader. According to the principle of preemption, no one other than IBM could possibly be identified as *the* computer company. So how did its stock fall from $130 in 1983 to barely $40 in 1993?

Obviously, the full picture is a book in itself, but advertising can still paint some useful broad strokes. Remember that in 1983 investors felt that IBM could do anything it wanted. The IBM PC, as introduced by the Charlie Chaplin "tramp" ads in 1981, was a runaway success. But even though it was the only such success of that decade (can you name any other memorable IBM campaigns?), investors extrapolated from the PC and assumed that IBM would dominate all niche markets. It didn't happen. As IBM expanded, it left behind the lucrative safety of good positioning for disastrous fragmentation.

The failure of the heavily promoted PCjr for the home market was perhaps IBM's most visible failure in a smaller market, but there were more to follow. Supercomputers, workstations, even mail order—all were dominated by the competition, not by IBM. The moral is that when industries fragment, the broad position (i.e., IBM = computer) can become less valuable than the niche positions.

Actually, for many IBM shareholders, the biggest tragedy was that they *weren't* investing in the specialty companies that were taking business from IBM: Sun Microsystems, Cray, Dell, to name but a few. These companies were not to be viewed as secondary or tertiary computer companies; they were to be viewed as leaders in their respective fields. That may sound like semantics, but it's a crucial distinction—one that many IBM shareholders failed to notice.

WHEN TO SELL

Most investors realize that knowing when to sell is every bit as important as knowing when to buy. But how do we know what to look for? What is our advantage over the other guy? In our search for clues, we'll find that the sell signals from advertising can take many different forms.

When a Position Gets Abandoned

Following their 1984 classic, "Where's the beef?," Wendy's was the hottest thing going in the fast-food business. These three words were enough to make Clara Peller a media superstar, to send Gary Hart to the sidelines of the 1984 presidential race, and to send Wendy's sales up 20 percent in the twelve months that followed. It was an extraordinary accomplishment for the number-three player in the fast-food field.

The underlying message was simple: If you want fast food, go to McDonald's or Burger King; if you want a real hot and juicy hamburger, come to Wendy's. People did. And Wall Street noticed: Within six months of the campaign's debut, Wendy's stock had risen 50 percent.

Obviously, you can't say "Where's the beef?" forever, so the company's challenge was to find new ways of conveying the "hot and juicy" position. That's where they went wrong.

The Wendy's advertising juggernaut moved on to "Parts is parts," an offbeat campaign about chicken sandwiches that only *seemed* to represent continuity (the ads, like "WTB," were produced by Chicago's innovative Joe Sedelmaier). By thinking that humor, not the product, was the key to success, Wendy's unwittingly abandoned its "better hamburger" position. Said one former Wendy's executive, "After 'Where's the beef?' the arrogance in the marketing department was unbelievable."

That arrogance proved costly because the company simply wasn't expecting revenues to level off, as they did beginning in 1985. Expenses were higher than ever, and earnings began a multiyear decline. The stock, which peaked at $18 in 1986 amid rumors that Anheuser-Busch was preparing a takeover bid, fell to just $4 in 1990 before recovering. (By the way, the timing of the recovery was widely attributed to ads featuring Wendy's affable, portly founder, Dave Thomas; the ads were as square as a Wendy's hamburger, but they made the company visible again and reintroduced the notion that Wendy's served a high-quality product.)

There is a tortoise-and-hare aspect to the Wendy's investment story. As Clara Peller was doing the talk show circuit in 1984, McDonald's was coming out with "It's a good time for the great taste of

McDonald's." The campaign was the heir to such tag lines as "Your kind of place," "You deserve a break today," and "You, you're the one." None of these slogans created a sensation along the lines of "Where's the beef?," but when you're the industry leader that's not necessary or even desirable. Once you're on top, quiet reinforcement can be the best strategy to keep you there.

As I've said before, it often makes sense to stick with the proven leader in the field, and this case was no exception. By early 1995, McDonald's shares were up over sixfold from the "Where's the beef?" year of 1984. Wendy's, with all its fits and starts, was up only 25 percent—and it was still trading below its 1986 high.

Wayward Corporate Pride and the Principle of Unicity

Remember the principle of preemption and how it protected companies like Federal Express and Philip Morris from me-too competitors? Well, the principle of unicity is really the same thing, except it's from the *competitor's* point of view. Unicity basically means uniqueness, except that it sounds a little snazzier. The principle of unicity means that one product or product name cannot stand for two different things. Companies that violate this principle eventually become sell candidates.

For example, Kleenex—although a trademark—is thought of as the generic facial tissue: to many people it *means* facial tissue. Even if the company's plants could just as easily produce notebook paper, a Kleenex notebook paper would never work because the image of blowing one's nose into one's notes would be unshakable. Fortunately, Kleenex has never made that particular mistake, but many companies have made similar ones, and they and their investors have paid a price.

This principle is not always well understood by the investment community. For example, when Black & Decker bought GE's household appliance business in 1984, many portfolio managers were excited about the growth potential of this business. Largely on the strength of institutional buying, Black & Decker shares, which had traded as low as $18 in 1983, hit $28 by early 1984.

However, the principle of unicity suggested that the optimism was overdone. How could one brand name produce Workmates, Air Stations, and power tools (thereby achieving an image of "toughness") and also be associated with toasters and irons? It doesn't work.

I happen to own a Black & Decker toaster. It works fine. It even looks fine. But its name still looks funny. Whereas the GE name was a natural for appliances, Black & Decker's wasn't. If you shunned Black & Decker shares because of misplaced investor enthusiasm, you made the right move. The $28 share price of early 1984 was its high for the decade.

Note that the Edsel ad of an earlier section was a clear violation of the principle of unicity and a gigantic clue that the car wouldn't live up to its hype. By trying to be both elegant and low-priced, Ford assured that the Edsel would be perceived as neither. Any investor with a sense of positioning theory would have been on the sidelines as Ford shares dropped to an all-time low in the wake of the Edsel fiasco.

More recently, General Motors handed investors a sell signal with its "This is not your father's Oldsmobile" campaign from the mid-eighties. The campaign itself was actually quite well put together. It featured some well-known fathers and their not-so-well-known children (or vice versa) driving some cars that looked far too sporty to have a name like Oldsmobile.

The only problem was, that *was* their name and they were stuck with it. The attempt to make the Olds dog do new tricks was an outright violation of the principle of unicity. How does a consumer respond when told "This is not your father's Oldsmobile."

In three words: "Yes it is."

Not surprisingly, the Oldsmobile division of GM proceeded to have some very difficult times, even though its cars were arguably better than ever. In 1985, there were over one million Oldsmobiles sold in this country. By 1992, that figure had dropped by 50 percent. General Motors was losing market share to Ford, Chrysler, and just about everybody else. GM stock traded in the mid-30s in 1985 and remained there into the next decade.

You may be wondering something. If the "This is not . . ." line was so bad for Oldsmobile, why in the world did the title of this book borrow the same idea? Well, it all boils down to perceptions. If you know what your father's Oldsmobile is, there's no point in trying to convince you that it has changed. But whether or not you know what your father's stockpicking book was, it should be clear that this one is different. Positioning a new product can be a whole lot simpler than repositioning an old one.

Besides, my editor and I thought the title captured the spirit of the book. And you bought it, didn't you? Didn't you?!

Long-term Marketing Blunders

Even worse than Edsel and Oldsmobile are cases where you see a company's ads stretching directly into someone else's territory. One such "dual" violator was Eastman Kodak. Kodak's marketing malapropisms go a long way toward explaining why its stock—one of the 30 Dow Jones Industrials—was a notable laggard in the historic bull market of the eighties.

Kodak's initial violation was its lamentable move into instant photography in 1976. The move is best known for the patent infringement lawsuit it inspired, which ultimately required Kodak to pay Polaroid a gigantic settlement. But lawsuit or no lawsuit, Kodak was not destined to win the marketing battle. Polaroid *means* instant photography, and, to the company's credit, its ads never let you forget it. The old James Garner/Mariette Hartley spots showed the Polaroids fully developed before the two had finished their playful banter. Years later, Polaroid found a new angle with the strawberry ice-cream cone that melted right on top of a developed picture of itself. Great ad. There has never been any question about who owned the instant photography position.

It's not that Kodak couldn't hurt Polaroid by treading on its territory. By competing aggressively on the basis of price, Kodak was able to send its rival's earnings into a prolonged tailspin beginning in 1979, and within a few years Polaroid was fighting for its independence. On that basis, you could even argue that Kodak's litigation penalty was money was well spent, because the whole effort served to cripple a competitor. However, the point is that *Kodak* didn't benefit from instant photography as much as investors believed it would back in the launch year of 1976. Within two years, its stock had dropped by 66 percent and it continued to flounder thereafter.

But unicity would strike again. In 1986, Kodak announced its intention to enter the battery market, where it would be going head-to-head with the likes of Duracell and the Energizer. The problem here was that Kodak means camera, *not* battery. The company could have expected decent battery sales in camera stores, but it was going to be much tougher going in the supermarket checkout lines. The result was that Kodak lost untold millions on batteries between 1986 and 1993.

The reason I'm being vague with these numbers is that Kodak's marketing blunders don't show up as neatly identifiable points on the company's stock-price chart. Perhaps a better way to express the problem is that the instant photography and battery ventures created a constant negative drag on the stock (and the curious acquisition of Sterling Drug in 1988 didn't help, either). In fact, when Kodak shares finally perked up in 1993 after years of underperformance, the gains came from investor excitement about the old management being thrown out.

The companion principles of preemption and unicity sound so obvious it's hard to believe that companies ever violate them, but they do. One very good reason is that sinister agent called corporate pride. Inside a company, promoting that company's name is almost always politically correct, and conquering a brand-new market is even better. Suggesting that some other company owns the territory is not a prescription for climbing the corporate ladder.

Sometimes the violations occur simply because management has gotten restless. When Federal Express founder Fred Smith moved his company into the international marketplace in the eighties, the fathers of positioning theory disapproved: Federal owned the "overnight" label in the delivery business, but DHL owned "worldwide." But what would you expect Smith to do? Pioneers don't sit at home collecting dividends. They seek new worlds to conquer, even if it isn't in the cards. Today, DHL owns over 40 percent of the air delivery market in Europe, while FedEx's share is stuck somewhere in low single figures. (The double whammy of such restlessness is that companies can fail to reinforce their original positions. When you think about it, the heyday of great FedEx ads ended circa 1983. Since that time, the company has lost some of its exclusivity, and its stock has lagged far behind the overall market.)

One final reason why companies disregard the principle of unicity is that they view their own market as having matured. And they may be right. However, if management feels that way, perhaps shareholders should listen. Any way you slice it, these ventures into dangerous terrain give shareholders a good reason to get out.

Rip-offs of Prior Successes

The unfortunate truth is that great ads, like great positions, are almost always preemptive—they don't work nearly as well the second time around. The strategy of mimicking a proven winner occasionally works for ad agencies, but it practically never works for investors.

The Iacocca ads of the early eighties have already been designated as one of history's greatest "investor's" campaigns. However, when Chrysler again found itself struggling in 1987, Iacocca's repeat performance fell flat. The fact that the novelty had worn off was no surprise —he had appeared in forty-six different commercials since 1981. As Iacocca himself admitted in *Automotive News,* "I think people are tired of me coming into their living rooms."

Without a second bolt of lightning, Chrysler could only watch its balance sheet deteriorate and its stock price fall—from $50 in 1987 to just $10 in 1990—before it revived again. No, the ads didn't *cause* the decline; that's not the point. The point is, they couldn't be expected to *prevent* it.

Iacocca's early success not only colored his subsequent efforts, it also put an unwanted me-too label on other would-be turnaround campaigns. Several years later, when Martin Shugrue (who?) tried to save bankrupt Eastern Airlines, the potential turnaround might have tempted investors looking for "the next Chrysler." Like Iacocca, Shugrue (Eastern's bankruptcy trustee) was portrayed as confident in the face of peril. The ads didn't lack for drama, what with an impassioned speaker, hundreds of workers in an airport hangar, a proud airline with its name on the aircraft and its legacy on the line. But they didn't work.

Given the severity of Eastern's financial crisis, there is of course no guarantee that *any* ad could have saved them. But Iacocca's preemption of the corporate savior role practically guaranteed that this particular ad would not, because when the viewing public says "I've seen this before," the effect is lost. The ultimate result was that Eastern folded, and Martin Shugrue quickly disappeared from the limelight. It was a good reminder to investors that no two situations are precisely alike.

I should point out that ripping off prior successes is at least an annual event. Every January, a lot of otherwise rational corporations spend millions trying to duplicate the success of Apple's "1984" Super Bowl ad—the one with the brazen red-clad vixen (Apple) hurling a sledgehammer through monolithic Big Brother (IBM). The mimicry is understandable because Apple's sales rose by more than 50 percent in the year following that memorable challenge to Big Blue. But that was 1984. Don't expect it to happen again.

Clever Competition

We have seen that even strong positions can outlive their usefulness on Wall Street. But the timing of the eventual decline doesn't have to be guesswork. When competition hastens the demise of a position, you sometimes don't have to leave your television set to see the transition in progress: American Express is a case in point.

Before introducing the ads that told you to sell AmEx shares before its early nineties swoon, I should acknowledge that American Express has a long history of brilliant advertising—from 1973's pathbreaking "Do you know me?" campaign to Karl Malden's fear-inspiring "Don't leave home without it" to the widely praised Annie Leibovitz "Portraits" campaign of 1987 and beyond. The idea of all these campaigns, of course, was to promote the American Express card as *the* prestige credit card, enabling the company to command a premium from merchants and a high annual fee from cardholders. These were the basic factors that enabled American Express's flagship Travel Related Services division to be so profitable for so many years. In particular, during the eighties—the decade of prestige—American Express shares rose 400 percent.

However, as the economy slipped into recession in 1990, the company was looking more and more vulnerable. Said John Keefe of Lipper Analytical Services, "The [credit card] market has changed. Competition is no longer based on prestige or image—the competition is based on cost." In that regard, Amex was particularly ill-suited because of its high merchant user fees. In April 1991, when a movement led by a pair of Boston-based restaurateurs forced American Express to lower the rates that merchants had been paying to feature the card, AmEx shares quickly dropped from $30 to $25.

I had been recommending the stock prior to that time, but as a positioning theorist I knew enough to sell despite the drop. Unicity being what it is, American Express couldn't very well claim that it didn't stand for prestige anymore. That, coupled with the company's problems at its Shearson subsidiary, suggested a long recovery period. By the end of 1991, the stock was at $18.

However, just when I was starting to feel smug about avoiding the second part of the decline, I realized that the warning signs had been in place for over six years. The year of the watershed ad was 1985. The scene was Rosalie's, a restaurant in Marblehead, Massachusetts, and the storyboard was unforgettable. "But if you go there, remember: Bring a big appetite, and bring your Visa card. 'Cause at Rosalie's they don't take no for an answer . . . and they don't take American Express."

Uh-oh. Even back then, Visa was winning merchants on price and customers on availability—from Rosalie's in Marblehead to Captain John's in Bermuda to Doyle's in Sydney Harbor—and its ads were positioning it accordingly. Between 1986 and 1991, Visa's worldwide market share rose from 44.3 percent to 50.9, while AmEx's share fell from 21.7 percent to 16.4. Remember that "sudden" change in AmEx's fortunes? There was nothing sudden about it.

As an important footnote, I should add that this lag time between a positioning problem and a stock's demise is not unusual, because the stock market doesn't really understand positioning theory—if it did, where would our advantage be? This means that you don't have to sell the first instant you smell trouble. But also realize that when the stock market finally sees the problem, it will have years of catching up to do —and the result is seldom pretty.

Positions Whose Time Has Passed

At some point, even the best positions can be brought down by social or technological change. The key for investors is to recognize when a company may be battling a lost cause.

When Wall Street Meets Madison Avenue **261**

A case in point is Wang Labs, which went from highflier to cellar dweller in a matter of a few short years. It's worth examining the blueprint of that descent because it happens over and over again. What we will discover is that *ads that don't say anything* can be the clue that a position is past its prime.

First, the background. Wang Labs made its real killing in the late seventies, when the company became the dominant force in office word processing systems. In our preferred jargon, they owned the "dedicated word processor" position, and it served them well for many years. Between 1977 and 1984, Wang's revenues increased from $134 million to $2.2 billion, for a compound annual growth rate of 49 percent. The stock rose more than twentyfold during those seven glorious years. (Money manager Robin Maynard gave me the idea back in 1978. Thanks, Robin.)

Unfortunately for Wang, as the personal computer came of age, word processing shifted from a hardware function to a software function. The concept of a dedicated word processor became a dinosaur, and Wang had nowhere to go. The company's peak earnings of $209 million in 1984 were never approached again. Losses started appearing in 1987 and became heavy losses in 1989–90. Wang ended up declaring bankruptcy in 1992, its share price having come full circle— from $2 to $40 down to $2 again.

The clues offered by Wang's advertising seemed faint but were actually quite powerful. Three separate campaigns from the mid-eighties did a wonderful job of exposing Wang's identity crisis.

First there was the short-lived print campaign that proclaimed "We're shooting bullets at IBM." The question was, With what? Never mind that IBM itself was becoming a downward-sliding target. Advertising that brags about becoming number one is one of the most worrisome types around. Products get you there, not aspirations, and this ad worked wonders in telling you about the new products that Wang *didn't* have.

Other ads were even more vague in their intent. There was the guy on a motorcycle with the Wang nameplate emblazoned on his helmet, symbolizing speed. Finally, there were the "compuspeak" ads, wherein office managers threw around technological buzzwords that meant nothing to the populace but were supposed to impress them anyway.

Where was Wang's position in all this? It had vanished. But before you criticize these vapid campaigns, realize that ad people aren't entirely stupid. They know when a message is tired, or ill suited to a company's future. Typically, when a company has nothing new to say the ad people will try a smoke-screen play, and draping Wang in "technology stuff" was the result. (What are they supposed to do, resign the account?)

The real problem was that Wang did not own the concept of technological superiority, and the ads certainly weren't about to give it to them. In general, one of the most gruesome mistakes investors can make with a once-successful company is separating the company (Wang) from the position that made it successful (the dedicated word processor). Somehow we believe that one will come back even when we know that the other won't. It can be a costly mistake.

Celebrity Ads

I couldn't let this section close without taking a brief jab at celebrity endorsements. They probably won't hurt your investments much, but they're not likely to help you out, either.

The problem boils down to common sense. If it isn't obvious that the celebrity uses the product in question, the ad is usually doomed to failure: Eleanor Roosevelt for Good Luck margarine, Joan Rivers for Faygo beverages, quasi vegetarian Cybill Shepherd for the U.S. beef association. And what about those Christmastime ads with Santa Claus for Norelco electric razors? When's the last time you saw him shave?

When evaluating celebrity ads, use the simple screen of believability. The American Express "Do you know me?" campaign worked because seeing was believing. We saw the name of the mystery celebrity typed right onto the card.

As it turns out, actors and actresses are more believable as pitchmen and -women when they appear in character! Gavin MacLeod was a perfect match for Princess Cruises, but only because viewers perceived him as Captain Merrill Stubing of *Love Boat* fame. Similarly, Tim Allen of *Home Improvement* was a natural to do ads for Builder's Square.

The best "in character" campaign was Nike's "Air Jordan" campaign of 1984, which launched the most successful product in the company's history and helped trigger a tenfold increase in its share price. Years later, when Spike Lee gaped at Jordan's leaping and suggested "It's gotta be the shoes," the idea seemed quite believable. He *was* wearing them! For that matter, Jordan did a pretty good job of pitching Gatorade.

But when Jordan signed a multimillion-dollar deal with Sara Lee in 1992, the synergy was less obvious, and the investment hopes nonexistent. "It's gotta be the pound cake?" Again, common sense prevails.

DIFFERENT ROUTES TO SUCCESS

In case you've grown weary of positioning theory, herewith a breather. It is possible to make money from some completely different categories of ads, many of which are neither creative nor effective—at least, not in the sense to which we have become accustomed. Here's what to look for in these nonstandard successes:

The Overly Proud Parent

Because we have been lauding companies with a sharply defined focus, as well as the advertising campaigns that reflect such a focus, conglomerates have been ruled out of our discussion. However, it turns out that there is a perfectly good model for an investor's conglomerate ad.

Remember "We're Beatrice!"? If you watched the 1984 Olympics you'd never forget it. Carl Lewis wins the long jump. Time for a commercial break. A close-up of a carton of Tropicana orange juice: A voice cries out "We're Beatrice!" Next commercial break—a snapshot of some Samsonite luggage. "We're Beatrice!" Et cetera. Ad nauseam.

The logic behind the Beatrice campaign sounded like it came from a boardroom pep rally. "We decided that strong corporate identification can do a lot to reinforce our brands, and our strong brands can help reinforce the Beatrice name," said Beatrice's director of marketing. In other words, once consumers realize that Beatrice makes all these wonderful products, they'll all be better off.

Yikes! Beatrice apparently didn't realize that the only way the campaign could have worked is if advertising in general did not work. Admittedly, it may be silly to associate Orville Redenbacher's Gourmet Popping Corn with a small-town entrepreneur instead of a large corporation, but surely the maintenance of that imagery has been crucial to the brand's success—likewise, the down-home folksiness of Keebler and Pepperidge Farm.

Unfortunately, "We're Beatrice!" was nothing but a reminder that all that imagery was bunk. *Madison Avenue* magazine realized the problem immediately. "People bought Fisher nuts, Swiss Miss Cocoa Mix and Samsonite luggage before they knew they were from Beatrice. Why not leave well enough alone?"

Indeed. Corporate pride notwithstanding, why spend all that money ($29 million) to make consumers aware of the name Beatrice when they couldn't go out and *buy* a Beatrice? Well, that was the one saving grace. The one place where you could buy a Beatrice was the New York Stock Exchange.

Remember, it was 1984, when betting on corporate takeovers was the investment game of choice. Beatrice, with a bunch of disparate divisions and a cheap stock price (*because* of all those disparate divisions), was a prime takeover candidate.

In that context, the Beatrice campaign brought the takeover game to the masses by unveiling the company's vast holdings for all to see. Rewards were fairly swift. Two years after the ads first aired, Beatrice was taken over by KKR (Kohlberg, Kravis, Roberts) for $50 per share, up 66 percent from the stock's levels of mid-1984. Just because an ad is lousy doesn't mean it can't make you money.

The Beatrice campaign was actually a corporate identity campaign, which is not unusual in and of itself. For example, when you see PepsiCo advertise on MacNeil/Lehrer, you'll find out that the company owns Kentucky Fried Chicken, Pizza Hut, Taco Bell, and Frito-Lay. *The Wall Street Journal* also houses many such corporate campaigns, because part of the idea of these campaigns is to stir up investor interest and get a company's stock price up. The consumer orientation of "We're Beatrice!" is what made it so different.

However, if we want to apply the Beatrice concept to future stock market successes—and we do—we need to look at a similar campaign that didn't work out as well.

When "It is ITT" debuted in 1986, it might have looked like Beatrice all over again. Following the Beatrice theme, the ads listed such holdings as Rayonier Timberlands, Hartford Insurance, and Sheraton Hotels—all safely nestled under ITT's corporate umbrella. Again, the message seemed to be that all of these individual units were somehow rendered superior by the ITT cachet. And, again, that was false. Do people really check in to a Sheraton because ITT owns it? It was Beatrice, stage two—except for one teensy-weensy detail.

The detail was that ITT, unlike Beatrice, wasn't a takeover candidate! At the same time that the "It is ITT" campaign was making its appearances in the media, ITT chairman Rand Araskog was busy penning a book called *How I Fought Off the Raiders* (published, ultimately, in 1988) in which he outlined the tactical maneuvers he employed to ward off such corporate predators as Jay Pritzker, Philip Anschutz, and Irwin Jacobs. Typical of the greedy eighties, however, the maintenance of ITT's independence was a defeat for shareholders; with the takeover possibilities gone, ITT stock went sideways for many years. Unless you bought shares early (the stock peaked in precrash 1987), you were out of luck.

Given that takeovers may never again be as prominent as they were in the eighties, we should broaden our scope when looking at conglomerates and their ads. Rather than relying on a takeover, one hope is that a conglomerate will either sell losing divisions or spin off winning ones.

Gerber and Xerox were stocks that benefited from outright sales of divisions. Gerber rose more than 150 percent in 1988–89 when the company's divestment of its furniture and transportation businesses led to a sharp rise in earnings. Xerox shares rose 10 percent in the first two months of 1993, after the company's announcement that it would sell its financial services unit, including its Crum and Forster insurance subsidiary. I can't help but point out that these actions were overdue from an advertising point of view: Xerox, after all, is "The Document Company," while Gerber has said for years that "Babies are our business, our only business." (Note: When Sandoz of Switzerland wanted to get into that business, they bought Gerber—at a substantial premium—in 1994.)

The appeal of spin-offs is that divisions of large corporations tend to be accorded higher valuations when they become freestanding entities—in other words, the sum of the parts can be worth more than the whole. Examples of this phenomenon at work would include Sears's 1993 spin-off of Dean Witter Discover, part of the dismantling of the company's ill-starred diversification into financial services. Sears stock had been a laggard for many years but advanced over 25 percent as the spin-off effort took shape. Sears stock also got a nice nudge in late 1994 upon announcing a similar spin-off of its Allstate Insurance subsidiary. Finally, when none other than ITT split itself into three companies—insurance, industrial products, and entertainment—in June 1995, its stock was up 30 percent for the first half of the year.

If I've just made conglomerate investing look ridiculously easy, let me set things straight. Obviously the major rub is that you don't know *when* these events are going to happen. Some investors wait years for corporate behemoths to "enhance shareholder value," during which time the stocks can go absolutely nowhere. It is therefore especially good news that advertising offers clues to the timing of these restructuring maneuvers. A good example is the corporate identification campaign of Greyhound/Dial.

The Greyhound Corporation used to be a full-fledged conglomerate. In addition to the bus lines that bore the house name, Greyhound also owned a manufacturing business, a financial subsidiary, and some well-known consumer brands (Dial soap, Brillo scouring pads, Purex bleach). The company's print advertising tried to remind people of this diversity, but the ads were a lost cause. Even after the company sold its then money-losing bus line in 1987, Greyhound still meant bus, period. Anyone who thought otherwise didn't understand the principle of unicity.

The ads started taking a new twist in February 1990, when the company changed its name from Greyhound to Greyhound Dial. The idea of the name change and the advertising was to call attention to the consumer division. A year later, the company shed the Greyhound name altogether and became simply Dial. I know it sounds horribly naive, but the stock could have been bought on the basis of the name changes alone. More than that, it *should* have been bought, because Dial shares doubled by early 1992. Was the company simply doing well? Maybe. But there was another important reason for the stock's rise.

To get to that reason, imagine you were the director of research at a Wall Street brokerage firm. When Greyhound was really a mishmash of very different companies, who would you hire to analyze it? Someone with a background in transportation? Airport services? Brillo pads? Who on earth is qualified to analyze all these businesses?

The answer is, not many. It is for that reason that conglomerates are often "undercovered" by Wall Street. But once Dial made a commitment to the consumer side (recall that no one believed it until the name was changed), the stock had two things going for it. First, consumer products companies are consistently valued higher relative to earnings than are conglomerates—or bus companies, for that matter. Second, Dial could now be covered by the same analysts who followed other household products companies, meaning that there would be more people to spread the story around. The dramatic increase in brokerage sponsorship of Dial was an important factor in the stock's ascent.

Note that Dial told you precisely what it was doing through its advertising. And remember for the future that a name change is never taken lightly within a corporation, because the change represents nothing less than a shedding of its heritage. As an investor, you can be certain that the company intends to make good on its newfound efforts to achieve focus.

Surprise Benefits from Industry Ad Wars

When we see two or more companies from the same industry paying big bucks to wage an advertising war, the natural question to ask is, "Who will win?" But investors shouldn't let their competitive streaks get the best of them. The more important underlying investment message may be that *the industry itself* holds great promise. The cola wars were a perfect example.

Recall that the modern-day Coke/Pepsi battle started in 1984, when Pepsi hired Michael Jackson, fresh from *Thriller* album superstardom, to do some television spots. This move was consistent with the youth position the company had staked out years before with "The Pepsi Generation." Nonetheless, Coke countered with a few celebrities of its own, and the battle was on.

The cola wars were a paradox. On the one hand, their believability was nil, as you'd expect from most celebrity campaigns. When *The*

Wall Street Journal challenged readers to match up stars like Art Carney, Vanna White, Madonna, and Billy Crystal with the soda brands they represented (Coke, diet Coke, Pepsi, and Diet Pepsi, respectively), the editors were rightly confident that readers didn't have a clue. However, even as the celebrity ads drew more and more criticism, a funny thing happened on the stock market: *Both* Coke and Pepsi won the war.

In the words of one Wall Street beverage analyst, "In the two-person debate between Coke and Pepsi, the onlookers forgot there was anyone else." Meaning that consumers didn't *buy* anything else. In effect, the celebrity dueling made cola hip, enabling both Coke and Pepsi to increase their already dominant market shares at the expense of weaker brands.

One of the victims was 7UP (Uncola, unhip?), whose share of the domestic soft drink market plummeted by more than one-third, from 7.0 percent to 4.2, between 1985 and 1990. Meanwhile, Coke and Pepsi's combined share went from 66.2 percent to 72.2. Within the decimal point angst of the market share game, these were huge shifts: Each percentage point represented almost 80 million cases of soda.

Couple that with international success (Coke) and impressive results in the restaurant business (Pepsi) and you had everything an investor could ask for. Coke and Pepsi each outperformed the Dow by nearly 3 to 1 between 1984 and the end of the decade. Rather than asking the question "Coke or Pepsi?," you could have bought both stocks and called it a day.

The same strategy could have been applied at one time or another to such famous battles as Apple versus IBM (early eighties) or Nike versus Reebok (mid-eighties and beyond). Remember, these battles were not price wars. The reason these battles occurred was that the industries in question offered tremendous growth opportunities. When that happens, there is a case for buying both stocks and holding on until the ads disappear. After all, the only time you really have to pick the best stock in an industry is when you've picked the wrong industry.

The Bad-Ad Rebound

Our final source of nonstandard successes arises from some truly bad campaigns—worse than the "Man from Glad," worse than "Ring around the collar." I'm not talking about flawed positioning campaigns, which can hurt a company for years. Instead, I'm talking about the sort of gaffe that can *temporarily* turn a perfectly respectable company into a national disgrace. Assuming you don't own the stock already, you could have a terrific opportunity on your hands.

Advertising gaffes go back to April 1954, when, on Westinghouse-sponsored *Studio One*, a refrigerator door refused to open on live TV. (You can be sure if it's Westinghouse?) Of course, the stock market doesn't necessarily care about such trivialities: People still placed Westinghouse buy orders on the trading floor the next day, stuck door or no stuck door.

However, we will see that embarrassing campaigns do have the power to bring a stock down in the near term. When that happens, by all means buy on weakness; the idea is that the flawed campaign will be short and that the stock will quickly return to where it was before the trouble started. These opportunities aren't exactly plentiful, but the following examples establish a nice pattern.

Sex and the Single Stock

In 1971, a stock market opportunity arose from an ad campaign that pushed women over the edge.

It's not that advertising had never demeaned women before. But the fifties and sixties passed with only transient dissatisfaction at the saccharine-sweet women who purveyed household wares on TV—from nameless housewives who saw white tornadoes to Carmelita Pope, the eternally perky spokesperson for PAM. Then came 1971, and adman Bill Free's infamous "Fly me" campaign for National Airlines.

"I'm Margie, fly me," cooed the stewardess. (Yes, stewardess. They weren't flight attendants yet.) In 1967, the campaign just might have worked. But by 1971, the women's movement had begun in earnest. *Ms.* magazine was launched the very next year, in some sense foreshadowed by the streams of protests that found their way to Bill Free's office. The stock market seemed ashamed: National shares lost one-third of their value between June and August of that year.

Funny thing, though. As off-putting as the campaign may have been, it worked. National, which earlier in 1971 had omitted its first-quarter dividend to save cash, enjoyed renewed profitability on sharply higher sales in the wake of "Fly me." For investors, this translated into a major opportunity: After its summer slide, National stock rose 150 percent between September 1971 and April 1972.

National's ascent finally fell victim to a prolonged decline in the overall market, but with any luck we would have been out of the stock by then. Remember, the idea of the rebound strategy is to profit from the stock's return to normal levels. Once that happens, it's time to say good-bye. (Incidentally, the final good-bye for National Airlines came in 1980, when it was acquired by Pan Am.)

Sage Herb

In the eighties, Burger King's "Herb" fiasco had no peers in the lousy campaign category, dwarfing even such forgettables as Reebok's 1989 "U.B.U." campaign and Max Headroom for the ill-fated New Coke (although, in Max's case, the *product* was the problem, not the messenger). The idea behind the Herb campaign was that customers would flock to Burger Kings across the country in hopes of seeing Herb, a nerdy fellow who looked disturbingly like Roxanne's first husband on *L.A. Law*. The campaign was a miserable failure.

But this created a buying opportunity, not for Burger King itself but for J. Walter Thompson, the publicly held agency that created the ad! J. Walter Thompson was already a struggling agency when the Herb ads hit the airwaves in 1986. Even the Burger King account, worth some $200 million in annual billings, couldn't prevent a sizable loss in the first quarter of 1987, and JWT stock sagged.

But when the "Herb" fallout led to Burger King's putting its account up for review in May 1987, JWT was particularly vulnerable to outside predators. Said Richard Morgan in *J. Walter Takeover*, "The Burger King review . . . provided the 'trigger point' for Martin Sorrell's successful takeover."

Martin Sorrell was CEO of Britain's WPP Group. The WPP, as it happens, stood for Wire and Plastic Products, but Sorrell had been introduced to the world of advertising by Charles and Maurice Saatchi, and, like the Saatchi brothers, he was intent on acquiring advertising companies.

Even though J. Walter Thompson wasn't earning any money, the stock had tremendous appeal as an asset play. The long and short of it is that in the summer of 1987, WPP Group gave JWT shareholders a present that they wouldn't lose in the stock market crash a few months later. WPP acquired J. Walter Thompson for $55 per share, twice the level JWT was trading at when Herb the nerd was being laughed off Madison Avenue.

Bear Trap

Personally, I didn't profit from either "Fly me" (before my time) or "Herb the nerd" (asleep at the switch). But the reason to study such examples is that they establish patterns. When Volvo came out with its disastrous "Bear Foot" campaign in 1990, I was ready.

As you may recall, the ill-starred campaign pictured an unscathed Volvo popping out from a row of cars that had been destroyed by an oversized truck named Bear Foot. The picture was vivid and awfully impressive—until the news broke that the resilient Volvo had been structurally reinforced. The company that for a generation had stood for safety and integrity saw its position tainted by fraud.

That year had already been a difficult one for Volvo. Automakers were quick to feel the global recession that began that summer, and Volvo's sales were down 11 percent in the first ten months of 1990. During this time, Volvo shares dropped precipitously, from $72 to $46. When the "Bear Foot" scam was unmasked in early November, the stock began yet another drop.

When was the right time to buy? When embarrassment was greatest, of course. By November 14, when the papers reported that ad agency Scali, McCabe, Sloves had resigned the Volvo account, the stock had dropped to $36.

A buying point anywhere near $36 would have worked out quite nicely. The agency took the rap for the flawed campaign, and Volvo never really lost the all-important "safety" position. By April 1991, Volvo shares were back up to $46 and beyond, even without a turn-around in the company's basic business. Consistent with Volvo's return to business as usual, later ads featured vignettes of people around the world who owed their lives to a Volvo. "Bear Foot" had lapsed into history.

That's the nature of the bad-ad rebound. The fundamental principle is that memories can be short. Whatever embarrassment the ads might have caused, there comes a day when people are willing to forgive and forget.

"Soft" Inferences

There is room for one more arrow in the ad investor's quiver, but you'll have to give me even more license than I've asked for already. In this section we will look for meaning in ads even when the immediate investment connection is far too weak to act on. These are what I call "soft inferences."

The reason soft inferences are important is that the stock market involves more "gray area" decisions than most people realize—and, alas, far more than you'll ever read about. Most articles and books on the stock market are sculpted to be as black and white as possible.

The problem with any black-and-white investment approach is that the real world isn't nearly that accommodating. Although you can make a lot of money by hitting the big moments right (Federal Express, 1978; Chrysler, 1981), these historic moments are by definition outnumbered by those occasions when an investor has to scratch and claw to come out ahead. My definition of scratching and clawing is seeing the bullish possibilities of some very faint clues.

Disney's "What's next?": A Role Model

In January 1987, it surely looked too late to buy shares in the Walt Disney Company. The Michael Eisner–led management team had already been in place for three years. Theme park ticket prices were 50 percent higher than they were in 1984. Income from filmed entertainment had surged from $2.2 million in 1984 to over $50 million in 1986. The stock had already tripled off its 1984 low.

In fact, the only thing that made January of 1987 at all special was that New York Giants quarterback Phil Simms introduced the phrase "I'm going to Disney World" after the Giants won Super Bowl XXI. But so what? You don't buy stocks because of some cute advertising gimmick.

Or do you? At a minimum, the campaign was an extraordinary public relations coup for Disney. Following the Simms inaugural, "What's next?" went on to L.A. Lakers heroes Magic Johnson and Kareem Abdul-Jabbar, figure skating gold medalist Brian Boitano, even to 1988 Miss America Gretchen Carlson.

Not everybody enjoyed this mousification of America. Wrote Tony Kornheiser of *The Washington Post,* "What's next for Disney? . . . Putting Mickey Mouse ears on NFL football helmets? . . . Racing the Absent Minded Professor's flubber sedan in the Indianapolis 500? . . . Entering 101 Dalmatians in the Iditarod?" In fact, Disney/Anaheim *would* later snag a National Hockey League franchise, the Mighty Ducks, named for a highly successful film from Disney's Touchstone division. Then came the purchase of a 25 percent stake in the California Angels, a follow-up to the 1994 hit *Angels in the Outfield.* What's next indeed.

But investors should take note of the "soft" inference: Such resentment wouldn't have been there if the Walt Disney Company hadn't been making money—a lot of money. In 1984, a down year, the company earned $98 million. By 1987, the take had risen to over $444 million.

The "What's next?" campaign crystallized the combination of commercialism and magic that the Walt Disney Company had always stood for, and there was no rule that said the magic had to end. As things turned out, Disney's corporate winning streak stayed intact until the EuroDisney debacle of 1992; by that time, the stock had tripled from its January 1987 level, and even then there were better times ahead.

This is not the time to get caught up in causality. I know that "What's next?" wasn't the *cause* of Disney's share-price rise, so please don't write. But if an ad like that doesn't make you curious about what lies behind it, well, you're not maximizing your precious ad-watching time.

Ideas from Ads That May Still Be Running

Remember, ads are always trying to tell you something. If you want to be a true ad investor, you have to start reading companies' minds as to why their advertising took the form it did. This isn't as hard as you think, as we'll see by quickly dissecting a few ad campaigns of the nineties.

AMERICAN AIRLINES.

"Going home, Mr. Reynolds?"

"I'm halfway there."

Remember that one? The U.S. businessman on assignment in South America. Day after day of meetings and deals. Finally, the return trip and the sight of the American Airlines jet. That's when he's halfway home.

The idea of the ad is simple: to increase American's share of overseas markets. Think about it. If you were planning a trip to Switzerland, wouldn't your first impulse be to go SwissAir? It sounds like much more fun than flying *American*. The same is true of British Airways to London or Qantas to Australia. Merely being the airline that is known for its destination will get you a lot of business. The bummer for American Airlines is that as long as there are round-trip tickets, the foreign carriers will get the return trip even though American has the name of the destination! The clever part of the ad was getting travelers to think of the return trip first.

It was no coincidence that American was targeting its South American routes, because at that time many U.S. carriers had been faring poorly with their international operations. For example, Delta bought Pan Am's transatlantic routes in late 1991 and proceeded to lose mightily, including a $400 million loss in 1993. Delta stock, which had risen from $60 to $75 in the months following the acquisition, fell to just $40 in early 1994 when the company announced a significant reorganization of its European operation.

Would we have lost money on Delta? I hope not. If an established international name like Pan Am couldn't prosper in the transatlantic market, what was Delta bringing to the party other than a name that didn't fit? As for American, its clever ad promised absolutely nothing in the way of investment returns, but it *did* suggest that investors should look to the international division for signs of improved performance. If the company thought the problem was important enough to tackle with its advertising, why shouldn't we follow its lead?

COOL MINT LISTERINE. The ads for Cool Mint Listerine debuted in 1992 with a lot of plusses. Set against an animated tropical backdrop, they showed a Caribbean blue Listerine bottle swinging through an iridescent green jungle, complete with Tarzan-like yells and a catchy theme song. The voice-over that added the words "Cooool Mint" was so rich in tone, so effortlessly mellifluous, you'd swear the guy had beaten out Pavarotti for the part.

A great new taste from Listerine? What could be better? We might think it would be successful, and we'd be right. In its first year, Cool Mint captured a more-than-respectable market share of 6.6 percent.

But which mouthwash brand was this new entry likely to be taking share from, Scope or the old Listerine? Clearly, the latter, if you know your ad history. Listerine's position was the original, and it owned the market for decades. Scope countered in the seventies by attacking Listerine as "medicine breath," thereby carving out the "good-tasting" position for itself. Listerine then re-countered with "The taste you hate, twice a day" (subtext: I wonder if that good-tasting mouthwash can really kill the germs that cause bad breath?).

But the name Cool Mint Listerine is basically an admission that Listerine tastes bad. In Cool Mint's inaugural year, sales of regular Listerine plunged 17 percent; Scope, with a 3 percent gain, went unscathed. Gulp.

If you missed that inference, you were protected by the "Speedy Alka-Seltzer" syndrome: Listerine accounts for only a small percentage of the sales of parent company Warner-Lambert, so even a serious loss of Listerine's market share wasn't likely to hurt Warner-Lambert's stock. But the next time you see a consumer company jeopardize its flagship product this way, you might consider hitting the sell button.

IBM AND INTEL.   Some ads say a lot just by being there. The "Intel inside" ads that debuted in 1992 were in that category, because they symbolized an enormous power shift within the personal computer industry.

Intel had first gained renown a decade earlier, when it was selected as the chip supplier for the IBM PC. But consumers didn't care about the chip makers back then. Thanks to IBM's massive marketing effort, the IBM name was really the value-added component.

Ten years later, the situation was reversed! Intel was trying to reorient computer purchases by calling attention to the nuts and bolts of the computer, never mind whose name was on the outside.

The reason these ads were a "soft" buy signal for Intel is that the company wouldn't have been advertising in this way if it didn't have a huge opportunity on its hands. The ads were brash, they were pre-emptive, and they helped set Intel apart from other chip makers. Intel shares were up 78 percent in 1992 alone. Inquisitive ad watchers could have helped themselves to at least part of that gain.

By the way, it was only fitting that 1992 was one of the worst years ever for IBM shares, which fell 43 percent.

IBM AND AMERICAN EXPRESS.   So what did IBM do following its worst year ever? It changed its advertising strategy. Yes, I know, it changed CEOs, too, but we're just looking at the ads, remember?

Anyway, as Lou Gerstner came in from RJR Nabisco to the top spot at IBM in 1993, IBM ads sought to improve the company's downtrodden image by aligning it with some successful companies that just happened to be IBM customers: Callaway Golf, Nintendo, Tower Records. Clearly, IBM felt that associating with these success stories might rub off.

The idea of IBM playing a latch-on game would have been unthinkable just years earlier, but it was worth noticing. It wasn't long before investors started hearing about "the new IBM."

As for IBM shares, they bobbed up and down for months after that but eventually broke out of their slump, jumping over 10 percent in one day in April 1994, upon the announcement of a surprising first-quarter profit. Lou Gerstner's cost cutting was paying off. The same thing happened in the second quarter, and so on. By the summer of 1995, IBM was pushing $100 per share, 150 percent higher than its interim low. The role of the ads was in telling you that IBM was a very different company.

At the same time, American Express was advertising in a very similar way. Obviously AmEx had more of a tradition of aligning themselves with famous people of one sort or another, but what distinguished the 1993 campaign from its predecessors was that corporate icons were used: leaders such as Anita Roddick of the Body Shop, Charles Lazarus of Toys "Я" Us, and Herb Kelleher of Southwest Airlines.

The similarity of the IBM and American Express ads was no coincidence, because both companies were in a transitional stage. Gerstner had replaced John Akers atop IBM, and Harvey Golub had replaced James Robinson atop American Express. Both companies wanted to salvage their names; both used the same technique; and, ultimately, both stocks rebounded from their multiyear downdrafts. Giving these turnarounds a final flourish was the fact that IBM and American Express shares outperformed virtually all of the high-flying companies they aligned themselves with in their advertising.

PUTTING IT ALL TOGETHER: FOURTEEN YEARS OF INVESTING IN LONG DISTANCE

By now I've told you everything I know about ad-based investing. But I thought I'd add one more section to see how our principles hold up in a real-time setting.

Our testing ground will be the long-distance industry, one of the most active advertising arenas in recent years. Since 1980, there have been many different occasions when advertising clues could have helped us out. As usual (boilerplate caveat coming up), advertising does not provide the basis for every single investment decision that has arisen among long-distance companies. But it holds a lot more answers than you might think. In fact, it starts with a bang.

1980–83: The Glory Years of MCI

MCI had been around for over a decade before it advertised on television. Described as "a law firm with an antenna on top" by tenacious founder William McGowan, MCI's early years amounted to one legal battle after another as the company sought the right to compete with AT&T, *the* phone company. But our story begins on March 3, 1980, when MCI unveiled the first-ever counterposition to AT&T in a test campaign in Denver, Colorado. What people saw was MCI's "split screen" ad, which showed two meters running during a phone call. When the call had ended, the AT&T meter was north of $6.00; the MCI meter came in at $3.07.

The campaign struck an immediate chord. Before the seventies, there was no alternative to a high phone bill. Now there was MCI. Even if it took some extra effort to make calls through MCI (twenty-two digits, at its worst), the idea of cheap long distance was a godsend. Within twenty-four hours of the ad's debut, MCI's Denver sales office received over a thousand inquiries. Management quickly scrapped a planned regional test and went national with the campaign. It was time to buy shares.

MCI had been a public company since 1972, so getting in in 1980 didn't seem early. But it seldom pays to do investment planning through the rearview mirror. Besides, the company's original thrusts were directed to business customers; the vast residential market represented a brand-new arena for growth, meaning that we ad-based investors had a real opportunity on our hands.

As is often true of niche positions, MCI's relatively small size was at the root of its investment appeal. If AT&T lost one-half of one percentage point of residential market share, so what? At MCI, though, gaining that half point could mean going from a 1 percent share to a 1.5 percent share—in other words, 50 percent revenue growth. As the following table shows, the company achieved that and more.

MCI REVENUES: 1979–83 ($ MIL)

1979	1980	1981	1982	1983
144	234	506	1,073	1,665

For most of this period, earnings per share were growing at an even faster clip than revenues. The beauty of the MCI investment story was that the stock was having some of its best years when the market as a whole was going absolutely nowhere. On March 3, 1980, the Dow Jones Industrial Average closed at 854.35. Two years later, it stood at 815.16, a decline of 4.6 percent. Meanwhile, shares of MCI moved from $6⅜ to $32⅞, a gain of over 400 percent. (The prices are not adjusted for subsequent splits.)

As these gains were being made, MCI's advertising changed, but only on the surface: The theme was always low costs. (Finding different ways to convey the same message is reminiscent of the Federal Express example, as it should be. Both accounts were handled by Ally & Gargano.)

First there was the famous "rocking chair" campaign. The plot was straightforward: Old lady sits comfortably in rocking chair; AT&T bill arrives; lady and chair fall to the floor.

Then there was the middle-aged man who sees his wife distressed after getting off the phone.

> HUSBAND: "Have you been talking to our son long-distance again?"
> WIFE: (She nods through her sobbing.)
> HUSBAND: "Did he tell you how much he loves you? And did he tell you how well he's doing in school? All those things are wonderful. What on earth are you crying for?"
> WIFE: (Finally, she breaks her silence.) "Have you seen our long-distance bill?!"

Finding fresh new ways to convey the same underlying message is the hallmark of great advertising, and this stuff was truly brilliant.

Working together, the ads made America know this company. Who knew that the initials MCI stood for Microwave Communications, Inc.? No one. Who knew that MCI *meant* cheap long distance? Everyone. As the tag line said, MCI was "the nation's long-distance phone company." *That's* a position.

The sobbing ad came in 1982, and MCI was still on a roll. Earnings per share for 1982 were up 85 percent from their levels of 1981. The stock, now a favorite of institutional money managers, tripled between March 1982 (where we last left it) and mid-1983. So far, so good.

1983-87: AT&T the Blue Chip

How long do you ride such positions? For as long as they hold up. As we've discovered, that decision can sometimes be a gray one, but in MCI's case it was clear.

MCI's rosy prospects came to an abrupt halt in July 1983 when the FCC ruled that the company would have to pay higher "access charges" (payments to local telephone networks to complete long-distance calls). Until then, MCI's access charges were less than half of what AT&T was required to pay, a key component of MCI's ability to charge less. (Note: Buying MCI shares because of the company's low-cost position was a good idea. Not knowing *why* they had the lowest costs was a bad idea.)

The published FCC ruling was released in late August. MCI shares, which had already been suspiciously trickling down from their high of $28, dropped 25 percent in one day, from $20⅜ to $15¼. (The stock had twice split 2-for-1 in the 1982–83 period.) But had the stock bottomed out? As with American Express and Wang Labs, the answer was no.

Those who knew the power of the low-cost position would have understood that the company was in for a difficult stretch. With its cost structure permanently altered, MCI found itself struggling to post a profit. Between 1983 and 1987, MCI's annual local interconnection expenses rose from $262 million to *$1.9 billion*. Earnings dropped from $0.84 per share in 1982 to $0.78 in 1983, to $0.38 in 1984, and all the way down to $0.06 per share in 1986. During this same time, the stock declined over 80 percent.

Also during this time, MCI's advertising provided valuable clues that the company had lost focus. For example, in late 1983, the company seemed to disregard the principle of unicity as it diverted its advertising dollars to MCI Mail, an ill-fated electronic mail venture. Then, in 1984, MCI turned to celebrity customers such as Joan Rivers, Merv Griffin, and Burt Lancaster to do TV spots for its residential service. These were a mixed bag: Lancaster turned out to be the public's favorite, Griffin the least effective, while Rivers's abrasive style played better in some parts of the country than others.

These spots were discontinued in 1986 in favor of ads that emphasized the quality and service aspects of the business. Then, as part of a companywide cost-cutting strategy in 1987, MCI sharply reduced its TV advertising budget. Together, these various campaigns showed a company that was struggling with its identity, on top of obviously struggling to keep costs in line.

To add insult to injury, investors who played it safe by sticking with AT&T made out like bandits. The uncertainty surrounding the divestiture of AT&T had caused its share price and the share prices of the seven Baby Bells to be artificially low immediately following the historic spin-off of January 1984, and, from these depressed levels, the stocks had a lot of catching up to do.

Although the divestiture was a much bigger news story than long-distance rulings, the dilution of MCI's price position was also an important factor in AT&T's rise. Now, for the first time, AT&T could advertise *its* price competitiveness, a swing of the pendulum that was in plain view for ad investors. AT&T shares rose a point and a half, from 65 to 66½, the day of the FCC decision that rocked MCI, but that was just the beginning. Starting with the divestiture month of January 1984, AT&T doubled in three years. Not bad for a blue chip.

1986–89: Sprint Joins the Fold—Good Times for All

As we've seen, being third-place in any industry can be rough sledding, and long distance was certainly no exception. Without a position, Sprint was doomed. What could they offer that AT&T and MCI could not?

The answer was voice clarity, and in July 1986 another watershed long-distance ad debuted—Sprint's "pin drop" campaign. Sprint may have been in third place in terms of market share, but it was the first long-distance company to have a 100 percent fiber optic network, making it the CD of the industry compared to everyone else's reel-to-reel. Sprint's lines sounded better and the pin drop ads told you just that.

Today, you can buy shares of Sprint directly, but in 1986, when Sprint long-distance service was a 50-50 venture between United Telecommunications and GTE, you didn't have the same pure play. So when I talk about buying Sprint back then, I'm technically on the wrong side of the law, because you couldn't do it. But you could have bought either of the parent companies, with United Telecom being the more direct play on "pin drop." (Sprint's stock symbol—FON, adopted in 1992—is one of the true greats and plays to the company's heritage. It simultaneously sounds like "phone" and stands for "Fiber Optic Network.")

Within two years of the pin drop ad's debut, Sprint's long-distance volume doubled—yet another beneficiary of low market share! And by the end of 1989, Sprint's share price had tripled from that of July 1986, never mind the October 1987 market crash. (Things would have been even better, except that Sprint's billing system wasn't up to speed with the rest of its technology. Some customers went without bills for three or more months at a time, creating a bloating of accounts receivable and, ultimately, a significant charge against earnings in 1988.)

Why didn't AT&T respond with ads of its own? Because it couldn't! The company's microwave technology was no longer state of the art, a fact that came up in virtually every AT&T corporate sales call. The soft yet vital inference from the Sprint ads is that AT&T's conversion to fiber optics would have to be accelerated, and that move was not going to come cheaply or without investor response. In 1988,

AT&T took a $6.7 billion charge against earnings as it jettisoned its old network. In the first half of that year, AT&T shares dropped 20 percent.

However, better days lay ahead. In terms of new opportunities, the 1988–89 period was one of the brightest times ever for all of the long-distance companies. There was the proliferation of 800 and 900 services. There was the fax boom. And there were new products such as MCI's "Vision" service for small businesses, which didn't show up in consumer advertising but which played a prominent role in the company's earnings recovery.

No, advertising didn't provide nearly enough clues to this industry upswing (other than the cola-wars analogy that the prominence of long-distance advertising suggested opportunities in the underlying business). At MCI in particular, the company's recovery was rooted in the major cost-cutting program of 1987 as well as its new billing system, and a full dissection of those efforts runs well outside my advertising boundaries. However, what I *can* say is that just when investors had become accustomed to these prosperous times throughout the industry, the ads started to suggest that the good times would be coming to an end.

1989–90: Time to Avoid Everyone

This stage of our investment story coincides with the most frenetic period of advertising in the industry's history. The big three—particularly MCI and AT&T—were entering a period of aggressive price competition in order to gain market share.

If it seemed as though the industry had become more visible on television, it was. In the first half of 1989, AT&T's television ad budget was $95 million; in the first half of 1990, just one year later, its budget had risen to $184 million. MCI's ad spending for the same period rose from $29 million to $43 million; Sprint's from $27 million to $41 million. Everybody wanted your business.

The ads embodied a theme we have seen before. By trying to win customers on price, the companies were good for their customers but lousy for their investors. Although the ads were pitched at only the residential side of the long-distance business, they accurately reflected the competitive environment in the other two main arenas—high-end business customers and small business. Importantly, the ad blitz was visible in the *first* half of 1990, just in time to make a nice sell decision; by the second half, the recession had set in and the long-distance companies' prospects had gotten even worse.

MCI, the company that had built the price position, was the main victim of the industrywide price war. AT&T ads reminded customers that their supposed price advantage with MCI wasn't nearly as great as they thought (subtext: So why bother?). MCI's share of the long-distance market dipped a full percentage point in 1990, from 14 percent to 13. The company let go a thousand workers. The stock dropped from its high of $48 in late 1989 to just $18 by January 1991, a loss of 62 percent.

MCI wasn't the only one hurt: Sprint shares dropped almost 50 percent during the same time. AT&T declined 33 percent. Recession and price wars are a devastating combination. When an industry's ads revolve around price competition, it's time to get out.

1991–93: The Friends and Family Rally

Whenever two stocks have declined, one more than the other, it is tempting to believe that the more downtrodden of the two will someday have the bigger rebound. That's precisely what happened to MCI and AT&T in 1991, but more than naive arithmetic was at work.

The first quarter of 1991 was a time of great strength for the entire stock market because of the good news coming out of the Persian Gulf. Between January and March, AT&T rebounded 15 percent from its low of 1990. During this same time, MCI rebounded 50 percent. So far, a victory for naive arithmetic. However, even as these gains were being consolidated, out came a whole new reason to own shares of MCI. In March 1991, MCI launched its Friends & Family program and with it created a brand-new opportunity for the ad-based investor.

Prior to Friends & Family, a long-distance bill didn't know the difference between your brother and the IRS. The idea behind the plan was to give 20 percent discounts for groups of MCI customers who phoned one another regularly. Suddenly the long-distance bill had a personal element to it. Not only was the pricing attractive, but the new program's name was far more personal than "MCI." It wasn't quite a name change on the order of Greyhound/Dial, but clearly MCI had created a new identity for itself.

Within three years of the 1991 launch, MCI had signed up over ten million people into the Friends & Family program. The company's residential market share grew by a whopping 7 percentage points—from 13 to almost 20—and the stock had more than doubled from its level of March 1991, when F&F debuted.

By now, we trained ad investors should be asking why AT&T had never tried the idea. The answer was that the company's billing system was routed through the local phone companies, making it an arduous process to link different accounts nationwide. MCI, with a national billing system of its own, was much better positioned.

What an ad investor *did* see was AT&T's attempt to counteract Friends & Family by making it seem like a violation of privacy. "Someone else is giving out my number," et cetera. But even in the politically correct nineties, these ads played like sour grapes. Eventually, AT&T tried its hand at a discounting gimmick with its "*i* Plan." It bombed, in the pattern of me-too products we have already seen—yet another reason to prefer MCI in the stock market.

Meanwhile, Sprint, fearful that the industry's proliferation of look-alike ads was chipping away at its identity, was hooking up with its now-famous corporate spokesperson, *Murphy Brown* star Candice Bergen. It was hard to tell if Bergen's favorable attributes—independence, candor, intelligence—belonged to her or to Murphy. Personally, I think it's another case of celebrities being more successful when in character. Sprint hoped that Murphy's tremendous public appeal would rub off on them, and it wasn't a bad short-term idea.

As we've seen, though, being defined by a corporate spokesperson isn't as effective as being defined by innovative new products. Although Candice Bergen is widely credited with stabilizing Sprint's consumer division, and although she is surely responsible for AT&T's decision not to advertise on *Murphy Brown,* she is not a position.

Her most believable and therefore most effective moment came in early 1994, when Bergen/Brown introduced the Voice Activated FON Card. This was innovation the likes of which the company hadn't seen since "pin drop." (It didn't hurt that Bergen had actually owned a FON

Card for two years prior to the ads, as part of the company's pilot program.)

Having recommended sale of Sprint in late 1993 at $36 per share —and having been rewarded in the near term by a fall to the $30 level —I watched with particular interest. The voice-activation campaign went on to such famous "voices" as Don Shula, Steve Young, and Beverly Sills, and met with a tremendous response. Partly on investor hopes for the FON Card, the stock made up its lost ground. In this case, though, the effect was brief: Sprint fell below $30 once again in the weak stock market of late 1994.

At this writing, it's still too early to gauge the ad's ultimate effect. What we can say is that Sprint, as the number-three player in the industry, must continue to innovate in this fashion if it wants to remain competitive. It is an extremely tough task.

1994 On: Whatever Happened to Positioning Theory?

Speaking of too early to gauge, in early 1994 MCI introduced its "information superhighway" ads—the ones with Anna Paquin of *The Piano* fame talking vaguely about the future of telecommunications. In terms of charm and execution, the ads couldn't have done better, and they won critical acclaim. But positionwise they said absolutely nothing, creating the disturbing possibility that MCI would lose its identity in the nineties and beyond. The ads were a far cry from the slogan "The nation's long-distance phone company" of the early eighties.

The superhighway ad was a message to the investing public that MCI's future lies outside of its current core business, and I wouldn't count them out just yet. But positioning theory makes it a safe bet that many companies that attempt to travel the information superhighway will be thwarted because they already own a different type of slot in the consumer's mind. These companies may end up wishing they had defended their original positions instead of abandoning them.

It was poetic justice that many of the ill-defined "superhighway" stocks that had soared in 1993 encountered rough sledding in 1994. If we've learned anything from this chapter, it's that you need a position to survive.

■ ■ ■

In some ways, this book only *seemed* to be about its five components of weather, television, fads, presidents, and advertising. As I look back, these five areas were in fact merely launching pads for the sort of information digging that any successful investor must learn to do, and that may be the most important message behind all the examples we have just looked at.

Frankly, I was surprised by how one question led to the next and, ultimately, how far you could get by taking a few simple concepts to their absolute limit. Sometimes we came up with well-developed strategies covering a broad range of securities; other times, we simply saw explanations for why individual stocks moved in the manner they did. Either way, I hope the stock market looks a little less mysterious than it did when we began.

INDEX

ABOUT THE AUTHOR

DERRICK NIEDERMAN is a contributing editor for *Worth* magazine. His investment writing experience includes the *Independent Investor* and *Sector Dynamics* newsletters and *Investment Vision* magazine. He is also a nationally recognized creator of crossword and cryptic puzzles, and is a former national squash champion. A graduate of Yale University, Niederman received a Ph.D. in mathematics from M.I.T. in 1981. He and his trusty sled team live in Newton Center, Massachusetts.